Basic English

by
Bonnie L. Walker

AGS®

American Guidance Service, Inc.
Circle Pines, Minnesota 55014-1796
800-328-2560

About the Author

Bonnie L. Walker taught for 16 years in secondary schools and college. She holds a Ph.D. in curriculum theory and instructional design from the University of Maryland, an M.Ed. in secondary education, and a B.A. in English. She studied psycholinguistics at the University of Illinois Graduate School and was a curriculum developer at the Model Secondary School for the Deaf at Gallaudet University. She is the author of *Life Skills English, Basic English Composition, Basic English Grammar,* and numerous curriculum materials in written expression, grammar, and usage. Since 1986, Dr. Walker has been president of a research and development company specializing in development of training and educational materials for special populations.

Photo Credits: Cover photos: left–©Barbara Haynor/Index Stock Imagery; upper right–©Dana White/PhotoEdit; lower right–©SW Productions/PhotoDisc; background and back cover–©Steve Taylor/Stone; pp. iii, 16–©Randy Allbritton/PhotoDisc; pp. iv, 86–©Shaffer-Smith/Index Stock Imagery; pp. vi, 194–©David Nardini/FPG International; pp. viii, 334–©Super Stock International; pp. 13, 75, 97, 196, 197, 325, 341, 372, 378–©David Young Wolff/PhotoEdit; p. 17–©Steve Holland/AP/Wide World Photos; p. 24–©D. Boone/Corbis; p. 32–©Bill Bachman/PhotoEdit; p. 36–©Jose Carrillo/PhotoEdit; p. 55–©Partnership for a Drug-Free America®; p. 58–©Art Wolfe/Stone; p. 67–©Rudi Von Briel/PhotoEdit; p. 101–©Kevin Hatt/Image Bank; p. 112–©Digital Vision Photography/Eyewire Collection; p. 118–©H. Armstrong Roberts; p. 121–©Mary Kate Denny/PhotoEdit; p. 138–©David Crow/PhotoEdit; p. 152–©Premium Stock/Corbis; p. 159–©Galen Rowell/Corbis; p. 170–©Pete Turner Inc./Image Bank; p. 176–©Tony Freeman/PhotoEdit; p. 185–©Tony Dizinno/AllSport USA; p. 197–©Ed Young/Corbis; p. 197–©Jon Feingersh/Stock Market; pp. 197, 232–©Michael Newman/PhotoEdit; p. 200–©Bob Daemmrich/Stock Boston; p. 216–©Andrew Yates Productions/Image Bank; p. 238–©Roman Soumar/Corbis; p. 250–©Color Day Productions/Image Bank; p. 270–©Joe McDonald/Corbis; p. 282–©Arthur Tilley/Stone; p. 292–©White, Packert/Image Bank; pp. 295, 314–©Eyewire Collection; pp. 299, 396–©Jeff Greenberg/PhotoEdit; p. 303–©Andy Whale/Stone; p. 316–©Barbara Stitzer/PhotoEdit; p. 321–©Steve Mason/PhotoDisc; p. 367–©Wolfgang Kaehler/Corbis; p. 384–©H. Richard Johnson/FPG International; p. 391–©Stone; p. 398–©D. Robert Franz/Corbis

Publisher's Project Staff

Director, Product Development:
  Karen Dahlen

Editor: Julie Maas

Development Assistant: Bev Johnson

Designer: Virginia Sutton

Design Manager: Nancy Condon

Desktop Publishing Manager: Lisa Beller

Desktop Publishing Specialists:
  Linda Peterson, Pegi Cull

Purchasing Agent: Mary Kaye Kuzma

Executive Director of Marketing:
  Matt Keller

Marketing Manager: Brian Holl

Editorial and production services provided by Creative Services Associates, Inc.

Printed in the United States of America

ISBN 0-7854-2905-0

Product Number 93440

A 0 9 8 7 6

Contents

How to
Use This Book:
A Study Guide

Welcome to a study of the English language. Everyone needs to learn how to read and write English. We use language every day in almost every aspect of life. We use it to communicate through writing, reading, and speaking.

As you read the chapters and lessons in this book, you will learn about the different parts of speech. You will learn about writing sentences, punctuation, and proper grammar. You will practice your vocabulary and spelling skills.

How to Study

• Plan a regular time to study.

• Choose a quiet desk or table where you will not be distracted. Find a place that has good lighting.

• Gather all the books, pencils, and paper you need to complete your assignments.

• Decide on a goal. For example, "I will finish reading and take notes on Chapter 1, Lesson 1, by 8:00."

• Take a 5- to 10-minute break every hour to stay alert.

• If you start to feel sleepy, take a short break and get some fresh air.

CHAPTER 1

Writing Sentences

E very day we need to communicate with other people. Sometimes we talk to express our ideas. Other times we write. There are other reasons to talk and write. We may need to write something down so that we can remember it. We may want to make a record of certain kinds of information. We communicate better with other people and ourselves if we understand our language better.

In Chapter 1, you will learn some basic rules about writing sentences.

Goals for Learning

▶ To identify complete sentences and sentence fragments
▶ To capitalize the first word and use end punctuation marks in sentences
▶ To identify the subject and predicate in simple sentences
▶ To recognize declarative, interrogative, imperative, and exclamatory sentences

Before Beginning Each Chapter

• Read the chapter title and study the photograph. What does the photo tell you about the chapter title?

• Read the opening paragraphs.

• Study the Goals for Learning. The Chapter Review and tests will ask questions related to these goals.

• Look at the Chapter Review. The questions cover the most important information in the chapter.

Note the Chapter Features

• **Writing Tip**—quick tips to help improve writing skills

• **Thumbtack Note**—brief bits of information about parts of speech or punctuation

• **Using What You've Learned**—an exercise that has students apply something taught in the chapter

Writing Tip

Using vivid action verbs adds interest and color to your writing. Substitute colorful verbs such as *stroll* and *dash* for ordinary ones such as *walk* and *run.*

Think about whether a noun is singular or plural. If it has an apostrophe, the noun is also possessive. A possessive noun shows ownership of another noun.

- **Vocabulary Builder**—vocabulary practice

- **Spelling Builder**—spelling practice

 • **Where to Find It**—information about various reference materials such as dictionaries, encyclopedias, and more

- **Writing Project**—writing practice

Before Beginning Each Lesson

Read the lesson title and restate it in the form of a question.

For example, Write: *How do you begin and end a sentence?*

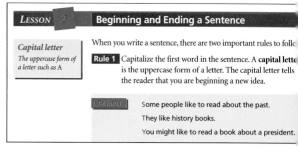

LESSON 2 | **Beginning and Ending a Sentence**

Capital letter
The uppercase form of a letter such as A

When you write a sentence, there are two important rules to follo

Rule 1 Capitalize the first word in the sentence. A **capital lette** is the uppercase form of a letter. The capital letter tells the reader that you are beginning a new idea.

EXAMPLE | Some people like to read about the past.
They like history books.
You might like to read a book about a president.

Look over the entire lesson, noting . . .

- bold words
- text organization
- exercises
- notes in the margins
- photos
- lesson review

As You Read the Lesson

- Read the major headings.
- Read the subheads and the paragraphs that follow.
- Read the content in the Example boxes.
- Before moving on to the next heading, see if you understand the concepts you read. If you do not, reread the section. If you are still unsure, ask for help.
- Practice what you have learned by doing the activities in each lesson.

Using the Bold Words

Sentence

A group of words that expresses a complete thought

Knowing the meanings of all the boxed words in the left column will help you understand what you read.

These words appear in **bold type** the first time they appear in the text and are defined in the paragraph.

A **sentence** is a group of words that expresses a complete thought.

All the words in the left column are also defined in the glossary.

Sentence—A group of words that expresses a complete thought (p. 8)

Word Study Tips

• Start a vocabulary file with index cards to use for review.

• Write one word on the front of each card. Write the chapter number, lesson number, and definition on the back.

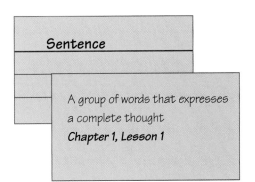

Sentence

A group of words that expresses a complete thought

Chapter 1, Lesson 1

• You can use these cards as flash cards by yourself or with a study partner to test your knowledge.

Using the Reviews

• Answer the questions in the Lesson Reviews.

• In the Chapter Reviews, answer the questions about vocabulary under Part A. Study the words and definitions. Say them aloud to help you remember them.

• Answer the questions under the other parts of the Chapter Reviews.

Preparing for Tests

- Complete the activities in each lesson. Make up similar activity questions to practice what you have learned. You may want to do this with a classmate and share your questions.
- Review your answers to lesson activities, Lesson Reviews, and Chapter Reviews.
- Test yourself on vocabulary words and key ideas.
- Use graphic organizers as study tools.

Using Graphic Organizers

A graphic organizer is a visual representation of information. It can help you see how ideas are related to each other. A graphic organizer can help you study for a test or organize information before you write. Here are some examples.

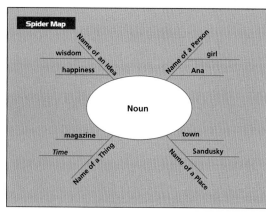

Spider Map

The Spider Map shown here can be used to connect related ideas to a central idea or concept. Write the main or central idea or concept in the circle in the center. Identify related ideas and write them on the lines that angle out from the circle. Write examples that support the ideas on the horizontal lines that are attached to the angled lines.

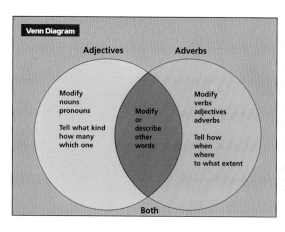

Venn Diagram

The Venn diagram shown here can be used to compare and contrast two things. For example, this diagram compares and contrasts adjectives and adverbs. List the characteristics for adjectives in the left circle. List the characteristics for adverbs in the right circle. In the intersection of the two circles, list the characteristics that both have.

Introduction

People need to know the basics of the English language to communicate effectively. Whether you are writing, reading, or speaking, you need to understand how words work in sentences.

This book will teach you the rules for putting words in the right places in sentences. The lessons will help you learn to speak and write more clearly. You will learn that each word in a sentence has a purpose. The English language has thousands of words. Each word fits into at least one of eight main groups. These groups are called *parts of speech.*

Parts of Speech

Nouns	Words that name people, places, things, or ideas.
Pronouns	Words that replace nouns.
Adjectives	Words that describe nouns and pronouns.
Verbs	Words that express action or a state of being in a sentence.
Adverbs	Words that tell about an action. They tell *how, when, where,* or *how much.*
Prepositions	Words that show a relationship between a noun and the rest of the sentence.
Conjunctions	Words that connect sentences or parts of a sentence.
Interjections	Words that express feelings.

In this book, you will learn the parts of speech. You will practice writing and punctuating sentences. The lessons will help you improve your vocabulary and spelling skills. You will also develop and improve your writing skills.

CHAPTER 1

Writing Sentences

Every day we need to communicate with other people. Sometimes we talk to express our ideas. Other times we write. There are other reasons to talk and write. We may need to write something down so that we can remember it. We may want to make a record of certain kinds of information. We communicate better with other people and ourselves if we understand our language better.

In Chapter 1, you will learn some basic rules about writing sentences.

Goals for Learning

▶ To identify complete sentences and sentence fragments

▶ To capitalize the first word and use end punctuation marks in sentences

▶ To identify the subject and predicate in simple sentences

▶ To recognize declarative, interrogative, imperative, and exclamatory sentences

Sentence

A group of words that expresses a complete thought

A **sentence** is a group of words that expresses a complete thought.

 EXAMPLE   Angela Choy is a high school student.

What sport does she enjoy most?

Get to practice now!

Sentence fragment

A group of words that does not express a complete thought

A group of words that does not express a complete thought is called a **sentence fragment.**

EXAMPLE   Plays baseball in the spring.

This group of words does not express a complete thought. It is a sentence fragment. What you need to know is "Who plays baseball in the spring?" *Armando* plays baseball in the spring.

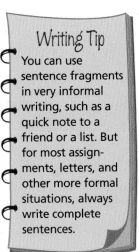

Writing Tip

You can use sentence fragments in very informal writing, such as a quick note to a friend or a list. But for most assignments, letters, and other more formal situations, always write complete sentences.

Activity A Read each group of words and write it on your paper. Write *S* if the group of words is a sentence. Write *F* if the group of words is a fragment.

1) Emily Watson likes to draw.

2) After school in the park.

3) Since she was seven years old.

4) Her favorite kind of paint is watercolor.

5) For her birthday she received a set of oil paints.

Activity B Write each group of words from Activity A that you marked *F* on your paper. Add words to each one to make it a complete sentence. Begin each sentence with a capital letter. Put a period at the end of each sentence.

For each item, write *S* on your paper if the group of words is a sentence. If the group of words is not a sentence, write it on your paper and add words to make it a complete sentence.

1) Emily likes to play the clarinet.

2) She is in the band at school.

3) Practices with the band three days a week.

4) She practices at home every night.

5) Good at playing the clarinet.

6) Michelle and Karl are in the band with Emily.

7) The band concert coming up soon.

8) Practice their songs.

9) The music not easy to learn.

10) A lot of fun playing their instruments.

Write each of the following groups of words on your paper. Add words to make each one a complete sentence.

11) Nathan outdoors.

12) To Yellowstone National Park.

13) Camp out near Old Faithful.

14) A book about Yellowstone.

15) Find out about caving sites in the park.

Capital letter

The uppercase form of a letter such as A

When you write a sentence, there are two important rules to follow.

Rule 1 Capitalize the first word in the sentence. A **capital letter** is the uppercase form of a letter. The capital letter tells the reader that you are beginning a new idea.

> **EXAMPLE**
>
> Some people like to read about the past.
>
> They like history books.
>
> You might like to read a book about a president.

End punctuation

A mark at the end of a sentence that tells the reader where a sentence ends:

• a period (.)

• a question mark (?)

• an exclamation mark (!)

Rule 2 Put an **end punctuation** mark at the end of the sentence. An end punctuation mark can be a **period,** a **question mark,** or an **exclamation mark.** It tells the reader where the sentence ends.

> **EXAMPLE**
>
> George Washington was the first president of the United States.
>
> Do you know who the second president was?
>
> Yes, I do!

Writing Tip

Be sure you leave a small space after end punctuation in each sentence you write. The space tells the reader that one thought is ending and another is beginning.

Activity A Find four sentences in each paragraph below. List them on your paper. Capitalize the first word in each sentence. Use an end punctuation mark at the end of each sentence.

the library has many history books some students like to read about the past other people like to read about the future those books are in the science fiction section

do you enjoy music many people listen to music on the radio others play their own favorite CDs what is your favorite album

Find the sentences in each paragraph. Write them on your paper. Capitalize the first word in each sentence. End each sentence with correct punctuation.

1) blues music can be very relaxing the guitar is one instrument in blues many people write their own blues music the songs of blues artists have good rhythms

2) Mr. Jackson is getting the band ready for a performance the concert is on Wednesday they have 10 songs to prepare do you think they will be ready in time

3) Angela is a very good athlete and likes to swim she is a fast swimmer her favorite event is butterfly maybe one day she will be fast enough for the Olympics

Write four sentences about your favorite kind of music. Begin each sentence with a capital letter. End each sentence with correct punctuation.

Spelling Builder

Words with Final e

Say the words *hid* and *hide.* When you hear a long vowel sound in a short word, you often see an *e* at the end of the word.

Add a final *e* to each word to make a word with a long vowel sound. Then write a sentence using the word.

1) plan   **4)** fin

2) not   **5)** cub

3) slid   **6)** tap

LESSON 3 The Subject and the Predicate

Subject

The word or words in a sentence that tell what the sentence is about

Every sentence has a **subject.** The subject is the part of the sentence that tells who or what the sentence is about.

  Emily enjoys oatmeal for breakfast.
Who enjoys oatmeal for breakfast?
Emily does.

Activity A Write these sentences on your paper. Underline the subject.

1) The school is on the corner of 5th and Main Streets.

2) Armando attends the school.

3) The bus goes to the school.

4) It arrives at 8:45 A.M.

5) School starts at 9:00 A.M.

The subject can be one word or many words.

  The French teacher gave the class a quiz.

She returned the quizzes the next day.

Activity B Write these sentences on your paper. Underline the subject. Ask yourself who or what the sentence is about.

1) The students wrote an essay about summer.

2) Summer is their favorite time of year.

3) They passed the essay in today.

4) The teacher will grade the papers tonight.

5) The entire class did the assignment.

Predicate

The word or words in a sentence that tell something about the subject; it always contains a verb

Verb

The word or words in a sentence that express action or state of being or link ideas

The **predicate** is the part of a sentence that tells something about the subject. It can be one word or many words and always contains a **verb**. A verb is the word or words in a sentence that express action or state of being. A verb can also link ideas. You will learn more about verbs in Chapters 5 and 6.

EXAMPLE

Angela swims.

Angela tried out for the swimming team.

She is one of the best swimmers on the team.

Activity C Write these sentences on your paper. Underline the predicate.

1) Swim practice begins at 3:00 P.M.

2) Angela practices every day after school.

3) She has a summer job at the YMCA.

4) She is a lifeguard at the pool.

5) The lifeguards had a picnic last weekend.

A picnic is just one of many summer activities.

Activity D Combine the subjects and predicates to write five different sentences. Write the sentences on your paper.

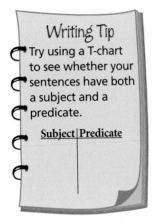

Subjects	Predicates
1) Angela and Nathan	wants a CD player for her birthday.
2) They	practices every day.
3) The swim team	got a new paint box.
4) Emily	is fun to play.
5) A clarinet	like to draw.

Activity E Here is a list of sentence fragments that contain subjects. Write them on your paper. Add a predicate so that each group of words expresses a complete thought. End each sentence with correct punctuation.

1) Every summer I

2) The book on the table

3) The first football game of the year

4) My friend from elementary school

5) My breakfast this morning

Activity F Here is a list of sentence predicates. Write them on your paper. Add a subject to make each group of words express a complete thought. End each sentence with correct punctuation.

1) go to the beach at least once

2) moved here from another town

3) went to the movies at 3:00 P.M.

4) got ruined in the wash

5) was late as usual

Write these sentences on your paper. Underline the subject.

1) A sentence has two parts.

2) Mary is an old friend of mine.

3) Her birthday is on August 7.

4) My friend would like a CD player.

5) I will give her a CD.

Write these sentences on your paper. Underline the predicate.

6) Mary and I met in middle school.

7) We rode the school bus.

8) She sat next to me.

9) The first day of school was on a Tuesday.

10) My friend and I are now in high school.

Each sentence is missing a subject. Add a word or words to make the sentence complete. Write the complete sentence on your paper.

11) _____ is the most interesting president to me.

12) _____ begins at 3:00 P.M.

13) _____ interests me very much.

14) _____ hangs on the wall of my bedroom.

15) _____ is playing on the radio.

Declarative sentence

A sentence that states a fact

There are four kinds of sentences.

A statement that gives information to another person is called a **declarative sentence.** It states a fact and ends with a period.

> EXAMPLE
>
> Nathan likes to read.
>
> He is interested in American history.
>
> John Adams was the second president of the United States.

Interrogative sentence

A sentence that asks a question

A question is also called an **interrogative sentence.** It ends with a question mark.

> EXAMPLE
>
> Who was the third president?
>
> What is Nathan reading about today?
>
> Why does Nathan like history?

Imperative sentence

A sentence that gives a command

A command or request is also called an **imperative sentence.** It tells someone to do something. It ends with a period.

> EXAMPLE
>
> Give me that book.
>
> Turn to page 200.
>
> Please read out loud.

Exclamatory sentence

A sentence that expresses strong feelings

An **exclamatory sentence** or exclamation expresses strong feelings. It ends with an exclamation mark.

> EXAMPLE
>
> This book is great!
>
> That was the best story ever!

Activity A Read these sentences. Write the kind of sentence each one is on your paper. Choose from the following:

Statement   **Question**   **Command**   **Exclamation**

1) Angela Choy is on her school's swim team.

2) She will swim in the state finals.

3) I really hope I will win a medal!

4) Will I make the Olympic team someday?

5) Hurry up, Angela.

6) Have you heard of Nashville, Tennessee?

7) Of course, I have!

8) Did you know it is one of America's largest cities?

9) Tell me about it.

10) Nashville is the home of the Grand Ole Opry.

Activity B Write five sentences about your town or city. Include at least one sentence that makes a statement, one that asks a question, one that gives a command, and one that expresses strong feelings.

Angela swims for the Wilson High School swim team.

Activity C We write to give information to others. Write three sentences about yourself. Begin each sentence with a different word. Capitalize the first word in each sentence. Put a punctuation mark at the end.

Example   My name is Armando.
                In the fall I play on the soccer team.
                Right now my favorite subject in school is art.

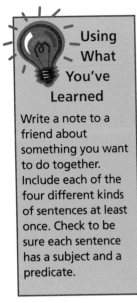

Using What You've Learned

Write a note to a friend about something you want to do together. Include each of the four different kinds of sentences at least once. Check to be sure each sentence has a subject and a predicate.

Command   You tell a person to do something.
Request   You ask a person to do something.
Question   You ask a person if he or she will do something.

Activity D Read these sentences. Decide the purpose of each one. Write whether it is a *command, request,* or *question.* Then write a command, request, or question to communicate that you want someone to show you how a computer program works.

   1) Please hand in your paper.

   2) Hand in your paper now.

   3) Will you hand in your homework?

   4) What is your name?

   5) Please give me your name.

We ask questions to get information. Always put a question mark at the end of a question. An answer is a statement. Use a period at the end of an answer.

Question   Who was the fifth president of the United States?
Answer   James Monroe was the fifth president.

Activity E Write five questions on your paper. Then write the answers. Begin every sentence with a capital letter. End every sentence with a punctuation mark.

LESSON 4 Review

Read these sentences. Write the purpose of each sentence on your paper. Choose from the following:

Statement   **Question**   **Command**   **Exclamation**

1) Practice starts in five minutes.

2) Are you going to be late again?

3) I am never late!

4) Are you sure about that?

5) Stop giving me a hard time.

Write five sentences about a topic of your choice. Include at least one statement, question, command, and exclamation. Be sure to begin each sentence with a capital letter and use an end punctuation mark.

Vocabulary Builder

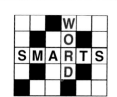

Antonyms

An **antonym** is a word with the opposite meaning of another word.

cold—hot   small—large   bland—spicy

Select the antonym for the first word and use it in a sentence. Write the sentences on your paper.

1) same   **a)** alike   **b)** nearly   **c)** different

2) problem   **a)** example   **b)** solution   **c)** obstacle

3) hostile   **a)** important   **b)** young   **c)** friendly

4) arrive   **a)** stay   **b)** leave   **c)** start

5) sharp   **a)** dull   **b)** pointed   **c)** colorful

Where to Find It

Dictionary

A dictionary lists the words in the English language in alphabetical order. Each word has an entry that gives you information about the word. Look at this sample entry.

> **jour•nal** \'jər•nəl\ *n* [ME, service book containing the day hours, fr. MF, fr. *journal,* adj., daily, fr. L *diurnalis,* fr. *diurnus* of the day, fr. *dies* day—more at DEITY] (15c) **1 a :** a record of current transactions, *esp:* a book of original entry in double-entry bookkeeping **b :** an account of day-to-day events **c :** a record of experiences, ideas, or reflections kept regularly for private use **d :** a record of transactions kept by a deliberative or legislative body **e :** LOG 3, 4 **2 a :** a daily newspaper **b :** a periodical dealing esp. with matters of current interest **3 :** the part of rotating shaft, axle, roll, or spindle that turns in a bearing

It tells you
- how to spell the word and divide it into syllables
- how to pronounce the word
- the part or parts of speech this word may be
- the word's history
- all the meanings the word may have

1) Suppose your teacher gives you this assignment:
   Pretend you are George Washington at Valley Forge. Write about the day in your journal. Which definition for *journal* is used here?

2) You are writing a paper. The word *journal* does not fit at the end of the line. Where do you divide or break the word?

3) What kind of sentences are used to write the assignment in 1?

4) What is the subject of this sentence?
   This journal gives my thoughts about life.

Use Complete Sentences to Express Your Ideas

Think about a time when you were especially happy. In this activity you will describe this time. Include the following points:

- What happened?

- Who else was there?

- Why was the event pleasant?

- What was it about the event that made it memorable?

Follow these directions:

1) List everything you remember about the event.

2) Write several complete sentences about the event.

3) Organize your sentences into a paragraph.

4) The first sentence should express the main idea.

5) The middle sentences should give examples and specific details.

6) The last sentence should sum up the main idea.

Example paragraph

When I was six, my parents gave me a birthday party. I was allowed to invite all of the kids in my neighborhood. It was summer. We had the party in our backyard. We played games and had ice cream and cake. All of the children brought me a present and a card. My aunt videotaped the event. I remember how special I felt that day.

WORD BANK

capital letter

declarative
   sentence

end punctuation

exclamatory
   sentence

imperative
   sentence

interrogative
   sentence

predicate

sentence

sentence fragment

subject

verb

Part A On a sheet of paper, write the correct word or words from the Word Bank to complete each sentence.

1) An _____ shows strong feelings.

2) A _____ is the uppercase form of a letter.

3) A _____ is a group of words that expresses a complete thought.

4) A sentence that states a fact is a _____.

5) An _____ gives a command.

6) The _____ in a sentence tells who or what the sentence is about.

7) A _____ does not express a complete thought.

8) A question is also called an _____.

9) The _____ in a sentence tells something about the subject.

10) A period, a question mark, and an exclamation mark are all _____ marks.

11) A _____ expresses action or state of being or links ideas.

Part B Read each group of words. Write *S* if the group of words is a sentence. Write *F* if the group of words is not a sentence.

12) During October, the students at Wilson High School celebrate Homecoming.

13) A Homecoming King and Queen.

14) Some of the teachers.

15) Homecoming was a huge success.

Part C Find the sentences in the paragraph. List them on your paper. Capitalize the first word in each sentence. Use an end punctuation mark at the end of each sentence.

16) it is almost Thanksgiving david is busy in his kitchen he is cooking a turkey he has made cranberry sauce and a pumpkin pie david invited six people to his Thanksgiving dinner

Part D Write these sentences on your paper. Circle the subject in each sentence and underline the predicate.

17) My favorite sweater is blue.

18) The school bus drove into a snowbank today.

19) My friends and I went skiing last weekend.

20) The field trip to the Colby Science Museum was fun.

Part E Read these sentences. Write the kind of sentence each one is on your paper. Choose from the following: *statement, question, command,* or *exclamation.*

21) You scared me!

22) Is this Ms. Benson's classroom?

23) Put your notebook away.

24) Go to the principal's office.

25) Mr. Jackson is the music teacher.

Test-Taking Tip When studying for a test, write your own test problems with a partner. Then complete each other's test. Double-check your answers.

Using Nouns in Sentences

Nouns are words that name people, places, things, and ideas. It is nearly impossible to talk about anything without using a noun.

Nouns surround us in everyday life. Look around and you will see thousands of nouns. The photograph on the opposite page shows raindrops as they splash into a puddle of water. The raindrops and the puddle of water are nouns.

In Chapter 2, you will learn about nouns. Each lesson tells about different kinds of nouns. You will learn how they are used in everyday speech and writing.

Goals for Learning

▶ To recognize nouns in sentences

▶ To capitalize proper nouns

▶ To spell the plural forms of nouns correctly

▶ To distinguish between plurals and possessives

Noun

A word that names a person, place, thing, or idea

A **noun** is a word that names a person, place, thing, or idea.

Persons	teacher, agent, aunt, worker, Harriet	
Places	state, theater, town, Washington	
Things	book, dish, apple, Liberty Bell	
Ideas	decision, thought, belief, amazement	

Activity A Write three nouns that belong in each group. Use the examples in parentheses as a guide.

1) sound   (noise, whisper)

2) event   (dance, party)

3) person   (nurse, neighbor)

4) quality   (strength, loyalty)

5) feeling   (joy, sadness)

A noun can be the name of a part of something.

EXAMPLE

A hand is part of a clock.

A mane is part of a horse.

Activity B Here is a list of nouns. Write words that name four parts of each thing. Use the example as a guide.

Example   house—roof, window, wall, porch

1) kitchen   **4)** car

2) tree   **5)** bicycle

3) ship

Collective noun

The name of a group of people, places, or things

A **collective noun** is the name of a group of people, places, or things.

EXAMPLE		
	Groups of people	group, audience, crowd, team
	Groups of places	nation, United States
	Groups of animals	herd, flock, swarm, pack
	Groups of things	collection, set, series

Activity C Read the paragraph. Write the nouns that name a group of people or things on your paper.

> The swim team practices every day. Angela's swim club meets weekly. The whole group went to the meet. The audience cheered for the athletes.

Compound noun

Two words joined together to form one new noun

A **compound noun** is two words joined together to form one new noun.

EXAMPLE	
	fire + fighter = firefighter
	black + bird = blackbird
	back + yard = backyard

Activity D Write a sentence using each of these compound nouns. Be sure to capitalize the first word and use end punctuation. Underline the nouns in your sentences.

1) earthquake

2) moonlight

3) thunderstorm

4) toothpaste

5) watermelon

Hyphen

A short dash between parts of a word

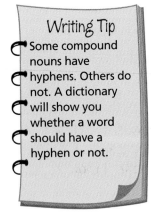

Writing Tip

Some compound nouns have hyphens. Others do not. A dictionary will show you whether a word should have a hyphen or not.

A noun can be a group of related words. Sometimes the word has a hyphen.

A **hyphen** is a short dash between parts of a word. We use a hyphen to join parts of words such as *mid-July* or *mother-in-law*.

Other groups of related words without hyphens are also nouns.

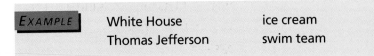

| EXAMPLE | White House | ice cream |
| | Thomas Jefferson | swim team |

Activity E Find 10 nouns in this paragraph and write them on your paper.

Emily thinks that a lily of the valley is the most beautiful flower. She brought a bouquet to her sister-in-law who was in the hospital. "These flowers smell so sweet," said Julie. "You are a good friend. I will ask someone to put them in water for me."

Activity F Find the nouns in these sentences and write them on your paper.

1) Nathan is a student in high school.

2) His favorite subject is history.

3) His family took a trip to a big city.

4) They saw a crowd of people in a park.

5) The people were looking at the Liberty Bell.

1) Write the nouns in this paragraph on your paper.

The United States has many national parks. Yellowstone National Park was the first one in the entire world. It has ten thousand geysers and hot springs. The most famous geyser is Old Faithful. The park also has spectacular waterfalls. If you go to this park, you might see grizzly bears, moose, and buffalo.

2) Write five sentences about a place you have visited. Be sure that each sentence begins with a capital letter and has correct end punctuation. Underline the nouns in your sentences.

Vocabulary Builder

Use Nouns to Improve Your Writing

A synonym is a word that has the same or almost the same meaning as another word. Many nouns have synonyms. For example:

    road—street   freedom—liberty

When you write, you want to choose words that most closely express what you want to say. You can make your writing more interesting by choosing interesting nouns.

Write this paragraph on your paper. Replace the nouns in bold with synonyms that you think are more interesting.

Angela would like to take a **trip** this **fall**. She wants to go to the **beach**. Her best **friend** Emily will go with her. They will drive in Emily's new **car**. On this **vacation**, the girls will stay in a **motel**.

Common noun

The name of a general type of person, place, thing, or idea

Proper noun

The name of a particular person, place, thing, or idea

A **common noun** is the name of a general type of person, place, thing, or idea. Capitalize a common noun only when it is the first word in a sentence or part of a title.

A **proper noun** is the name of a particular person, place, thing, or idea. Always capitalize a proper noun.

EXAMPLE

Common Nouns	Proper Nouns
president	Andrew Jackson
mountain	Mount Everest
house	White House

Activity A Write these common nouns on your paper. Write a proper noun next to each common noun.

Example   street   Howard Street
             city   Minneapolis

1) country   4) television show

2) state   5) month

3) movie

Activity B Write these proper nouns on your paper. Write a common noun next to each proper noun.

Example   Georgia   state
             Abraham Lincoln   president

1) Los Angeles

2) *Star Wars*

3) "The Star-Spangled Banner"

4) Mars

5) Spain

Capitalizing Names of Places

The name of a particular place is a proper noun. The name of a country, state, city, or building is a proper noun.

EXAMPLE	Common Nouns	Proper Nouns
	city	Philadelphia
	building	Empire State Building
	high school	Wilson High School

Activity C Write these sentences on your paper. Capitalize the proper nouns. Every sentence has at least one proper noun.

My friend angela loves to swim. Her favorite swimmer is janet evans. Janet won three individual gold medals in the 1988 summer olympics. Those games took place in seoul, korea. Janet also won a fourth gold medal at the 1992 olympics in barcelona, spain.

The names of parts of the country are proper nouns. When compass directions are used as nouns, they are common nouns.

EXAMPLE	Part of the country	Nathan visited the East with his family.
	Direction	The plane flew toward the east.

Writing Tip
When you write about the seasons of the year, do not capitalize them. The seasons are common nouns, not proper nouns. *Cara's favorite season is spring, but she also likes summer.*

Activity D Write these sentences on your paper. Capitalize the proper nouns. Not every sentence has a proper noun.

1) jennifer took a trip to the south.

2) On the first day, she drove 200 miles southeast.

3) She began in springfield and went to tennessee.

4) The next day she headed south toward alabama.

5) She liked the south very much.

The name of a language is a proper noun. The name of a particular course in school is a proper noun. The name of a subject is a common noun.

EXAMPLE	Proper Nouns	Common Nouns
	English, French	language
	History I, Algebra II	history, math

Activity E Read each pair of sentences. Write the one with the correct capitalization on your paper.

1) a) Meg is in the Band.

   b) Meg took Beginning Band this year.

2) a) Next year Nathan is taking a history class.

   b) Next year Nathan is taking a History class.

3) a) Angela enjoys her physical education class.

   b) Angela enjoys her Physical Education class.

4) a) All of the students take english.

   b) All of the students take English.

5) a) Emily plans to study french next year.

   b) Emily plans to study French next year.

Meg plays the saxophone in the school band.

Capitalizing Abbreviations of Proper Nouns

An **abbreviation** is a short form of a word. If the word is a proper noun, capitalize its abbreviation.

Abbreviation

A short form of a word

EXAMPLE	Proper Nouns	Abbreviations
	Maryland	MD
	Doctor Turner	Dr. Turner
	Franklin Drive	Franklin Dr.

People have used abbreviations for thousands of years. Ancient tombs and coins include abbreviations. Hundreds of years ago, people wrote books by hand. They used abbreviations to save time and space.

Activity F Most of the words in an address are proper nouns. Write these addresses on your paper. Capitalize the proper nouns. Use abbreviations when you can.

1) ms. julie choy
2760 west 86th avenue
apartment #9
westminister, colorado 80030

2) mrs. lenora gomez
2138 whitehall court
crofton, maryland 21114

3) mr. dan connell
923 barnett drive
starkville, mississippi 39759

4) mr. hak lee
6884 johnson way
apartment 11
lanham, maryland 20706

5) doctor aziza alam
nassau professional building
suite 102
nassau, delaware 19969

Write these nouns on your paper. Capitalize the proper nouns.

1) donald duck

2) england

3) river

4) math

5) spring

6) valentine's day

7) ocean

8) park

9) new york city

10) history 101

Number your paper from 11 to 15. Read each of the following sentences. If the sentence is correct, write *Correct* after the number. If the sentence has a capitalization mistake, write the sentence correctly.

11) Emily enjoys her english class at Wilson High School.

12) Armando's favorite holiday is halloween.

13) The school mascot is a leopard.

14) We have relatives who live in the West.

15) Nathan went to Philadelphia to see the liberty bell.

Using What You've Learned

Write your own address. Put each part of your address on a separate line. Be sure to capitalize the proper nouns.

Concrete noun

A word that names something you can see or touch

Abstract noun

A word that names something you cannot see or touch

Nouns can be abstract or concrete. A **concrete noun** is a word that names something you can see or touch. An **abstract noun** is a word that names something you cannot see or touch. You can think about it or talk about it.

EXAMPLE

Concrete Nouns	Abstract Nouns
money	expense
clock	minute
college	education

Activity A Read each pair of nouns. On your paper, write the abstract noun in each pair.

1) day   sun   **4)** justice   judge

2) winter   ice   **5)** bank   security

3) rain   weather

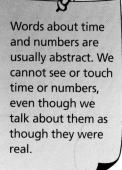

Words about time and numbers are usually abstract. We cannot see or touch time or numbers, even though we talk about them as though they were real.

Abstract nouns are the most difficult nouns to recognize. Two abstract nouns that you will often see in sentences are *kind* and *type*.

Kind is a noun that means a certain group or a certain manner. *Type* is a noun that means a group that has characteristics or features in common.

EXAMPLE

What kind of ice cream do you like?
I like chocolate. (Chocolate is a "kind" of ice cream.)

What type of shoes do you prefer?
I like comfortable shoes. (A characteristic of a certain group of shoes is that they are comfortable.)

I like sandals. (Sandals are a certain type of shoe with open toes and heels.)

Activity B Write these sentences on your paper and underline the nouns.

1) What type of dessert do you like? Sweet or crunchy?

2) What kind of shoes do you prefer?

3) A comedy is my favorite type of movie.

4) What kind of book do you like?

5) There are many kinds of apples.

Activity C Find the nouns in these sentences. Write them on your paper. Identify each one as *abstract* or *concrete*.

1) Nathan wants to buy a car.

2) He has been thinking about the type he would like.

3) Nathan saw an ad in the newspaper.

4) He liked the car, but the price was not right.

5) Maybe next time his luck will be better.

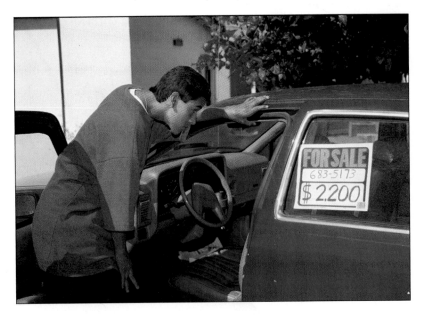

Nathan liked the car, but not the price.

On your paper, write a sentence using each abstract noun. Underline the nouns you use.

1) year

2) happiness

3) bravery

4) springtime

5) energy

6) beauty

7) reading

8) friendship

9) love

10) conversation

Find the nouns in these sentences. Write them on your paper. Identify each one as *abstract* or *concrete*.

11) The party was a total surprise for Michelle.

12) What was Michelle's reaction when she saw the package?

13) She kept looking at her new watch and telling us the time.

14) The cheers of the crowd filled the stadium.

15) The player showed his appreciation by tipping his cap.

On a sheet of paper, write a few sentences about your best friend. Describe his or her characteristics. When you are finished, go back and underline the nouns. Identify each one as *abstract* or *concrete*.

Singular noun

The name of one person, place, thing, or idea

A **singular noun** is the name of one person, place, thing, or idea.

A **plural noun** is the name of more than one person, place, thing, or idea.

Most plural nouns end in *-s*.

Plural noun

The name of more than one person, place, thing, or idea

EXAMPLE	Singular Nouns	Plural Nouns
	flower	flowers
	tree	trees
	mouth	mouths

Activity A Write the plural forms of these nouns on your paper.

1) apple

2) boy

3) toe

4) desk

5) computer

Activity B Find the plural nouns in this paragraph. Write them on your paper.

> Wilson High School has computers for the students to use. They are in the media center. Nathan and his friends go there after school. They use the equipment to write their papers. Nathan also likes to play computer games in his free time.

Add *-es* to nouns that end in *s, z, x, ch,* or *sh* to form the plural.

EXAMPLE	Singular Nouns	Plural Nouns
	pass	passes
	quiz	quizzes
	wish	wishes

When a plural noun ends in -es, the word has an extra syllable. You can hear the difference if you say the singular and plural forms out loud.

Activity C Write the plural form of each of these singular nouns on your paper. Add either -s or -es. Say the plural out loud. You will hear the extra syllable when the plural noun ends in -es.

1) tax   4) printer

2) path   5) dish

3) peach

Nouns That End with *y*
Some nouns that end with *y* become plural by changing the *y* to *i* and adding -es.

Some nouns that end with *y* become plural by adding -s.

Study the two examples. What is the difference between the two groups of words? Say the plural forms in both groups out loud.

EXAMPLE	Change *y* to *i* / Add -es		Add -s	
	city	cities	key	keys
	lady	ladies	alley	alleys
	spy	spies	boy	boys

Here are the rules for making the plural forms of nouns that end with *y*.

Rule 1 The letter before the *y* in *key, alley,* and *boy* is a vowel. These nouns become plural by adding -s.

Rule 2 The letter before the *y* in *city, lady,* and *spy* is a consonant. These nouns become plural by changing the *y* to *i* and adding -es.

Activity D Using the rules you have learned, write the singular and plural forms of these nouns on your paper.

Example **Singular Noun**   **Plural Noun**
monkey   monkeys

1) baby   **4)** turkey

2) toy   **5)** country

3) penny

Nouns That End with *o*

If a noun has a vowel before its final *o,* you add *-s* to make the noun plural.

EXAMPLE	Singular Nouns	Plural Nouns
	radio	radios
	studio	studios
	trio	trios

If a noun has a consonant before its final *o,* you usually add *-es* to make the plural.

EXAMPLE	Singular Nouns	Plural Nouns
	potato	potatoes
	echo	echoes

To make the plural forms of many musical words that end with *o,* you add *-s.*

EXAMPLE	Singular Nouns	Plural Nouns
	piano	pianos
	solo	solos

Activity E Complete each sentence using the plural form of the noun shown in parentheses. Write the plural noun on your paper.

1) Emily bought ____ at the store. (tomato)

2) Angela went to a store that sold ____. (radio)

3) Nathan's mother serves ____ every night at dinner. (potato)

4) At the beginning of the song, the ____ sang alone. (soprano)

5) Janet Evans is one of Angela's ____. (hero)

Nouns That End with *f* or *fe*
Nouns that end with *f* or *fe* often sound different in their plural forms. Say these words out loud. Listen to how they sound.

   cliff   cliffs   roof   roofs

You form the plural of some nouns that end with *f* or *fe* by adding -*s*. You form the plural of others by changing the *f* or *fe* to *v* and adding -*s* or -*es*.

EXAMPLE	Singular Nouns	Plural Nouns
	safe	safes
	life	lives
	belief	beliefs
	leaf	leaves

Activity F Say each word in the list out loud. Then write its plural form on your paper.

1) calf   4) knife

2) thief   5) chief

3) chef

Irregular Plurals

Sometimes the singular and plural forms of a noun are the same.

EXAMPLE	Singular Nouns	Plural Nouns
	one deer	a herd of deer
	one sheep	many sheep
	a trout	a school of trout

Activity G Find the spelling mistakes in this paragraph. Write the correct spellings of the words on your paper.

> Armando and his family drove out to the country. They went past a field of deers. They saw several farms with flocks of sheeps and herds of cows. They stopped at a lake in a state park to fish. Armando caught three trouts. Everyone enjoyed the day.

Some plural nouns are spelled very differently from their singular forms. You change letters in the words or add other letters to make the words plural.

EXAMPLE	Singular Nouns	Plural Nouns
	child	children
	foot	feet
	ox	oxen
	mouse	mice
	man	men

Activity H On your paper, write the plural form of each of these nouns in a sentence.

1) child   **4)** tooth

2) woman   **5)** mouse

3) foot

Write the plural forms of these nouns on your paper.

1) goose   **4)** lady

2) mouth   **5)** deer

3) monkey   **6)** ox

Each of these sentences has one mistake. Find the mistake. Then write the sentence correctly on your paper.

7) Evans won four individual gold medales in the Olympics.

8) Mrs. Langston says we will have to make several speechs next semester.

9) One of her beliefes is that speaking in front of an audience is good for students.

10) Emily sings with the altoes in the choir.

Spelling Builder

Plural Nouns

If you write about more than one thing, you need to use the plural form of the word. Most plurals are spelled by adding -s or -es to the words. The following hints can help you spell the plural forms of most nouns.

- Add -s to most nouns: *rule—rules.*
- For nouns that end with *s, z, x, sh,* and *ch,* add -es: *fox—foxes.*
- For nouns that end with a consonant before a *y,* change the *y* to *i* and add -es: *country—countries.*
- For some nouns that end with *f* or *fe,* change the *f* or *fe* to *v* and add -es: *leaf—leaves.*

Write the plural forms of these nouns.

     penny   wish   house   life

More About Plural Nouns

Plurals of Proper Nouns

We form the plurals of most proper nouns by adding -s to the singular forms. If a proper noun ends in *s* or *z*, add -es to make it plural.

EXAMPLE	Singular Proper Nouns	Plural Proper Nouns
	the Jones family	the Joneses
	Hernandez	the Hernandezes

Activity A Make each of these family names plural and use the plural form in a sentence.

1) Williams

2) Martinez

3) Choy

4) Weiss

5) Okada

Activity B Fix the mistakes in this paragraph. Write the plural forms of the words in bold on your paper.

The **Wozniak** are having a party. They invited all their neighbors. The **Takahara** are bringing a noodle dish. The **Vargas** said they would bring enchiladas. The **Davis** plan to make a huge vegetable salad. Music will be provided by the **Perez.** They will play guitars and sing. Everyone is looking forward to the party.

Plurals of Numbers, Dates, and Letters

Make a number, date, or letter plural by adding -s.

> **EXAMPLE**
> The 1990s were years of great changes in technology.
>
> Angela got two As on her report card.
>
> Several papers got scores in the 90s.

Activity C Find the mistake in each sentence. Write the correct word on your paper.

1) In the 1960's the Beatles were popular.

2) Last semester Meg got two C's on her report card.

3) The teacher hoped that all the students' test scores would be in the 70's or higher.

4) Put all of the B's and C's in a column.

5) I know my ABCS.

Activity D Fix the mistakes in this paragraph. Write the plural forms of the words in bold on your paper.

My grandmother was born in the **1940.** She went to college in the **1960.** She was in her **20** then. In college she made mostly **A** and **B.** She says she had a lot of fun in college. Now she is in her **60** and still has a lot of fun.

Find the mistake in each sentence. Write the sentence correctly on your paper.

1) Armando and Nathan are both hoping for A's on their report cards.

2) "The Hernandezs are having a party," said Armando.

3) The music teacher is teaching them songs from the 1960's.

4) The boys packed a cooler of sandwichs for the fishing trip.

5) They met the O'Hara's at the pond.

On your paper, write the plural form of each of these words in a sentence.

6) Williams

7) 1920

8) Hudson

9) quiz

10) ABC

Possessive noun

A word that shows ownership or a relationship between two things

A **possessive noun** shows ownership or a relationship between two things. It always has an **apostrophe** ('). An apostrophe is a punctuation mark. It is often used to indicate that a noun is possessive.

EXAMPLE

Where are Angela's goggles?
(The goggles belong to Angela.)

Angela's swim team won its meet.
(Angela is part of the team.)

The team's score is 2.
(The team has a score of 2.)

Apostrophe

A punctuation mark that indicates a noun is possessive

Rules for Forming Possessives

Rule 1 Make a singular noun possessive by adding an apostrophe and -s ('s).

EXAMPLE

Angela's team   Nathan's guitar

the school's motto   the computer's keyboard

Rule 2 When a singular noun ends in s, add an apostrophe and -s ('s).

EXAMPLE

the boss's day off   Gail Russ's book

Rule 3 Make a plural noun possessive by adding only an apostrophe (').

EXAMPLE

the trains' routes   the trumpets' sounds

Rule 4 If a plural noun does not end in *s*, add an apostrophe and *-s* (*'s*).

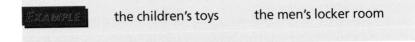

EXAMPLE   the children's toys   the men's locker room

Activity A Read the sentences. Write the words in bold on your paper. Add an apostrophe if the word shows ownership. If the word is plural, write *plural* next to it.

1) All of the teams met at the **citys** new stadium.

2) The **swimmers** were there for the meet.

3) Everyone on **Angelas** team was ready for the competition.

4) The **coachs** last words were to try their best.

5) The winner of the meet will go to the state **finals.**

Activity B On a sheet of paper, make the four columns shown here. Write the headings at the top of the columns. Write the correct forms of the nouns in the columns. Use the information in Lessons 4 and 5 to help you with plurals.

Singular	Singular Possessive	Plural	Plural Possessive
1) team			
2) wolf			
3) man			
4) Jones			
5) city			

Use an apostrophe in phrases such as *one dollar's worth* or *a week's vacation*. If the word is plural and ends in *s*, add only an apostrophe.

EXAMPLE	Singular	Plural
	one cent's worth	ten cents' worth
	a month's vacation	two months' vacation

Activity C Read each pair of sentences. Choose the correct sentence in each pair and write it on your paper.

1) a) Nathan likes to put in his two cents' worth.

   b) Nathan likes to put in his two cent's worth.

2) a) Please give me two dollar's worth of stamps.

   b) Please give me two dollars' worth of stamps.

3) a) You will only have a minute's wait.

   b) You will only have a minutes' wait.

4) a) The week's activities were posted on the bulletin board.

   b) The weeks activities were posted on the bulletin board.

5) a) The snow caused an hours delay.

   b) The snow caused an hour's delay.

Recognizing Plurals and Possessives

Look carefully at the two words in red type below. How are they different? What does each word mean?

EXAMPLE	Plural	There were six teams at the meet.
	Possessive	The team's prize was a trophy.

Activity D Read Angela's report. Find the plural nouns. Write them on your paper in one column. Then find the possessive nouns. Write them in a second column. The first two sentences are done for you.

The Swim Meet
by Angela Choy

The school's most recent swim meet was last Friday. The swimmers' nerves were on edge. Everyone had high hopes about doing well. Teams from several schools met in the school's stadium. Our coaches were very supportive. They told us to do our best. There were several events. Our team's best event is the relay. We have good individual swimmers also. Our goal was to win the meet and go to the state finals. The referee's whistle signaled the start of the first race. The swimmers dove into the water. I could write many stories about the exciting match-ups. The short answer is that Wilson's team won. We are going to the state finals!

Plurals	Possessives
nerves	school's
	swimmers'

Read each pair of sentences. Pick the correct one and write it on your paper.

1) a) Where are Armando's running shoes?

   b) Where are Armandos running shoes?

2) a) All of the team's were ready for the swim meet.

   b) All of the teams were ready for the swim meet.

3) a) My neighbor's dog ran away.

   b) My neighbors dog ran away.

4) a) Learning to proofread improved the students' grades.

   b) Learning to proofread improved the students grades.

5) a) Mrs. Langston looked everywhere for her car keys'.

   b) Mrs. Langston looked everywhere for her car keys.

6) a) Everyone had high hopes at the swim meet.

   b) Everyone had high hope's at the swim meet.

7) a) A good writer makes sure the words are spelled right.

   b) A good writer makes sure the words' are spelled right.

8) a) There was cheering in Wilson Highs locker room.

   b) There was cheering in Wilson High's locker room.

9) a) Emily's job is at a music store.

   b) Emilys job is at a music store.

10) a) Her hours are from 3:00 to 6:00 P.M.

   b) Her hour's are from 3:00 to 6:00 P.M.

A Noun Can Be a Title

Books, songs, movies, and stories are some of the things that can have a title. A title is a proper noun. Capitalize the first word and all of the important words in a title.

Writing Tip
When you write a title on your paper, underline it. In a book or other printed material, a title is often set in italic type. See the examples of italic type on this page.

EXAMPLE		
	Song	"America, the Beautiful"
	Movie	*Star Wars*
	Book	*The Red Pony*
	Play	*Romeo and Juliet*
	Story	"To Build a Fire"

Underline the title of a movie, book, magazine, opera, or play.

Put quotation marks around the title of a song, poem, or short story.

Activity A Write each of these titles on your paper. Capitalize the first word and all of the important words. Underline or use quotation marks for the titles.

1) the sound of music

2) the wizard of oz

3) the perfect storm

4) there's no business like show business

5) beauty and the beast

A person's name is a proper noun. People also can have titles. Capitalize a person's title.

EXAMPLE	Rev. Robert Stetler	Dr. Jacquelyn Montoya
	Mr. Hak Lee	Professor Eve Rice

On your paper, write sentences using these nouns and titles. Be sure to capitalize proper nouns and underline the titles.

1) mrs. langston

2) the pigman by paul zindel

3) new york giants

4) roots by alex haley

5) the lion king

6) independence hall

7) mr. thomas

Write these sentences on your paper. Capitalize any proper nouns. Underline or use quotation marks for the titles.

8) Emily is doing her book report on the invisible man, a novel by ralph ellison.

9) My favorite play by william shakespeare is hamlet.

10) One of the most popular short stories is the lady, or the tiger? by frank stockton.

11) Home alone was a hit movie in 1990.

12) Our dentist's name is dr. richard harp.

13) Dr. albert einstein taught at princeton university.

14) The star-spangled banner is hard to sing.

15) Well-known weekly magazines are time and newsweek.

Where to Find It

Library Catalog

Suppose you wanted to find information about dogs in the library. Information appears in many different forms in a library. Of course, there are books. There are also magazines, videos, and special reference books on many subjects.

You can find the information you need by using a card catalog. The catalog includes entries for each item in the library, filed by subject, author, and title. Today most library card catalogs are online. You use a library computer terminal to search for information. You type in a subject, author, or title. The online catalog lists the library resources that match your request. For example, you might choose *subject* from the computer menu and type in *dogs.* A list of library resources about dogs will appear on the computer screen. Each entry will show where to find the resource in the library.

You can also search by author or title. However, you will probably most often search by subject. To conduct a search by subject, use a common noun or a proper noun. A search of the subject *pets* may give you hundreds of sources. You might narrow the subject further to *dogs* and even further to a breed, such as *collie.*

Title Keywords		New Search
Subject Keywords	collie	Additional Searches
Author (Last Name, First Name)		Previous Searches
Search Clear Close		Guided Search

1) What subject would you like to research? Write the name of the subject on your paper. Tell whether you have used a common noun or a proper noun to describe your subject.

2) Here are three general subjects: weather, sports, birds. Write two more specific subjects for each. Choosing more specific subjects can help narrow your search when you are using a library catalog.

3) Use a library catalog to find three sources of information on the subject you chose in exercise 1 above. Write the titles and authors of the sources. Be sure to use capitalization correctly.

Writing Project

Use Nouns to Create an Advertisement

Part A Find the nouns in the public service announcement below. Identify each noun as abstract or concrete, common or proper, and singular or plural. Write these four headings on your paper: *Nouns, Abstract/Concrete, Common/Proper, Singular/Plural.* List each noun under the correct heading.

Nouns	Abstract/Concrete	Common/Proper	Singular/Plural

Part B Choose an interesting advertisement in a newspaper or magazine. Find the nouns in the advertisement. Identify each noun as abstract or concrete, common or proper, and singular or plural. Write these four headings on your paper: *Nouns, Abstract/Concrete, Common/Proper, Singular/Plural.* List each noun under the correct heading.

Part C In a group or individually, think up a name for a new singing group or band. Design an advertisement to promote this new group. Find the nouns in your advertisement. Identify each one as abstract or concrete, common or proper, and singular or plural. Write these four headings on your paper: *Nouns, Abstract/Concrete, Common/Proper, Singular/Plural.* List each noun under the correct heading.

ENCOURAGE YOUR KID'S HABIT.

KIDS NEED SOMETHING BETTER TO DO THAN DRUGS. LIKE SPORTS. DANCE. OR MUSIC. BECAUSE GOOD THINGS CAN BE HABIT-FORMING, TOO. SO GET THEM INTO A GOOD HABIT. TODAY. OR THEY MAY GET INTO A VERY BAD ONE.

Office of National Drug Control Policy
Partnership for a Drug-Free America®

For more information, visit our websites at
www.projectknow.com, www.drugfreeamerica.org or call 1-800-788-2800.

WORD BANK

abbreviation

abstract noun

apostrophe

collective noun

common noun

compound noun

concrete noun

hyphen

noun

plural noun

possessive noun

proper noun

singular noun

Part A On a sheet of paper, write the correct word or words from the Word Bank to complete each sentence.

1) A _____ is a word that names a person, place, thing, or idea.

2) A _____ is the name of a particular person, place, thing, or idea and is always capitalized.

3) An _____ is the short form of a word.

4) A _____ names only one person, place, thing, or idea.

5) An _____ names something you cannot see or touch but can think or talk about.

6) The name of more than one person, place, thing, or idea is a _____.

7) A _____ is made from two words.

8) A _____ is the name of a general type of person, place, thing, or idea.

9) An _____ indicates a noun is possessive.

10) A _____ names a group of people, places, or things.

11) A short dash between parts of a word is called a _____.

12) A _____ names something you can see or touch.

13) A _____ indicates ownership or a relationship between two things.

Part B On a sheet of paper, write the nouns in these sentences.

14) Emily wants to ride her bike.

15) It is a lovely day to take a trip.

16) Emily decides to take a friend along.

17) Angela says she will meet Emily at her house.

Part C Write these sentences on a sheet of paper. Capitalize the proper nouns.

18) On saturday armando visits aunt edna.

19) She just moved to town from houston, texas.

20) She used to teach at the university of florida.

21) She was a professor of american history.

Part D On a sheet of paper, make the four columns shown here. Write the headings at the top of the columns. Write the correct forms of the nouns in the columns.

Singular	Singular Possessive	Plural	Plural Possessive
22) lady			
23) wolf			
24) deer			
25) child			

Test-Taking Tip If you know you will have to define certain terms on a test, write the term on one side of a card. Write its definition on the other side. Use the cards to test yourself or work with a partner.

Using Pronouns in Sentences

When we speak or write, we identify the person or thing that we are talking about. The word we use to name the person or thing is a noun. After we say or write the noun, we replace the name with a pronoun.

The photograph on the opposite page shows a school of Pacific double-saddle butterfly fish. When writing or talking about this school of fish, we might describe them using both nouns and pronouns. For example: This photograph shows a large school of Pacific double-saddle butterfly fish. *They* all have yellow, black, and white stripes. The word *they* is a pronoun.

In Chapter 3, you will learn about pronouns and how to use them in sentences.

Goals for Learning

▶ To identify pronouns in sentences

▶ To identify the antecedents of pronouns

▶ To identify the type of pronoun such as personal, interrogative, indefinite, relative, and demonstrative

▶ To identify correct usage of pronouns in sentences

▶ To write contractions with pronouns

What Is a Pronoun?

Pronoun

A word that replaces a noun

A **pronoun** is a word that replaces a noun.

> EXAMPLE   Armando is a senior. He writes for the school
> newspaper. His column appears in every issue.

The pronoun *he* replaces the proper noun *Armando*. The pronoun *his* replaces the possessive noun *Armando's*. The noun that the pronoun replaces is called the **antecedent.**

Antecedent

The noun that a pronoun replaces

Activity A Write each underlined pronoun on your paper. Then write the antecedent that the pronoun has replaced.

Example   Emily is a student.   <u>She</u> is in the band.
Pronoun—she   *Antecedent—Emily*

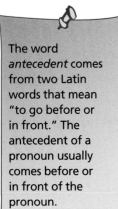

The word *antecedent* comes from two Latin words that mean "to go before or in front." The antecedent of a pronoun usually comes before or in front of the pronoun.

Armando and Joe are both seniors. <u>They</u> are friends. Mrs. Benson is one of <u>their</u> teachers. <u>She</u> teaches journalism. Brittany Francis is also in the class. Joe has known <u>her</u> for years. <u>They</u> were in the same elementary school.

Why are pronouns important? Without pronouns, we would have to repeat the same nouns over and over again.

> EXAMPLE   Nathan said that Nathan was going to call
> Nathan's mother.
>
> Nathan said that he was going to call his mother.

Activity B List the underlined words on your paper. Next to each noun, write a pronoun that could replace it.

Armando looked for <u>Armando's</u> new class. Armando had signed up for a journalism class. <u>Armando</u> walked up to the second floor. In the class, Armando found an old friend. <u>Armando and Armando's friend</u> had both signed up for the class.

Find the seven pronouns in the paragraph. List them in order on your paper. Write the antecedent next to each one. Remember that the antecedent is the noun that the pronoun replaces.

1)   Armando is on the soccer team. He asked Angela and Nathan to come to his game on Tuesday. They both came and cheered loudly for Armando. He scored one goal. After the game, they all went to Tony's to celebrate. Nathan was glad he had come to the game. Angela said she had a good time too.

Write each underlined pronoun on your paper. Then write the antecedent next to each one.

2) Emily and Angela like school, and <u>they</u> enjoy history class.

3) Emily was glad that <u>she</u> had studied for the test.

4) Angela and I studied together, so <u>we</u> did well on the test.

5) Since Mr. Thomas just gave a test, <u>he</u> will start a new unit next week.

Vocabulary Builder

			W	
			O	
S	M	A	R	T	S
			D	

Root Words

The root word *cast* first appeared in the 13th century. The word means "to make something move or to send something forth."

Here are four words that contain the root word *cast*: *forecast, newscast, outcast, telecast*. Write their meanings on your paper. Then check the accuracy of your meanings with the definitions in a dictionary.

Find three other words that contain the root word *cast*. Write the meanings of the words on your paper. Use a dictionary to check your meanings.

Personal pronoun

A pronoun that refers to a person or a thing

Personal pronouns refer to people or things. They refer to the person who is speaking and to the person who is spoken to. They also refer to the person or thing that is being talked about.

A **first-person pronoun** refers to the person who is speaking.

> EXAMPLE I am ready.

First-person pronoun

A pronoun that refers to the person who is speaking

A **second-person pronoun** refers to the person you are speaking to.

> EXAMPLE You are ready.

Second-person pronoun

A pronoun that refers to the person who is being spoken to

A **third-person pronoun** refers to the person or thing you are talking about.

> EXAMPLE He is ready.   She is ready.   It is ready.

Third-person pronoun

A pronoun that refers to the person or thing that is being talked about

Personal pronouns can be singular or plural. A singular pronoun refers to one person or thing. A plural pronoun refers to more than one person or thing.

> EXAMPLE **Singular** I am happy.   She is happy.
>
> **Plural** We are happy.   They are happy.

We use personal pronouns in different ways in a sentence.
          As the **subject** of a sentence
          As the **object** of a verb or preposition
          As a **possessive** that shows ownership

Depending on how it is used in a sentence, a personal pronoun may change its form.

EXAMPLE

He is in my math class.	*He* is the subject of the sentence.
Emily knows him.	*Him* is the object of the verb.
That is his desk.	*His* is possessive.

Here is a chart showing all of the personal pronouns.

Personal Pronouns			
	Subject	**Object**	**Possessive**
Singular			
First Person	I	me	my, mine
Second Person	you	you	your, yours
Third Person	he, she, it	him, her, it	his, her, hers, its
Plural			
First Person	we	us	our, ours
Second Person	you	you	your, yours
Third Person	they	them	their, theirs

Activity A Identify these pronouns. Write them on your paper. Use the chart above.

1) third person, plural, subject

2) second person, singular, object

3) second person, plural, subject

4) third person, singular, object

5) first person, plural, object

Possessive pronouns replace possessive nouns. The possessive noun is the antecedent of the possessive pronoun. Possessive pronouns never have an apostrophe.

> **EXAMPLE**
>
> Armando's baseball cap is blue and white.
> His baseball cap is blue and white.
> The antecedent of *his* is *Armando's*.
>
> John brought his own baseball bat to the game.
> "Where is yours?" he asked Armando.
> The antecedent of *yours* is *Armando's bat*.

Activity B On your paper, make a list of the personal pronouns in these sentences. Next to each pronoun, write its antecedent.

1) Mrs. Benson says, "Students, please listen to me."

2) Emily takes good care of her clarinet.

3) Angela tells the swim coach, "I want to swim in the Olympics someday."

4) Mr. Thomas asks Joe, "Is this book yours?"

5) Armando left a sketchbook at practice, but it was still there when he went back.

Writing Tip

Always capitalize the pronoun *I*.

Activity C Write the sentences on your paper. Use a pronoun to replace the underlined word or words.

Example   Emily works at the store. <u>Emily</u> enjoys her job.
Emily works at the store. She enjoys her job.

1) Angela hangs up <u>Angela's</u> bathing suit to dry.

2) Mrs. Young says to Nathan, "<u>Nathan</u> should get ready for school."

3) The coach asks Armando, "Is this <u>Armando's</u> soccer ball?"

4) Emily asks Mr. Jackson, "Would you like <u>Meg and me</u> to pass out the sheet music?"

5) Meg is in the band. <u>Meg</u> plays the saxophone.

We make **compound personal pronouns** by adding -*self* to singular personal pronouns and -*selves* to plural personal pronouns.

-*self* Pronouns		
	Singular	**Plural**
First Person	myself	ourselves
Second Person	yourself	yourselves
Third Person	himself, herself, itself	themselves

Activity D On your paper, write the -*self* pronouns in these sentences. Next to each one, write *singular* or *plural*.

1) Angela's boss at the YMCA makes the work schedule himself.

2) As he always says, "Someone has to be there because the pool doesn't open itself."

3) Angela's students push themselves to swim better and faster.

4) The students say, "If we practice by ourselves, maybe we can be as good as Angela!"

5) When they say that, Angela feels proud of herself.

Write the antecedent of each underlined pronoun.

1) "I am playing tennis for a USTA team," said Julie.

2) Julie said, "The United States Tennis Association has ranked me as a 3.5."

3) "The USTA has a ranking system so that I can compete with people at my level," Julie added.

4) "It is a very good system."

5) "John has a 3.5 ranking too. We sometimes play doubles against other pairs," said Julie.

Write the personal pronouns in these sentences on your paper. Write the antecedent next to each pronoun.

6) Armando saved his allowance for three months.

7) Armando and Nathan went to the sports store. They wanted to look at tennis rackets.

8) The manager greeted them. Armando asked, "Do you have any tennis rackets?"

9) "This racket is my favorite," said the manager. "Would you like to try it?"

10) Armando swung the racket and said, "It is just like my father's!"

11) Nathan asked Armando, "Did you buy your last racket too?"

12) "No," said Armando, "my parents bought the racket for me."

13) Armando asked Nathan, "Do you like this racket?"

14) Armando paid for the racket with his own money.

15) Nathan looked at Armando's new racket and said, "It looks ready to go!"

Relative pronoun

A pronoun such as who, whom, whose, which, that, *and* what

The **relative pronouns** are *who, whom, whose, which, that,* and *what.*

> *Who, whom,* and *whose* refer to people.
>
> *Which* and *what* refer to things.
>
> *That* refers to people or things.

Activity A Write these sentences on your paper. Circle the relative pronouns.

1) Emily likes musicians who play jazz.

2) The clarinet that Emily bought was expensive.

3) Emily's mother, who was a flute player, enjoys classical music.

4) She says it is music that speaks to her heart.

5) Emily says the same thing about jazz, which is very different from classical music.

The word *jazz* was first used in 1913 as the name of a kind of American music that developed from African American spirituals and folk music.

Emily enjoys playing her clarinet in the band.

Like personal pronouns, relative pronouns have antecedents. Remember, an antecedent is the noun that the pronoun replaces.

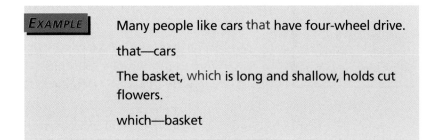

EXAMPLE

Many people like cars that have four-wheel drive.

that—cars

The basket, which is long and shallow, holds cut flowers.

which—basket

Activity B Write the relative pronouns in these sentences on your paper. Write the antecedent next to each pronoun.

1) The man who owns the music store sells CDs and audiocassettes.

2) There is the customer whom Emily met last week.

3) Emily wants the book that is on the table.

4) Emily's dog, which is a poodle, likes to eat noodles.

5) Her dog prefers Thai food, which is very spicy.

Compound relative pronoun

A pronoun such as whoever, whomever, whichever, *and* whatever

---

The **compound relative pronouns** are *whoever, whomever, whichever,* and *whatever.*

    Whoever and *whomever* refer to people.

    Whichever and *whatever* refer to things.

The antecedent of a compound relative pronoun is not stated in the sentence. The antecedent is a group of people or things that the listener or reader knows.

EXAMPLE

"Whoever wants to read this book may borrow it," said the teacher.

"Blue shoes or black shoes—choose whichever you want," said Emily's mother.

Activity C Write the compound relative pronouns in these sentences on your paper.

1) Here are several books. Choose whichever you want for a book report.

2) Do whatever you think should be done.

3) Invite whomever you want to the party.

4) I have lots of CDs. Take whichever you like best.

5) Whoever wants this sandwich can have it.

Activity D On a sheet of paper, make the two columns shown below. Label one column *Personal Pronouns*. Label the other column *Relative Pronouns*. Write each of the following pronouns in the correct column.

Personal Pronouns	Relative Pronouns
we	whose

1) which

2) mine

3) who

4) whatever

5) you

6) its

7) that

8) he

9) herself

10) us

11) whom

12) me

13) she

14) what

15) your

Make a list of the relative pronouns in these sentences on your paper. Write the antecedent next to each pronoun.

1) Nathan wants the new stamps that the post office just issued.

2) The bandleader is Mr. Jackson, who played the trumpet in college.

3) Emily went to the library, which is next to the post office.

4) Angela, whose bookbag is on the table, is late for school.

5) She is the woman whom I talked to in the office.

6) He wants to buy the CD that he saw last week.

Write the correct pronoun on your paper.

7) You may read (whichever, whoever) of these books you like.

8) He is the teacher (whose, which) class I enjoy the most.

9) Otto is the dog (what, that) I have had since I was born.

10) Angela gives lessons to children (who, whom) don't know how to swim.

Write the compound relative pronouns in these sentences on your paper.

11) Whoever made that mess should clean it up.

12) Please do whatever you can to help us.

13) We will ask whomever we want to the concert.

14) You may have whichever of the desserts you like.

15) Whoever answered the phone sounded excited.

Pronouns That Ask Questions

Interrogative pronoun

A pronoun that asks a question

The **interrogative pronouns** are *who, whom, whose, which,* and *what.* They are called interrogative pronouns because they are used to ask questions.

> Who is planning the party?
>
> Whom did you call?
>
> Whose is this hat?
>
> Which of these movies do you like?
>
> What is your telephone number?

To *interrogate* means to examine by asking questions. When police officers interrogate suspects, they ask the suspects questions about where they were and what they were doing at the time of the crime.

Some interrogative pronouns can also be used as relative pronouns. *Who, which,* and *what* are interrogative pronouns only when they ask a question.

EXAMPLE

| **Interrogative** | Who is going to the party? |
| **Relative** | Greg asked a girl who is in his class. |

You can use an interrogative pronoun to ask a question directly or indirectly.

EXAMPLE

Direct question	What are you wearing to the party?
Indirect questions	He asked what you are wearing to the party.
	Tell me what you are wearing to the party.

Activity A Write the interrogative pronouns in these sentences on your paper.

1) Which is your favorite holiday?

2) Who is your best friend?

3) What is the answer to the question?

4) Which do you prefer—bagels or muffins?

5) Do you know who will be at the party?

Unlike personal and relative pronouns, interrogative pronouns do not have antecedents that can be stated. Their "antecedents" are the answers to the questions they ask.

Who refers to a person or persons.
> **Who** is your swimming coach?
> **Who** are the teams in the Super Bowl this year?

What refers to things, places, or ideas.
> **What** is the name of your town?
> **What** is your favorite fruit?

Which can refer to people or things. Use *which* when the answer is a choice between two or more definite things.
> **Which** of the teams will win the game?
> **Which** will you choose for dessert—cake or ice cream?

Whose is a possessive pronoun. Use *whose* to show possession or ownership.
> **Whose** is this car?

You can find the answers to questions such as "What is the capital of Denmark?" in an almanac, a geographical dictionary, an atlas, or an encyclopedia.

Activity B Write the correct pronoun on your paper.

1) (Which, What) of the books is longer?

2) (Which, What) is the capital of Denmark?

3) (Which, What) of these movies would you rather see tonight?

4) (Who, Whose) knows how to speak Chinese?

5) Do you know (who, whose) left me this note?

Write the interrogative pronouns in these sentences on your paper.

1) What does Angela do after school on Fridays?

2) Who said, "I have a dream"?

3) Whose was the big blue boat?

4) What did Mr. Thomas just say?

5) Which of the fruits is your favorite?

On your paper, write the interrogative pronoun in each question. Then identify the question as *direct* or *indirect*.

6) Who else is on the baseball team?

7) She asked which of the books he liked best.

8) Whose was the science project with the plants?

9) Tell me what the names of Emily's pets are.

10) I know who Neeru can call for help with her homework.

Write the pronouns in these sentences on your paper. Next to each pronoun, write whether it is *personal*, *relative*, or *interrogative*.

11) Neeru is a new student who goes to Wilson High School.

12) Which is her hometown—Bombay or Calcutta?

13) She lived in Calcutta, which is in India.

14) Who is her homeroom teacher?

15) She is in Mrs. Benson's class with Emily and me.

Demonstrative pronoun

A pronoun that points out a particular person or thing

Demonstrative pronouns point out particular persons and things. The demonstrative pronouns are *this, these, that*, and *those*.

This and *that* are used with one person or thing. *These* and *those* are used with more than one person or thing.

EXAMPLE		
Singular	This is my house.	
Plural	These are my pencils.	
Singular	That is my high school.	
Plural	Those are my cousins.	

This and *these* point out people and things that are close by.

EXAMPLE	
	This is a pen I have in my hand.
	These are new shoes I have on my feet.

That and *those* point out people and things that are farther away.

EXAMPLE	
	That is my friend Angela standing over there.
	Those are my books by the door.

Activity A Write these sentences on your paper. Circle the demonstrative pronouns.

1) Is that your room?

2) No, this is my room.

3) This is my desk.

4) Are those your books?

5) Yes, these are my books.

Activity B Write the correct pronoun on your paper.

1) Was (this, that) a shooting star that I saw?

2) Is (this, that) your sheet music that I have, Emily?

3) (These, Those) are my favorite rings. I wear them all the time.

4) Here are your notebooks. (These, Those) over there are mine.

5) I found a pen. Was Nathan looking for (this, that)?

Activity C Write the demonstrative pronouns in these sentences on your paper. Next to each one, write whether it is *singular* or *plural.*

1) Is this the right assignment for history class?

2) These are roses from Mrs. Choy's garden.

3) Is that the shirt Armando wore to practice yesterday?

4) This is the auditorium where the Drama Club performs.

5) Are those Emily's clarinet reeds?

Activity D Write a sentence using each of the demonstrative pronouns *that, this, these,* and *those.* Try to write both statements and questions.

Armando scored two goals during soccer practice.

Write the demonstrative pronouns in these sentences on your paper.

1) Whose paper is this?

2) That is a very ugly car.

3) These are the football team's new uniforms.

4) Do you know if this is Angela's jacket?

5) Those are my parents standing by the door.

Write the pronouns in these sentences on your paper. Next to each pronoun, write whether it is *personal, relative, interrogative,* or *demonstrative.*

6) Which is the lane that Angela will be swimming in?

7) Mrs. Benson, who teaches journalism, is our advisor.

8) Is this Nathan's book? No, that is his over there.

9) Tell me which of the movies you liked best.

10) Armando's dog, which sleeps under his bed, snores loudly.

Spelling Builder

Doubling Consonants

Read these words: *hottest, hopping.* Note the double consonants before the *-est* and *-ing* endings. The endings *-est* and *-ing* begin with vowels. To add an ending that begins with a vowel to a consonant-vowel-consonant word, first double the final consonant. Then add the ending.

Add *-est* to *wet* and *red.* Add *-ed* and *-ing* to *tap* and *jog.* Use each new word in a sentence.

Indefinite pronoun

A pronoun that does not refer to a specific person or thing

Indefinite pronouns do not refer to specific people or things. So they do not have clear antecedents.

Most indefinite pronouns are singular. A few are plural.

Indefinite Pronouns		Plural
Singular		**Plural**
another	neither	all
anybody	nobody	both
anyone	no one	few
anything	nothing	many
each	one	several
each other	one another	
either	somebody	
everybody	someone	
everyone	something	
everything		

Writing Tip

To help you remember that indefinite pronouns such as *everybody* and *something* are singular, think of them as two words: *every body* and *some thing. Body* and *thing* are singular words.

Activity A Find the indefinite pronouns in these sentences. Write them on your paper.

1) Everyone at Wilson High School attended the band concert.

2) "I see someone I know," said Angela.

3) Angela and Emily waved at each other.

4) Many of the songs were familiar.

5) Everybody cheered for the band.

An indefinite pronoun can be the antecedent for another pronoun. Use plural possessive pronouns with plural indefinite pronouns. Use singular possessive pronouns with singular indefinite pronouns.

EXAMPLE   Both brought their books.

Each of the girls has her book.

One of the boys lost his book.

When you don't know if the person is male or female, you may use *his or her* or you can rewrite the sentence using plural pronouns.

EXAMPLE   Everyone played his or her own instrument.

All of the students played their own instruments.

Activity B Write the correct pronoun on your paper.

1) Everyone should turn in (his or her, their) paper.

2) Several gave (his or her, their) parents the newsletter.

3) Everyone must take off (his or her, their) shoes.

4) Few could identify (his or her, their) bags.

5) Someone left (his or her, their) lights on.

Activity C Use each of these pronouns in a sentence. Underline all the pronouns in your sentences. Use two underlines for the indefinite pronouns.

1) all   **4)** each

2) someone   **5)** several

3) everything

Find the indefinite pronouns in these sentences. Write them on your paper.

1) There is nothing I like more than a good movie.

2) Somebody is at the door.

3) Is anyone listening to me?

4) Neither knows the answer.

Find the pronouns in these paragraphs and write them on your paper. Next to each pronoun, write whether it is *personal, relative, interrogative, indefinite,* or *demonstrative.*

5)   After school, everyone likes to go to Tony's. Emily enjoys seeing many of her friends who meet there. They think that Tony's has the best French fries in town.

"What can I get you?" asks the waitress.

Emily can't decide between French fries and a milkshake. "I would like a vanilla shake, please," she says.

"Those are great," everyone tells her.

"What did you order, Neeru?" asks Emily.

Neeru points to a picture of an ice cream sundae on the menu and says, "I asked for that."

Nathan asks, "Which of the 25 flavors of ice cream do you like best?"

Neeru tells him that chocolate is her favorite flavor.

Using What You've Learned

Write a set of directions for working together successfully in a group. Use as many indefinite pronouns as you can. Make sure any possessive pronouns agree with their antecedents.

Contraction

Two words made into one by replacing one or more letters with an apostrophe

In Chapter 2, you learned how to use an apostrophe (') to show possession in nouns.

> **EXAMPLE**   Emily's dog   The students' instruments

We also use an apostrophe in a contraction. A **contraction** is two words made into one by leaving out one or more letters. An apostrophe is used in place of the missing letter(s). All of these contractions are made from a pronoun and a verb.

Common Contractions	
I'd = I would, I had	who's = who is
I'll = I will	we'll = we will
I'm = I am	we're = we are
I've = I have	we'd = we would, we had
you'll = you will	we've = we have
you're = you are	they'd = they would, they had
you've = you have	they're = they are
he's = he is, he has	they've = they have
she's = she is, she has	that's = that is
it's = it is, it has	what's = what is
let's = let us	

Writing Tip

We use contractions in informal writing, such as a friendly letter or a note to a friend. We also use contractions in everyday speaking. But we don't use contractions in formal writing.

Activity A Find the contractions in this paragraph. Write each contraction as two words on your paper.

I'd like to tell you an interesting story about something that's important. It's about the invention of the radio. We'd not have a radio without the invention of the microphone and the Audion tube. You're probably asking, "What's an Audion tube?" Well, I'll tell you. It's a tube that makes electrical impulses louder and sends them through the air. Without Audion tubes, radio would be impossible.

Remember that a contraction has an apostrophe to stand for missing letters. Find the contractions in these sentences and write them on your paper. Then rewrite each contraction as two words.

1)   You've probably heard people talk about yoga. It's something people have been doing for three thousand years. If you took a yoga class, you'd find that yoga is more than exercise. Its benefits are for the mind and body. The yoga student's first job is to learn how to breathe.

     "I've always known how to breathe," you'll probably respond. But complete yoga breathing is very different from regular breathing.

Write this paragraph but make each contraction two words.

2)   What do you know about Robert Frost? He's one of America's most famous poets. If you've read "The Road Not Taken," you'll know why he's so popular. President John F. Kennedy asked Frost to read a poem at his inauguration. What's the name of the poem Frost read? Its title is "The Gift Outright." During his lifetime, Robert Frost won the Pulitzer Prize for poetry four times.

Where to Find It

Book of Quotations

You can use a book of quotations to find interesting quotations for your writing. There are several popular books of quotations. One in particular is *Bartlett's Familiar Quotations.* You can find it in the reference section of the library. There are two ways to find quotations in Bartlett's.

1) Look up a specific person in the author index at the beginning of the book. Suppose you want a quote by John F. Kennedy. The index lists quotes by Kennedy. You might find the quotation "And so, my fellow Americans, ask not what your country can do for you; ask what you can do for your country."

2) To find a quote on a particular subject, look for the subject in the keyword index at the back of the book. For example, the following is part of the index entry for *weather.* Each listing gives a phrase from a quotation (using *w.* for *weather*), the page number on which it is found, and its listing number on that page. You might find this quote about weather by Mark Twain: "Everybody talks about the weather, but nobody does anything about it."

> **Weather,** always fair w., 589: 3
> appeared when w. cleared, 545: 3
> both with anxiety about w., 589: 3
> clear w. spreads cloudless, 53: 9
> cloudy was the w., 792: 17
> come wind come w., 272: 29

1) Write the quotations by Kennedy and Twain on your paper. Underline each pronoun. Write what kind of pronoun each is.

2) Use a book of quotations to find a quote by a person you have learned about in American history. Then find a quote on a subject that interests you. Write each quotation and its author on your paper.

Writing Project

Using What You Know About Antecedents

When you write, you often use pronouns to replace nouns. Make sure that it is clear to your reader what the antecedent of each pronoun is.

In this writing activity, you will practice using pronouns. Read this sentence.

Brenda's favorite activity is riding her bike.

What is the pronoun in this sentence?

What noun does the pronoun replace?

(The possessive pronoun *her* replaces the possessive noun *Brenda's. Brenda's* is the antecedent of *her*.)

Read the following story and identify the antecedents of these pronouns: *I, she, them, herself, me, we.* Does the writer make it clear what the antecedents are?

The Day I Met Mary
By Emily Watson

When I was twelve, I moved to Lewisdale, Maryland. On the first day of junior high school, I walked to the bus stop. Mary was standing with a group of other kids from the neighborhood. She walked away from them and introduced herself to me. We sat together on the bus and talked. From that day until now we have been good friends.

Write a paragraph that tells about how you met one of your friends. After you finish, list all the pronouns and write their antecedents. If any of the antecedents seem unclear, revise your paragraph to correct the problem. Then make another list of the pronouns and have a classmate read your paragraph. Ask the classmate to identify the antecedent of each pronoun on the list.

WORD BANK

antecedent

compound
   personal
   pronoun

compound relative
   pronoun

contraction ✓

demonstrative
   pronoun

first-person
   pronoun

indefinite pronoun

interrogative
   pronoun

personal pronoun

pronoun

relative pronoun

second-person
   pronoun

third-person
   pronoun

Part A On a sheet of paper, write the correct word or words from the Word Bank to complete each sentence.

1) A _____ is two words made into one by replacing one or more letters with an apostrophe.

2) An _____ asks a question.

3) A _____ is a pronoun such as *whoever, whomever, whichever,* and *whatever.*

4) A _____ refers to the person who is speaking.

5) A _____ refers to a person or thing.

6) An _____ does not refer to a specific person or thing.

7) A _____ refers to the person or thing being talked about.

8) A _____ combines a singular personal pronoun and *-self* or a plural personal pronoun and *-selves.*

9) An _____ is the noun that the pronoun replaces.

10) A _____ points out a particular person or thing.

11) A _____ refers to the person who is spoken to.

12) A _____ is a word that replaces a noun.

13) A _____ is a pronoun such as *who, whom, whose, which, that,* and *what.*

Part B Write the pronouns in these sentences on your paper. Write the antecedent next to each pronoun.

14) Nathan said he called Emily.

15) Angela was glad she went to the game.

16) Michelle left her notebook here.

17) Mrs. Benson likes students who ask questions.

18) Emily played a song she really likes.

Part C Write the pronouns in these sentences on your paper. Next to each pronoun, write whether it is *personal, relative, interrogative, demonstrative,* or *indefinite.*

19) I don't like people who interrupt.

20) That is one of my pet peeves.

21) Everybody in the class likes math because it challenges them.

22) What are some of the classes that you enjoy?

Part D Write the correct pronoun for each sentence on your paper.

23) Armando went to see a trainer (whom, what) he had met through a friend.

24) "I want to make (my, mine) arms stronger," he said.

25) Looking at the machines, Armando asked, "What do (this, these) do?"

26) "(This, Those) works your triceps," said the trainer, pointing to a machine.

27) People (which, who) exercise want to stay fit and feel healthy.

28) Everyone wants to look (his or her, their) best.

Part E On your paper, write each contraction as two words.

29) I'll let you know when we're ready to go.

30) That's the only route they've taken.

Using Adjectives in Sentences

Sometimes just naming the person, place, or thing is not enough. We want to describe it in more detail. We want to talk about its size, its color, or our feelings about it. We may want to compare it to something else. For these purposes, we often use adjectives. Adjectives are words that we use to describe nouns and pronouns.

Look at the photograph on the opposite page. How would you describe what you see in the photograph? You might say that you see one green apple surrounded by lots of red apples. The words *green* and *red* are both adjectives. They describe the word *apple*. We frequently use adjectives in our sentences to describe the world around us.

In Chapter 4, you will learn about adjectives and how to use them in your writing.

Goals for Learning

▶ To recognize adjectives in sentences and identify the nouns they describe

▶ To recognize articles and numbers

▶ To recognize and capitalize proper adjectives

▶ To recognize demonstrative pronouns and possessive nouns used as adjectives in sentences

▶ To use adjectives to make comparisons

What Is an Adjective?

Adjective

A word that describes or tells about a noun or pronoun

An **adjective** is a word that describes or tells about a noun or pronoun. An adjective may tell what kind, which one, how many, or how much. Usually the adjective comes before the noun it is describing.

What kind?	Angela enjoys the fall weather.
Which one?	I saw the pinto pony.
How many?	We planted two trees.
How much?	The dress cost thirty-five dollars.

Activity A Write the adjectives in bold on your paper. Next to each adjective, write the noun the adjective describes.

Example Angela bought a **new** swimsuit.
new—swimsuit

1) The suit matches her **blue** goggles.

2) She dives into the **chilly** pool in the morning.

3) Angela takes her **old** towel to swim meets for **good** luck.

4) She swims in **two** races.

5) Angela brings home a **blue** ribbon for **first** place.

You can use more than one adjective to describe a noun.

EXAMPLE   Wednesday was a crisp, cool, windy fall day.
(*Crisp, cool, windy,* and *fall* all describe the day.)

Activity B Write these sentences on your paper. Add one or more adjectives to describe the underlined noun.

1) Emily sits on the <u>couch</u>.

2) Nathan's family took a <u>vacation</u>.

3) Nathan played a <u>game</u>.

4) Neeru wore her <u>clothes</u> from Calcutta.

5) We all drank mugs of <u>cocoa</u>.

Word Order in Sentences
Most adjectives come before the noun they are describing. Adjectives sometimes come after the noun. Then they are set off from the rest of the sentence with commas.

The enthusiastic and excited football players took the field.
The football players, enthusiastic and excited, took the field.

Predicate adjective

An adjective that comes after the noun or pronoun it describes

A **predicate adjective** comes after the noun or pronoun it describes in the predicate part of the sentence.

EXAMPLE
The sky was cloudy. (*Cloudy* describes the sky.)
The students were happy. (*Happy* describes the students.)

Activity C Write the adjectives in these sentences on your paper. Next to each adjective, write the noun or pronoun the adjective describes.

1) Mr. Jackson is the band teacher.

2) He is great at playing the trumpet.

3) His students always have a fall concert and a spring concert.

4) Mr. Jackson tells the noisy students to quiet down.

5) He stands, quiet and patient, until the students are ready.

LESSON 1 | *Review*

Write the adjectives in bold on your paper. Next to each adjective, write the noun or pronoun the adjective describes.

1) Angela is **athletic.**

2) She has **strong** arms and legs from **swim** practice.

3) Neeru is **petite.**

4) She has **long black** hair.

5) Nathan is **stocky** and **strong.**

6) He has **thick, wavy** hair and a **nice** smile.

Rewrite these sentences on your paper. Add as many adjectives as you can to each sentence. Underline all the adjectives in the sentences.

7) Michelle drives a car.

8) Emily plays a song.

9) Armando kicked the ball.

10) We looked at the clouds in the sky.

Definite article
The word the, which is used to talk about a particular person or thing

Indefinite article
The word a or an, which is used to talk about a general group of people or things

The articles *a, an,* and *the* are always adjectives. We place them before nouns in sentences.

Definite article—*the*
Use the definite article when you are talking about a particular person or thing.

    Emily wanted the book about frogs.
(Emily wants a particular book. It must be the book about frogs.)

Indefinite articles—*a, an*
Use an indefinite article when you are talking about a general group of people or things.

    Nathan was looking for a book.
(Nathan does not have a particular book in mind. Any book will do.)

Activity A Write these sentences on your paper. Underline all the articles.

1) The English teacher made an assignment.

2) The assignment was to read a book.

3) The students had to write a report.

4) To receive an A, the students must write a report.

5) In the report they must tell why the book is popular.

Use the article *a* before a word that begins with a consonant sound. Use the article *an* before a word that begins with a vowel sound.

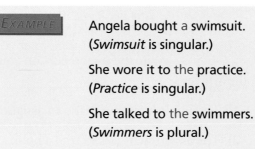

| EXAMPLE | a book | a hard assignment |
| | an apple | an early assignment |

Activity B On your paper, write the article that correctly completes each sentence.

1) Yesterday was (a, an) eventful day.

2) "I need (a, an) explanation," said the teacher.

3) All of the students raised their hands to offer (a, an) answer.

4) New shoes can be (a, an) big expense.

5) Michelle wanted (a, an) new pair of shoes.

Use the articles *a* and *an* only with singular nouns. You can use the article *the* with singular and plural nouns.

EXAMPLE	Angela bought a swimsuit.
	(*Swimsuit* is singular.)
	She wore it to the practice.
	(*Practice* is singular.)
	She talked to the swimmers.
	(*Swimmers* is plural.)

Activity C On your paper, write the article that correctly completes each sentence.

1) Galileo is (a, an) famous astronomer.

2) He was (a, an) astronomer who lived in the sixteenth century.

3) He studied (a, the) stars and planets.

4) Do you enjoy looking at (a, the) sky?

5) Nathan's science class is (a, the) first one of the day.

On your paper, write the article that correctly completes each sentence. Decide whether you need a definite or indefinite article. If you need an indefinite article (*a* or *an*), ask yourself if the word immediately after it begins with a vowel sound.

1) Emily brought (a, an) pear in her lunch.

2) She sat on (a, the) bench closest to the door.

3) Mr. Thomas gave (a, the) assignments for tomorrow.

4) Armando and (a, the) soccer team played a great game.

5) We waited for over (a, an) hour.

6) (A, An) actor came to talk to the Drama Club.

7) He has (a, the) cast on his broken leg.

8) Nathan put (a, the) stamps in the drawer.

9) There was (a, an) one-hour break between games.

10) Armando put (a, an) ice pack on his bruised knee.

Write five sentences about today's weather. Underline all the articles in your sentences.

Spelling Builder

Contractions vs. Possessives

Read this sentence:
    This is (you're, your) book.
Which word do you use—*your,* the possessive or *you're,* the contraction? Check by changing *you're* into the words that form the contraction: *you are.*

Write sentences for the words in these sets:
    they're/their   who's/whose

Proper adjective

A proper noun used as an adjective, or the adjective form of a proper noun

Proper adjectives are proper nouns that we use as adjectives. Proper adjectives can also be adjective forms of proper nouns.

EXAMPLE		
	Proper Noun	Emily speaks English.
	Proper Adjective	Emily speaks the English language.
	Proper Noun	Nathan would like to visit Spain someday.
	Proper Adjective	Nathan would like to see the Spanish countryside.

Activity A Write the word in bold in each sentence on your paper. Decide whether it is a noun or an adjective. If it is an adjective, write the noun it describes next to it.

Example Our family likes to eat in **Mexican** restaurants.
Mexican, adjective—restaurants

1) Angela is learning to speak **Chinese.**

2) Have you ever read any **Chinese** literature?

3) I read a book about **China** by Pearl Buck.

4) Pearl Buck won the **Nobel** Prize for literature.

5) She was the first **American** woman to win this prize.

Activity B Use these proper adjectives in sentences. Write the sentences on your paper. Draw an arrow from the proper adjective to the word it describes.

1) American   **4)** African

2) Spanish   **5)** Chinese

3) French

Noun or Adjective?

A proper noun is the name of a particular person, place, thing, or idea. A proper adjective is a proper noun that you use as an adjective.

Capitalize both proper nouns and proper adjectives.

EXAMPLE

Proper Noun	Jeong Chang lives in Hollywood. (the name of a particular place)
Proper Adjective	Curtis bought a Hollywood bed. (tells what kind of bed)

Activity C Write the words in bold on your paper. Next to each word, write *noun* or *adjective*. If a word is an adjective, write the noun that the adjective describes.

Example Nathan goes to **Wilson High School.**
Wilson High School, noun

He is a **Wilson High School** student.
Wilson High School, adjective—student

1) We are reading **Shakespeare** in English class.

2) *Romeo and Juliet* made me a **Shakespeare** fan.

3) I drive an **American** car.

4) This vase is from **Ireland.**

5) Neeru is glad she moved to **America.**

6) Mr. Thomas visited **Great Britain** last summer.

7) In 2000 the **Republican** convention was held in Philadelphia.

8) Did you see **Angela** swim last night?

9) Mrs. Young made **French** toast for breakfast.

10) Do you have a map of **France?**

Write these sentences on your paper. Capitalize all the proper adjectives. Then draw an arrow from the proper adjective to the noun it describes.

1) Michelle wanted to buy towels at the january sale.

2) One of the tallest trees in the world is the california redwood.

3) The republican senator voted for the bill.

4) The waitress brought us our belgian waffles.

5) The wilson high school athletes attended an awards banquet.

6) The actor's shakespearean costume was very accurate.

7) Emily has a project due in her french class.

8) I ordered a ham and swiss cheese sandwich at Tony's.

9) The video on african safaris was excellent.

10) The tuesday assignment is three pages long.

Write a sentence using each of these proper nouns as a proper adjective. Draw an arrow from the proper adjective to the noun that it describes.

11) German

12) Rome

13) August

14) Asian

15) Maryland

We can use common nouns as adjectives. To decide whether a word is a noun or an adjective, look closely at how it is used in the sentence.

EXAMPLE		
	Noun	Emily likes music.
	Adjective	She works at a music store. (What kind of store? A music store.)
	Noun	I saw a movie yesterday.
	Adjective	We went to a movie theater.

Activity A Write the words in bold on your paper. Next to each word, write whether it is a noun or an adjective. If a word is an adjective, write the noun that the adjective describes.

Example   The school is having a **talent** show.
                      talent, adjective—show

1) Emily will play her **clarinet.**

2) Neeru walks to **center** stage and begins her song.

3) Nathan and Armando are acting out a **movie** scene.

4) When Neeru is finished, the **audience** claps loudly.

5) The show is a huge **success.**

Neeru likes to sing for an audience.

Find all the adjectives in these sentences and write them on your paper. Next to each adjective, write the noun it describes. Be sure to include articles and proper adjectives.

1) Angela wore a shiny blue swimsuit to the pool.

2) I left the keys to the car on the kitchen table.

3) The assignment for Spanish class was long and detailed.

4) Armando had a glass of orange juice and French toast.

5) Angela practices speaking the Chinese language.

Write these sentences on your paper and add as many adjectives as you can. Add at least one adjective to each sentence.

6) I have a car.   **9)** Nathan took a test.

7) Jesse just got a kitten.   **10)** Emily ate a muffin.

8) The radio station plays music.

Vocabulary Builder

Powerful Words

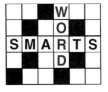

We can say so much with just one word if it is the right word. Read the sentence. Write the meaning of the underlined word on your paper.

> Emily is a <u>meticulous</u> person. She works slowly so she won't make even one mistake.
> **a)** sloppy   **b)** brilliant   **c)** unusually careful

Use a dictionary to find 10 adjectives that you have never used before. Write the adjectives and their meanings on your paper. Then write a sentence for each adjective. Read your sentences to a classmate. Ask your classmate to tell the meanings of the adjectives.

Some adjectives are possessive nouns or pronouns that you use to describe nouns in sentences.

Possessive Nouns as Adjectives

 Emily's dog is a poodle.
(The possessive noun *Emily's* is used as an adjective. It describes the noun *dog*.)

Activity A Write each possessive adjective in bold on your paper. Then write the noun it describes next to it.

Example   **Neeru's** family moved to the United States.
Neeru's—family

1) The **neighbor's** dog has pointed ears.

2) Emily likes **Angela's** perfume.

3) My **mother's** ring is missing.

4) Where is **Armando's** soccer ball?

5) The **band's** album hit the top of the charts.

Activity B Use the following possessive nouns as adjectives in sentences. Draw an arrow from each possessive adjective to the noun it describes.

Example   book's
The book's cover is torn.

1) band's   3) team's   5) world's

2) the teacher's   4) student's

Possessive Pronouns as Adjectives

> Her team is competing today.
> (The possessive pronoun *her* is used as an adjective. It describes the noun *team*.)

Activity C Write the possessive adjectives in bold on your paper. Next to each possessive adjective, write the noun it describes.

1) **Our** puppy likes to play tug-of-war.

2) **My** car is red and white.

3) **His** idea worked great for the project.

4) Michelle likes **her** new computer.

5) The students worked on **their** assignment.

Its and *It's*

Its is a possessive pronoun that we use as an adjective.
> **Its** bark is too loud. (Whose bark? Its bark.)

It's is a contraction of the words *it is*.
> **It's** a nice day. **It is** a nice day.

Activity D On your paper, write the word that correctly completes each sentence.

1) Have you seen (its, it's) cover?

2) The fax machine is beeping. (Its, It's) out of paper.

3) The television show has lost (its, it's) audience.

4) That movie has not lost (its, it's) appeal even after several viewings.

5) The puppy is barking. I think (its, it's) hungry.

Writing Tip

How can you determine whether you should write *its* or *it's*? Use *it is* in place of *it's* in the sentence to see if that makes sense. If not, then the spelling should be *its*.

Possessive nouns may be common or proper nouns. Possessive nouns are usually used as adjectives.

The high school's swim team is going to the state finals.
(Which swim team?)

That is my sister's class.
(Whose class?)

Nathan's friends go to Wilson High School.
(Whose friends?)

Activity E Write the possessive adjectives in these sentences on your paper. Next to each possessive adjective, write the noun it describes.

1) A few of Emily's friends came by the music store.

2) The football team's record was 6 and 2.

3) Nathan's father gets two weeks' vacation every year.

4) Tony's restaurant has the best French fries in town.

5) Armando heard the song playing on his brother's CD player.

Emily's friends came to the music store to buy CDs.

Find the possessive adjectives in this paragraph. Write them on your paper in order. Next to each possessive adjective, write the noun it describes. (Hint: Look for possessive nouns and pronouns.)

1) Nathan and his older brother David went to the presidential inauguration. David drove them to Washington, D.C., in his car. They went to their representative's office to pick up their tickets. The president's inauguration ceremony began at 11:30 A.M. Nathan and David brought their father's binoculars so they could see better from their seats on the Mall. After the new president's speech, Nathan and David went sightseeing.

Find all the adjectives in this paragraph. Write them on your paper in order. Next to each adjective, write the noun or pronoun it describes. Be sure to include articles. Some adjectives will appear more than once. (Hint: There are 25 adjectives.)

2) After their exciting day in the nation's capital, Nathan and David called their parents to say they were on their way home. David needed to fill their car's gas tank, so they stopped at a gas station. Since the windshield was dirty, Nathan washed it. After they were on the road again, they spotted a restaurant. Nathan said he was hungry, so they stopped and ate a quick dinner. After their tasty and filling meal, the boys got back on the road to finish their long trip home.

We can use numbers as adjectives. A number tells us how many.

> Nathan and his brother drove four hundred miles.
>
> It took them eight hours.

We can also use indefinite pronouns as adjectives. They tell how many, but the number is not exact. Remember, an indefinite pronoun refers to a noun that is not named.

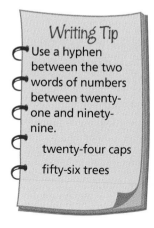

> Several people wanted to go on the trip.
>
> Few students were able to go.

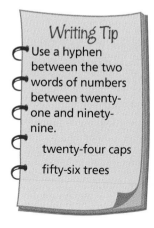

Writing Tip
Use a hyphen between the two words of numbers between twenty-one and ninety-nine.

   twenty-four caps

   fifty-six trees

Activity A Find the numbers or indefinite pronouns used as adjectives in these sentences. Write them on your paper. Next to each one, write the noun it describes.

1) The concert was three hours long.

2) Many people got there early.

3) There were a few songs Nathan recognized.

4) There were thirty people in the band.

5) The drive home took Nathan's family fifteen minutes.

Activity B Use each of these words as an adjective in a sentence. Draw an arrow from the adjective to the noun it describes.

1) twelve   **4)** six

2) several   **5)** few

3) one

Adjective or Pronoun?

A word is an adjective if it describes a noun or pronoun. A word is a pronoun if it replaces a noun in a sentence.

EXAMPLE	Pronoun	Many people clapped, and several cheered. (The antecedent is an unknown number of the people.)
	Adjective	Several families were there. (The word *several* tells how many families.)

Activity C Write the words in bold on your paper. Next to each word, write *adjective* or *pronoun*.

1) **Everyone** was excited about the dance.

2) When the band started playing, **most** people danced.

3) When the dance was over, **no one** wanted to go home.

4) **Some** people went to Tony's afterwards.

5) **Others** went bowling.

Activity D Find all the words used as adjectives in this paragraph. Write each adjective on your paper. Next to it, write the noun or pronoun it describes.

Thanksgiving dinner at Emily's house is busy. All her favorite relatives come to visit. There are twelve people staying in the little house! Emily's mom cooks the turkey, and it is always juicy and delicious. Emily's aunt makes the mashed potatoes and the green beans. Everyone loves the delicious desserts too.

LESSON 6 | *Review*

Write the number words and indefinite pronouns used as adjectives in these sentences. Next to each one, write the noun or pronoun it describes.

1) Most people enjoy going to the movies.

2) Tony's has several kinds of sandwiches.

3) Soccer season lasts three months.

4) Math class is fifty minutes long.

5) My room is two doors down on the right.

Complete each sentence by adding a number word or indefinite pronoun used as an adjective. Write the sentences on your paper. Underline the number words.

6) The rain fell for _____ hours one day.

7) The recipe calls for _____ eggs.

8) The speed limit here is _____ miles per hour.

9) I invited _____ people to the movies.

10) _____ students attend Wilson High School.

Using What You've Learned

Write a journal entry. Describe a natural scene that you especially enjoy. Use a variety of adjectives to make your description vivid and specific.

Demonstrative adjective

The word this, that, these, *or* those *used as an adjective*

You can use demonstrative pronouns as adjectives. The **demonstrative adjectives** are *this, that, these,* and *those.*

EXAMPLE		
	Pronoun	That is a long book.
	Adjective	That book is long. (Which book?)

Activity A Write the demonstrative words in bold on your paper. Next to each word, write *adjective* or *pronoun.*

1) **Those** are good hiking boots.

2) **That** is a beautiful painting.

3) I like the way **these** pens write.

4) **This** book is very funny.

5) Did you see **that** shooting star?

6) **Those** are Armando's poems.

7) Angela uses **that** locker in the gym.

8) **These** are the rules to the game.

9) **This** was a fun day.

10) Nathan has **those** stamps already.

Activity B Write five sentences describing things in the room you are in. Use a demonstrative adjective in each sentence.

Example   **This** desk is mine.
The light is coming in **that** window.
Those people are in my class.

Find the demonstrative adjectives in these sentences. Write them on your paper. Next to each one, write the noun it describes.

1) We had a very strange day this week.

2) Yes, that Wednesday is one I will remember.

3) First, this new bell system rang every other minute.

4) No one knew whether those bells meant to change class or not.

5) Then the cafeteria served these odd sandwiches.

6) Whoever heard of that combination—bananas and peanut butter?

7) This sandwich was a first for me!

8) Some people like these two foods together.

9) I like those tastes separately.

10) Perhaps I will try that mixture again.

Write a paragraph about the clothes you are wearing today. Underline all the adjectives you used, including articles. Then list each adjective and write the noun it describes next to it.

Adjectives describe people or things. You can also use adjectives to compare two or more people or things. Adjectives have three forms—the positive form, the comparative form, and the superlative form.

Positive form

The form of an adjective used to describe people or things

EXAMPLE	Positive	Comparative	Superlative
	fast	faster	fastest
	pretty	prettier	prettiest
	new	newer	newest

Comparative form

The form of an adjective used to compare two people or things

Forming Comparisons

Rule 1 Use the *positive form* to describe one thing.
That car is **fast.**

Rule 2 Use the *comparative form* to compare two things.
That car is **faster** than this car.

Superlative form

The form of an adjective used to compare more than two people or things

Rule 3 Use the *superlative form* to compare more than two things.
Of all the cars I have driven, this one is the **fastest.**

EXAMPLE		
	Comparative	Amanda's pet is cuter than mine.
	Superlative	Amanda has the cutest pet of all.

Activity A On your paper, write the form of the adjective that correctly completes each sentence.

1) Who is (older, oldest)—Nathan or Armando?

2) Mrs. Choy grows the (lovelier, loveliest) roses.

3) Neeru is the (kinder, kindest) of all my friends.

4) Chocolate ice cream is (sweet, sweeter).

5) I think chocolate is (sweeter, sweetest) than vanilla.

Comparative and Superlative Forms

Many adjectives form their comparative by adding -er. They form their superlative by adding -est.

Positive	Comparative	Superlative
tall	taller	tallest
young	younger	youngest

The positive form of some adjectives ends in *y*. For these adjectives, you change the *y* to *i* and add -er or -est.

Positive	Comparative	Superlative
happy	happier	happiest
lonely	lonelier	loneliest

Longer adjectives use the words *more* and *less* to form the comparative. They form the superlative by using *most* or *least*.

Positive	Comparative	Superlative
boring	more boring	most boring
talented	more talented	most talented
generous	less generous	least generous
anxious	less anxious	least anxious

Some adjectives do not have logical comparative and superlative forms. A painting cannot be the *most perfect*. An object is either perfect or not. However, it may be *more nearly perfect* than another. The word *unique* is similar, since it means "having no equal."

Activity B Write these adjectives on your paper. Next to each one, write its comparative and superlative forms.

1) expensive

2) comfortable

3) slow

4) early

5) successful

6) lovely

7) careful

8) blue

9) sweet

10) popular

Activity C Use each adjective form correctly in a sentence.

1) funny

2) oldest

3) longer

4) less famous

5) most entertaining

Irregular Adjectives
Some adjectives have completely different words for their comparative and superlative forms. You need to memorize these words or look them up in a dictionary to be sure.

Positive	Comparative	Superlative
good	better	best
bad	worse	worst
little	less	least
many	more	most

Activity D Write the correct form of the adjective for each sentence.

1) Jesse thinks Daniel Defoe is a (good, better) writer.

2) Nathan is watching (less, least) television lately.

3) He is doing (more, most) reading.

4) "The writer I like (better, best)," said Emily, "is Anne Tyler."

5) "*The Accidental Tourist* is the (funnier, funniest) book I ever read," said Nathan.

Double the Final Consonant

Some words double the final consonant to form their comparative and superlative forms. Double the final consonant when you add an ending to a word that has one syllable, ends in one consonant, and has one vowel before the final consonant.

EXAMPLE

Some words in which you double the final consonant
    big + -er = bigger   big + -est = biggest
    sad + -er = sadder   sad + -est = saddest

Some words in which you do not double the final consonant
    short + -er = shorter   short + -est = shortest
    fast + -er = faster   fast + -est = fastest

Activity E On your paper, write the form of the adjective in parentheses that correctly completes each sentence.

1) Angela wants to be the _____ swimmer in school. (fast)

2) Nathan's backpack is _____ than Armando's. (big)

3) Yesterday was the _____ day of the year. (hot)

4) Michelle is the _____ swimmer on the team. (short)

5) Monday was _____ than Tuesday. (hot)

Activity F Write the adjective forms in bold on your paper. Identify each one as *positive, comparative,* or *superlative.*

1) Nathan is a **friendly** person.

2) Everyone says he has the **nicest** smile.

3) Nathan is **taller** than Armando.

4) Armando is the **most successful** hitter on the baseball team.

5) He is **more successful** this year than he was last year.

Fewer and *less* are two important comparative adjectives. Many people mix up *fewer* and *less*. *Fewer* refers to a number of items that can be counted. *Less* refers to an amount or quantity.

We have fewer apples today than yesterday. (comparative form—apples are items that can be counted)

There is less applesauce in the jar than I thought. (comparative form—applesauce is a quantity; it cannot be counted)

Remember: If you can count individual items, then you use *few* or *fewer*.

Activity G On your paper, write the adjective that correctly completes each sentence.

1) Nathan has (fewer, less) books than Emily.

2) Emily drinks (fewer, less) tea than Neeru.

3) Do you drink (fewer, less) water than you should?

4) Angela sees (fewer, less) movies than Michelle.

5) The team scored (fewer, less) points in the second half.

We can see fewer hot air balloons today.

LESSON 8 | *Review*

Write the adjective forms in bold on your paper. Next to each one, write *positive, comparative,* or *superlative.*

1) Many readers think *Treasure Island* is the **most exciting** adventure story of all. They love its **colorful** cast of characters. Old Pew is a horrible creature, but even **more frightening** is Long John Silver. Have you read the book? Which character do you think is the **most memorable** one? Why do the characters seem **more vivid** than others you have read about?

Read each pair of sentences. Write the correct sentence on your paper.

2) a) Old Pew is one of the meanest men around.

b) Old Pew is one of the most mean men around.

3) a) Which of those two ships can sail faster?

b) Which of those two ships can sail fastest?

4) a) Long John Silver hopes to be richer soon.

b) Long John Silver hopes to be more rich soon.

5) a) *Treasure Island* is the goodest book I have read.

b) *Treasure Island* is the best book I have read.

On your paper, write the adjective that correctly completes each sentence.

6) Today was (hoter, hotter) than yesterday.

7) Last Friday was the (wetest, wettest) day so far.

8) I have (fewer, less) CDs than Armando.

9) Armando spends (fewer, less) money than Nathan.

10) We saw (fewer, less) people today than yesterday.

Thesaurus

Adjectives can make your writing interesting and specific. However, you may find yourself often using common adjectives such as *big, good,* and *pretty.* A **thesaurus** is a reference book of synonyms. In a thesaurus, you can find precise adjectives to use in your writing.

One popular thesaurus is *Roget's Thesaurus.* It is arranged in categories. You may find a thesaurus arranged in dictionary form easier to use. Words are listed in alphabetical order. They are followed by synonyms and sometimes by antonyms too. Here is a listing similar to one found in *Roget's College Thesaurus in Dictionary Form.*

> **nice,** *adj.* pleasing, agreeable, attractive, enjoyable; tasteful, proper, genteel; precise, accurate, exact, meticulous; delicate, fine, sensitive, appealing; overrefined, critical, squeamish. See PLEASURE, TASTE.

Suppose you wrote the sentence "The birthday party was very nice." What synonym for *nice* would make the sentence more colorful and specific? You might choose the synonym *enjoyable* from the listing above. Notice that some of the synonyms for *nice* would not make sense in your sentence. For example, the word *precise* would not make sense in the context of your sentence. If you look up *precise* in a dictionary, you will find it is a synonym for another meaning of *nice.* Before using a synonym from a thesaurus, be sure to look up its meaning in a dictionary. Make sure its meaning fits in your sentence.

1) Use a thesaurus to find a synonym for *great* in this sentence: *The concert was great.* Write the sentence with the synonym. Then choose one synonym from the *great* thesaurus listing that would not make sense in this sentence.

2) Use a thesaurus to find a synonym for each of the following adjectives. On your paper, write a sentence using each synonym you find.

   large   funny   smart   cold

Writing Project

Using Adjectives to Compare and Contrast

In this writing activity, you will practice using adjectives
to compare and contrast.

1) Think about a business you might like to start. You will need to sell something
or provide a service.

   Some possible businesses:
   - We Do It Better Painting Company
   - Top of the Line Greeting Cards
   - English Tutoring
   - Best Pet Sitting
   - Green Thumb Gardening
   - Quality Lawn Care
   - Happy Home Housecleaning
   - Daily Dog Walking
   - Creative Childcare

2) Write a letter to a bank. Tell the bank about your business. Ask the bank to
loan you money to start your business. Use adjectives to compare your new
business to other similar businesses.

   Include the answers to these questions in your letter:
   Why is your product or service better than others already on the market?
   Why would people choose your company instead of other companies?
   Why will your company do a better job than other companies?

3) Write a paragraph to use in an advertisement for your business. Be sure to tell
what makes your business different from other similar businesses.

4) Make a poster to put in a local store. Describe your business. Tell why you are
better than or different from other similar businesses. Be sure to give the
location of your business.

5) Write a thank-you note to your first customer.

WORD BANK

adjective

comparative form

definite article

demonstrative
adjective

indefinite article

positive form

predicate adjective

proper adjective

superlative form

Part A On a sheet of paper, write the correct word or words from the Word Bank to complete each sentence.

1) The _____ is the word *the,* which is used to talk about a particular person or thing.

2) A _____ is a proper noun used as an adjective, or the adjective form of a proper noun.

3) The form of an adjective used to compare two people or things is the _____.

4) A _____ is an adjective that comes after the noun or pronoun it describes.

5) The form of an adjective used to describe people or things is the _____.

6) An _____ is the word *a* or *an,* which is used to talk about a general group of people or things.

7) The form of an adjective used to compare more than two people or things is the _____.

8) A word that describes or tells about a noun or pronoun is an _____.

9) A _____ is the word *this, that, these,* or *those* used as an adjective.

Part B Find 22 adjectives in this description of Long John Silver from *Treasure Island* by Robert Louis Stevenson. Be sure to include articles and possessive pronouns.

10) Stevenson describes Long John as "a tall, strong, heavy, nut-brown man; his disorderly pigtail falling over the shoulders of his soiled blue coat; his hand ragged and scarred, with black, broken nails; and the saber cut across one cheek, a dirty, livid white."

Part C Write the adjectives in bold on your paper. Next to each adjective, write the noun it describes.

11) **The** sailor kept as clean as a **new** pin.

12) He had **good** schooling in **his** young days.

13) The sailor, **silent** and **cool,** stood and watched us.

14) **One** man ran through the **rough** thicket.

15) We had **a** long day of **hard** work ahead of us.

Part D On your paper, write the form of the adjective that correctly completes each sentence.

16) Emily's soup is (hoter, hotter) than mine.

17) Last Monday was (a, an) eventful day.

18) The program on (african, African) wildlife was interesting.

19) We like to order pizza at (Tonys, Tony's) restaurant.

20) (Its, It's) three days until Thanksgiving.

21) Did you see (that, those) bluebirds?

22) (Those, These) houses across town are new.

23) Jesse saw (fewer, less) television programs last week.

24) This book is the (better, best) one I have read this year.

25) Nathan's joke was (funnier, more funny) than Armando's.

Test-Taking Tip Effective studying takes place over a period of time. Spend time studying new material for several days or weeks before a test. Don't try to learn new material the night before a test.

Using Action Verbs in Sentences

Every sentence has a verb. It is the one part of speech that every sentence must have. To make your writing vital and exciting, you will want to choose your verbs carefully. Verbs express action or state of being.

Study the photograph on the opposite page. What do you see? The frog is leaping to grab its food from the branch. The word *leap* is an action verb. It expresses the frog's action. What other verbs could you use to express the frog's action?

In Chapter 5, you will learn about action verbs. Verbs have many different forms. You will learn how to use different verb forms in sentences.

Goals for Learning

▶ To identify verb phrases in sentences

▶ To identify the correct form of verbs in sentences

▶ To understand verb tense and use tense consistently in sentences

▶ To recognize the past and past participle forms of irregular verbs

Action verb

A word that tells what someone or something does, did, or will do

An **action verb** tells what someone or something does, did, or will do. Find the verb in a sentence by asking yourself two questions:

- Who or what is doing something? The answer is the subject of the sentence.

- What are they doing? The answer is the verb.

> EXAMPLE
>
> Every morning Mr. Choy makes coffee.
>
> Who is doing something?   Mr. Choy (subject)
>
> What does Mr. Choy do?   makes (verb)

Writing Tip

Using vivid action verbs adds interest and color to your writing. Substitute colorful verbs such as *stroll* and *dash* for ordinary ones such as *walk* and *run*.

A sentence can have more than one verb.

> EXAMPLE
>
> Mrs. Choy prepares breakfast and packs lunches.

A verb can tell about action you can see. You can see a person preparing breakfast or packing a lunch. A verb can also tell about action you cannot see.

> EXAMPLE
>
> Mr. Choy likes coffee.

Activity A   Write the verbs in these sentences on your paper.

Example   Students choose their own books.

            choose

1) The students at Wilson High School keep a reading log.

2) They read every day for 30 minutes.

3) Angela prefers biographies.

4) She found a biography of Janet Evans, the swimming star, and wrote a report about that book.

5) Nathan likes history books and reads a lot of them.

Activity B Write the verbs in these sentences on your paper.

Example   The students hurry to the cafeteria.
             hurry

   1) They form a line in front of the door.

   2) Angela chooses an apple and a slice of pizza.

   3) Armando puts a carton of milk on his tray.

   4) Angela and Armando pay for their lunches and look
          for a table.

   5) They sit at the table with Nathan and Neeru.

Activity C Write a paragraph about a sport or an activity you
enjoy. Use an action verb in each sentence.

The students stand
in line to buy lunch.

Find the verbs in the sentences in the paragraph. List them on your paper.

1)   In 1965 Frank Herbert wrote *Dune,* a science-fiction book. People purchased millions of copies of this book. During World War II Herbert served in the U.S. Navy. Later, he worked in many jobs. He operated a television camera. He delivered the news on the radio. Herbert reported the news for several papers. He authored many books. People still enjoy his books.

Write the verb in each of these sentences on your paper.

2) Angela walked down the crowded hallway.

3) She looked at the artwork on the walls.

4) She saw a large colorful poster.

5) Angela really liked the poster.

6) Armando made that poster.

7) He worked hard on the design.

8) Everyone stops in front of the poster.

9) Armando received the first-place prize.

10) Angela congratulated Armando on his award.

Verbs Express Tense

Tense
The time when an action takes place

Simple tenses
Present, past, and future forms of verbs

Infinitive
To plus the present tense of a verb

Helping verb
A verb that combines with a main verb to form a verb phrase

The verb in a sentence can describe action. Verbs also express **tense** (time). A verb tense tells when an action takes place.

Simple Tenses

Verbs can express three **simple tenses**—present, past, and future. Use the present tense when the action is happening now or usually happens. Use the past tense when the action has already happened. Use the future tense when the action will happen in the future.

The **infinitive** form is *to* plus the present tense of a verb.

Verbs use endings, **helping verbs,** or both to express tense. A helping verb combines with a main verb to form a verb phrase. You will learn more about helping verbs and verb phrases later in this chapter.

EXAMPLE		
	Present Tense	Angela looks for the poster. (the verb or the verb plus -s)
	Past Tense	Angela looked for the poster. (Add -ed or -d to the present form.)
	Future Tense	Angela will look for the poster. (Add the helping verb will or shall.)

Activity A Write the verbs in bold on your paper. Identify the tense of each verb as *present, past,* or *future.*

1) The band **marched** onto the field.

2) They **will play** the school song at the rally.

3) The students **gathered** for the rally.

4) The players **look** forward to this game.

5) The students **will support** their team.

Perfect Tenses

Perfect tenses

Present perfect, past perfect, and future perfect forms of a verb

The three **perfect tenses** of a verb are present perfect, past perfect, and future perfect.

The perfect tenses use the helping verb *have* with the past tense of a verb.

> **EXAMPLE**
>
> **Present Perfect**
> Neeru has joined the school choir.
> (shows an action that took place in the past and continues to the present)
>
> **Past Perfect**
> Neeru had belonged to a choir in India before joining the Wilson High School choir.
> (shows that one action was completed before another action began)
>
> **Future Perfect**
> By November she will have belonged to the choir for a month.
> (shows an action that will be completed before a certain time in the future)

Use the different forms of *have* to write the perfect tenses.

Verb Forms of *Have*		
Present tense	(singular)	Armando's team **has** the ball.
	(plural)	They **have** three goals so far.
Past tense		The team **had** the lead a minute ago.
Future tense		They **will have** practice tomorrow.
Present perfect tense	(singular)	Armando **has had** a good game so far.
	(plural)	The players **have had** chances to score.
Past perfect tense		They **had had** many victories before today.
Future perfect tense		They **will have had** a winning season.

Verb phrase

A main verb plus a helping verb

A **verb phrase** is a main verb plus a helping verb.

> **EXAMPLE**
>
> **Present Perfect**   Jim has talked to the team about practice.
>
> **Future**   Emily will take a vacation with her family.

Activity B Find the verb phrase and write it on your paper.

1) Neeru has performed in choirs before.

2) Neeru will tour with the choir.

3) The choir has been on tour before.

4) The singers had recorded their last concert.

5) They will sell their new CD.

The verb *have* can be a main verb or a helping verb.

> **EXAMPLE**
>
> I have art class today.   (main verb)
>
> I have scored a goal.   (helping verb)

Activity C Decide whether *have* is the main verb or the helping verb in each sentence. Write *main verb* or *helping verb* on your paper.

1) Armando **has** worked hard today.

2) He **has** soccer practice after school.

3) That band **has** a new CD.

4) The singer **has** a hit song.

5) **Has** she recorded a new CD?

Activity D Change the verb to the tense given and use it in a sentence. Underline the verb or verb phrase.

Example   fish—past perfect
                Armando <u>had fished</u> for an hour before he
                caught anything.

1) wonder   present

2) express   future

3) require   present perfect

4) fill   past perfect

5) select   future perfect

Activity E Write the verb or verb phrase in bold on your paper. Next to each one, write the tense of the verb.

Example   Emily will take clarinet lessons.
                will take—future

1) Emily **enjoys** the school band.

2) She **had joined** the band a year ago.

3) The other clarinet players in the band **welcomed** Emily.

4) The band **had held** a concert in the spring.

5) Emily **will practice** every day.

Write the verb or verb phrase in bold on your paper. Identify the tense of the verb as *present, past, future, present perfect, past perfect,* or *future perfect.*

1) Nathan and his friends **had planned** a special trip.

2) They **will write** about the trip for the school newspaper.

3) They **traveled** to a park with caves.

4) They **visited** a limestone cave during the trip.

5) Their safety gear **included** helmets and headlamps.

6) "**Carry** a flashlight at all times, too," said the cave guide.

7) "We **will hike** a mile to the cave's opening," the guide told them.

8) Nathan and his friends **crawled** through tunnels.

9) "I **have talked** about this trip for a long time!" said Nathan.

10) By next week the group **will have told** everyone about the trip.

Write the past and future tenses of each of these present tense verbs.

11) move   **16)** click

12) burn   **17)** type

13) look   **18)** close

14) ask   **19)** plan

15) clean   **20)** pick

Past participle

The verb form used to form the perfect tenses

Regular verb

A verb whose past tense and past participle are formed by adding -ed or -d

Irregular verb

A verb whose past tense and past participle are formed in different ways

Verbs have three main forms—infinitive (present), past, and **past participle.** The past participle is the verb form we use to form the perfect tenses. **Regular verbs** form their past and past participles by adding *-ed* or *-d.*

EXAMPLE

Infinitive	Present	Past	Past Participle
look	look, looks	looked	(has) looked
jump	jump, jumps	jumped	(has) jumped

Irregular verbs do not follow the usual rules. Sometimes the past and past participles are different. In a few cases, even the present tense has different forms. The verbs *be, have,* and *do* are examples of irregular verbs. We use them as helping verbs and main verbs. Two other common verbs that have unusual forms are *eat* and *go.*

Some Irregular Verbs			
Infinitive	**Present**	**Past**	**Past Participle**
to be	am, is, are	was, were	(has) been
to have	has, have	had	(has) had
to do	do, does	did	(has) done
to eat	eat	ate	(has) eaten
to go	go	went	(has) gone

Activity A Choose the form of the verb in parentheses that correctly completes each sentence. Write the verb in its correct form on your paper.

1) Mrs. Langston _____ the science teacher for two years. (be)

2) The students have already _____ their dinner. (eat)

3) Emily has _____ her job for nearly a year. (have)

4) They already _____ their homework. (do)

5) Armando has _____ to soccer practice. (go)

For some irregular verbs, the past tense and past participle are the same.

Irregular Verbs with Same Past Tense and Past Participle		
Present	**Past**	**Past Participle**
bend (s)	bent	(has) bent
bring (s)	brought	(has) brought
buy (s)	bought	(has) bought
catch (es)	caught	(has) caught
dig (s)	dug	(has) dug
feed (s)	fed	(has) fed
get (s)	got	(has) got (gotten)
hear (s)	heard	(has) heard
keep (s)	kept	(has) kept
lead (s)	led	(has) led
leave (s)	left	(has) left
lose (s)	lost	(has) lost
make (s)	made	(has) made
mean (s)	meant	(has) meant
send (s)	sent	(has) sent
sit (s)	sat	(has) sat
swing (s)	swung	(has) swung
teach (es)	taught	(has) taught
think (s)	thought	(has) thought
weep (s)	wept	(has) wept
win (s)	won	(has) won

Activity B Change each verb in bold to either the past tense or past participle form to correctly complete the sentence. Write the new sentences on your paper. Identify the tense of the verb phrase.

1) Neeru **think** about joining the basketball team.

2) Mrs. Benson has **teach** journalism for several years.

3) Has the soccer team **win** its game yet?

4) Has Armando **buy** the paint he needs?

5) Nathan **catch** trout at his favorite stream.

For some irregular verbs, the past tense and past participle are different. Study the irregular verbs in the following chart.

Irregular Verbs with Different Past Tense and Past Participle		
Present	**Past**	**Past Participle**
begin (s)	began	(has) begun
break (s)	broke	(has) broken
choose (s)	chose	(has) chosen
drive (s)	drove	(has) driven
fall (s)	fell	(has) fallen
fly (flies)	flew	(has) flown
forget (s)	forgot	(has) forgotten
give (s)	gave	(has) given
grow (s)	grew	(has) grown
hide (s)	hid	(has) hidden
know (s)	knew	(has) known
ride (s)	rode	(has) ridden
ring (s)	rang	(has) rung
see (s)	saw	(has) seen
swim (s)	swam	(has) swum
take (s)	took	(has) taken
wear (s)	wore	(has) worn
write (s)	wrote	(has) written

Activity C On your paper, write the form of the verb in parentheses that correctly completes each sentence.

1) Armando has _____ Nathan for many years. (know)

2) Angela _____ in the state meet. (swim)

3) Neeru has _____ her cousin in India a letter. (write)

4) The cup _____ when it fell off the shelf. (break)

5) Nathan has _____ that movie twice. (saw)

For some irregular verbs, the past tense and past participle are the same as their present tense.

More Irregular Verbs		
Present	**Past**	**Past Participle**
burst (s)	burst	(has) burst
cost (s)	cost	(has) cost
cut (s)	cut	(has) cut
hit (s)	hit	(has) hit
put (s)	put	(has) put
read (s)	read	(has) read
set (s)	set	(has) set

Writing Tip
When you are unsure of the correct past or past participle form of a verb, look up the word in a dictionary. These forms are listed at the beginning of an entry for an irregular verb.

We pronounce the past tense and past participle of the verb *read* differently. I wear glasses when I **read** (rēd). I **read** (red) yesterday. When a verb does not change its form, you must look at the other words in the sentence to determine the tense.

Activity D Read these sentences. Decide whether the verb in bold is present, past, or future tense. Write the verb tense on your paper.

1) I **will read** that book next week.

2) We **cut** our grass once a week in the summer.

3) Emily **put** a napkin on her lap at the restaurant.

4) Armando **hit** a home run during the last inning.

5) Last year a bucket of French fries **cost** two dollars at Tony's.

Activity E Find the verb error in each sentence. Write the sentence using the correct verb form.

1) Nathan has went to the store for his mother.

2) That is not what I meaned to do.

3) The fan keeped the room cool.

4) The plants have grew since yesterday.

5) I seen that movie already.

The verb in bold in each sentence is incorrect. Write the correct form of the verb on your paper.

1) Emily **bringed** a chocolate cake to the party.

2) The teacher **begin** to speak.

3) The bottle in the freezer **bursted.**

4) I **buyed** these shoes a week ago.

5) The wind has **blow** that tree down.

6) The airplane has **flew** to New York and back.

7) Angela **swum** her lap in record time.

8) "My fingers are **froze**," said Nathan.

9) "I hope you have **forgave** me," said my cousin.

10) "You **done** a fine job on that lesson," said Efran.

Use each of the verbs or verb phrases correctly in a sentence. Pay attention to the tense.

11) have grown

12) took

13) are

14) do

15) has thought

16) stood

17) had seen

18) sent

19) have known

20) will catch

Progressive Verb Phrases

Present participle

A verb form that shows continuing action

Progressive verb phrase

The form of a verb that ends in -ing *and uses a form of* be *as a helping verb to show continuous action*

The **present participle** expresses continuing action. Add -*ing* to the present tense of the verb to form the present participle. To form **progressive verb phrases,** use the helping verb *be* plus the present participle.

EXAMPLE
Present	Emily practices her clarinet every day.
Present Progressive	Emily is practicing her clarinet right now.

Activity A Write the progressive verb phrase in each sentence on your paper.

Example   Mrs. Choy is shopping for a new sweater.
    is shopping

1) Armando is designing a poster.

2) "I am working at the music store," said Emily.

3) Angela is swimming in the pool.

4) They are going to the library.

5) Neeru is singing her favorite song.

Use the correct form of the helping verb *be* to form progressive verb phrases.

EXAMPLE

Present Progressive	She is running.
Past Progressive	She was running.
Future Progressive	She will be running.
Present Perfect Progressive	She has been running.
Past Perfect Progressive	She had been running.
Future Perfect Progressive	She will have been running.

Activity B Identify the tense of each verb in bold.

1) Nathan **is going** to the library.

2) Emily **will be meeting** him there.

3) They **have been looking** for a book.

4) They **will have been looking** for this book for a week.

5) He **had been expecting** the best.

Verb Forms of *Be*		
Present tense	(singular)	I **am** on the team with Armando.
	(singular)	Armando's team **is** on the field.
	(plural)	They **are** in the lead.
Past tense	(singular)	The team **was** in the lead a minute ago.
	(plural)	The players **were** near the goal.
Future tense		We hope that they **will be** the winners.
Present perfect	(singular)	It **has been** a good game so far.
	(plural)	The players **have been** eager to score.
Past perfect		They **had been** the winners before.
Future perfect		They **will have been** on the field for an hour.

Activity C Write a sentence using each subject and verb shown. Write the progressive verb form shown in parentheses. Use the forms of *be* shown above.

1) students go (past progressive)

2) I work (present progressive)

3) cats play (present progressive)

4) flower grows (present perfect progressive)

5) James runs (past progressive)

Find the progressive verb phrase in each of these sentences.
Write it on your paper.

1) Armando has been playing soccer for many years.

2) They have been thinking about a new car.

3) In the library, Nathan was looking for a book about caving.

4) Emily is planning a visit to an art gallery.

5) Are you going to the gallery this weekend?

Identify the tense of the progressive verb phrase in bold in each
sentence. Write it on your paper.

6) Mrs. Watson **is enjoying** music.

7) She **was listening** to a CD player.

8) Emily's mother **had been waiting** for her to come home.

9) Mrs. Watson **has been wondering** where she is.

10) Emily **will be working** at the music store all day.

Vocabulary Builder

Vivid Verbs

Verbs express action. Good writers use verbs
that have very specific meanings. They do this to draw
readers into a story.

Ordinary verbs	Vivid verbs
catch	snag
see	witness
eat	devour
walk	saunter

Use each vivid verb in a sentence. Then try to think of other
vivid verbs to use in your writing.

A verb must agree in number (singular or plural) with its subject. The present tense of a regular verb has two forms. We use one form with a singular subject. We use another form with a plural subject.

Add -*s* or -*es* to the present tense of the verb when the subject is a singular noun.

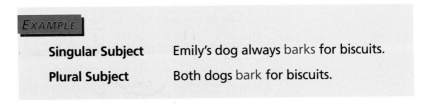

EXAMPLE

Singular Subject   Emily's dog always barks for biscuits.

Plural Subject   Both dogs bark for biscuits.

When the subject is a singular pronoun (*he, she, it*), add -*s* or -*es* to the verb.

Add -*es* to verbs that end with *s, z, x, ch,* or *sh*. Armando **catches** a lot of fish at his favorite pond.

When a verb ends in *y* and the letter before the *y* is a consonant, change the *y* to *i* and add -*s* or -*es*.
I **worry** sometimes. Nathan **worries** about the weather.

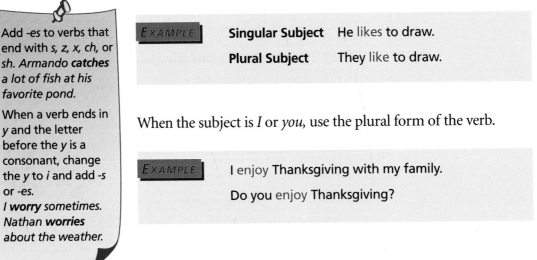

EXAMPLE   **Singular Subject**   He likes to draw.

Plural Subject   They like to draw.

When the subject is *I* or *you*, use the plural form of the verb.

EXAMPLE   I enjoy Thanksgiving with my family.

Do you enjoy Thanksgiving?

Activity A Write these sentences on your paper. Choose the verb that correctly completes each sentence.

1) Armando (hope, hopes) to win the contest.

2) They (enjoy, enjoys) art class.

3) I (want, wants) a new set of paints.

4) Neeru (watch, watches) television after school.

5) The bird (fly, flies) to its nest.

Most indefinite pronouns are singular even though their meanings are plural. They take a singular form of the verb.

EXAMPLE	Correct	Everyone goes to the beach in the summer.
	Incorrect	Everyone go to the beach in the summer.

Some indefinite pronouns may be singular or plural depending on their use. They are *all, any, most,* and *none.*

EXAMPLE	Singular	All of the money is safe in the bank.
	Plural	All of the boys are going to the concert.

Activity B Write the verb that correctly completes each sentence.

1) All of the fruit (look, looks) fresh.

2) Anyone (is, are) welcome at the concert.

3) Most of the students (go, goes) to Tony's for snacks.

4) All of the students (attend, attends) the band concert.

5) None of us (are, is) going.

Some indefinite pronouns are always plural: *both, many, few, others, several.* A plural indefinite pronoun takes a plural form of the verb.

EXAMPLE   Several **of the people** want **fruit for dessert.**

Writing Tip

Hearing the correct verb forms as they are spoken can help you write them correctly. Read the correct sentences aloud so that you begin to "hear" the sound of correct usage.

Activity C Write the verb that correctly completes each sentence on your paper.

1) Everyone (is, are) coming to the dance.

2) Both of the girls (seem, seems) happy to help.

3) Few of them (was, were) prepared for the test.

4) Nothing (sound, sounds) as noisy as a basketball game.

5) Several dance committee members (decorate, decorates) the gym every year.

The dance committee decorates the gym for the spring dance.

Activity D Write the present tense form of the verb in parentheses that correctly completes each sentence.

1) Neeru _____ many relatives in India. (have)

2) They _____ letters all the time. (write)

3) Everyone _____ to get a letter in the mail. (like)

4) Most of my letters _____ from my cousin. (be)

5) She _____ in northern California. (live)

Spelling Builder

Understanding Syllables

A syllable is a part of a word that has one vowel sound. A word can have one syllable or many syllables.

teach (one syllable)

teaching (two syllables)

The vowels are *a, e, i, o,* and *u. Y* can also be a vowel when it sounds like *e* or *i.*

Y as a consonant	Y as a vowel
young	baby
yet	cry

Count the syllables in these words and write the numbers on your paper. You may use a dictionary.

1) decorate

2) explore

3) listening

4) celebrate

5) teaches

Write the verb that correctly completes each sentence on your paper.

1) Motor vehicle accidents (causes, cause) many injuries.

2) Some people (injures, injure) themselves in falls.

3) Most people who fall (is, are) over age 75.

4) The National Safety Council (records, record) these facts.

5) The Council (reports, report) the number of accidents.

6) Everyone (needs, need) ways to find information.

7) Almanacs (provides, provide) many kinds of information.

Find the mistakes in these sentences. Then write the sentences correctly on your paper. (Hint: Look for spelling and usage mistakes.)

8) Angela teachs children to swim at the YMCA.

9) Several of her friends wants to be teachers.

10) Both hopes to go to college.

11) Angela visit the community college.

12) She are thinking about a career.

13) Angela like children.

14) She also enjoy art class.

15) I enjoys ice cream cones.

The verb *to do* can be a main verb or a helping verb. The main verb *do* means "to perform an action."

> EXAMPLE   Neeru does her chores on the weekend.
> (main verb)
> She did vacuum the bedrooms. (helping verb)

We use the helping verb *do* for emphasis, with the word *not,* and in questions. Notice the word order in questions.

> EXAMPLE   Armando did enjoy the game. (emphasis)
>
> The soccer team does not practice on Fridays.
> (with word *not*)
>
> Do you enjoy soccer? (question)

Activity A   A form of the verb *to do* is bold in each sentence. Write it on your paper. Decide whether it is the main verb or a helping verb. Write that on your paper.

Example   After dinner Neeru **did** her math homework.
did—main verb

1) Neeru **does** her homework in the evening.

2) On weekends the family **does** housework.

3) They **do** the work together.

4) Her brother **did** not want his dessert.

5) "**Do** you like chocolate pudding?" he asked.

Verb Forms of *Do*		
Present tense	(singular) (plural)	Michelle **does** her homework after school. The students **do** their research in the library.
Past tense		Michelle **did** her report on Cesar Chavez.
Future tense		She **will do** another report on farm workers.
Present perfect tense	(singular) (plural)	Armando **has done** three reports for the class. The students **have done** several reports this year.
Past perfect tense		They **had done** research on the Internet.
Future perfect tense		They **will have done** a total of six reports by the end of the year.

Activity B Write the verb in each sentence on your paper. Write the tense of the verb next to it.

1) Efran does his research at the library and on the Internet.

2) He did his last report on Neil Armstrong.

3) He has done two reports on the space program this year.

4) Emily had done her first report on Wolfgang Amadeus Mozart.

5) She will do her next report on Mary Chapin Carpenter.

Activity C Write five sentences about tasks you do each week. Use the verb *do* in your sentences.

Example   I do the dishes after dinner every night.

Write the verb or verb phrase in each of these sentences on your paper. Next to each verb or verb phrase, write its tense.

1) Did Columbus land in the Americas in 1492?

2) Yes, he did explore the Americas then.

3) Do you know the exact date?

4) No, I do not know.

5) According to the almanac, Columbus's crew did sight land on October 12.

6) We do celebrate that day as a holiday.

7) What land did Columbus actually see?

8) He actually did explore the Bahamas.

9) Have you done your history homework?

10) I will have done it soon.

Use each of these verbs or verb phrases in a sentence on your paper. You may add *not* to the verb phrase. You may split up the verb phrase to form a question.

11) will have done

12) did go

13) will do

14) does play

15) do

Some helping verbs put a condition on an action. We use them to express possibility or necessity. These verbs are *may, might, can, could, shall, should, will, would,* and *must.*

EXAMPLE	may—might	Nathan may visit Mammoth Cave. Armando might get a job.
	can—could	Neeru can sing very well. Angela could win a gold medal.
	shall—should	Emily shall go to work. Mrs. Choy should finish her work.
	will—would	The team will practice after school.
		They would like to win their next game.
	must	We must leave soon. Nathan must return his book.

Look at the main verbs in the verb phrases above. They are all in the present tense.

Activity A Write the verb phrase in each sentence on your paper.

1) Emily can play the clarinet quite well.

2) They must get to class on time.

3) Would you like some dessert?

4) Neeru will sing a solo in the spring concert.

5) *Jane Eyre* may be my favorite book.

The helping verbs *may, might, can, could, shall, should, will, would,* and *must* may be combined with the perfect tenses.

EXAMPLE	
Present Perfect	The band may have gone.
Past Perfect	The band could have gone.
Present Progressive	The band may be going.
Past Progressive	The band would be going.

Activity B Write the verb phrase in each sentence on your paper. Write the tense next to each one.

Example   You must like that ice cream.
                   must like—present

1) Miguel's poster might win the contest.

2) He could have won last year.

3) The teacher may hang the poster in the school corridor.

4) Miguel could have used brighter colors.

5) Should he try again?

6) Neeru might be the best singer in the choir.

7) I would like that book.

8) You could have gone with me to the library.

9) Emily might walk her dog.

10) Nathan would walk with her to the corner if he had time.

You can avoid a common mistake that writers often make. Sometimes people write, "I should *of* done that," when they mean "I should *have* done that."

 I should have done that.

I must have done that.

Activity C Write the verb or verb phrase that correctly completes each sentence.

1) Howard (should have, should of) done his homework.

2) Emily practices her clarinet every day if she (can, could).

3) If she (would have, had) joined the band, she would have practiced more.

4) Armando (must have, must of) heard Emily play.

5) Nathan went fishing whenever he (can, could).

Do you know the difference between *may* and *can? Can* suggests the ability to do something. *May* asks for permission.

 I can swim a mile in 30 minutes.
May I go swimming now?

Activity D Write the word that correctly completes each sentence.

1) Neeru wondered, "(Can, May) I hit those high notes?"

2) Nathan asked, "(Can, May) I check out this book?"

3) Armando said that he (can, may) kick a soccer ball a mile.

4) Emily asked the director, "(Can, May) I switch to the flute?"

5) "(May, Can) I have your attention?" asked Mr. Jackson.

Write the verb or verb phrase that correctly completes each sentence.

1) Emily (should have, should of) practiced her clarinet longer.

2) "(Can, May) I play the solo in this piece?" asked Emily.

3) The students played popular songs when they (could, can).

4) Miguel visits the art gallery whenever he (could, can).

5) If he (would have, had) gone Friday, he would have seen Armando.

6) Neeru (must of, must have) seen the car.

7) I (like, would like) some dessert.

8) (May, Can) you hear that sound?

9) Angela (may, can) swim the backstroke.

Use each of these helping verbs in a sentence. Write the sentences on your paper.

10) may

11) might

12) can

13) would

14) should

15) must

Using What You've Learned

Write a memo asking your boss for a raise or promotion or asking your teacher how to improve your grades. Or write a memo to suggest a theme for a school celebration. Use at least two helping verbs from the Example box on page 144.

Newspapers

Maybe you read a newspaper every day. If so, you know that the newspaper is a great source of information. In newspapers you can find everything from the daily movie listings to stories about important events.

Large city newspapers provide many different kinds of articles. You will find stories on international, national, and local events. Newspapers make an excellent historical record because they provide many details about events. You can look up articles on the Presidential election of 2000, the moon walk of 1969, or the end of World War II in 1945. You will find newspaper articles written at the time each event occurred. Here is the beginning of a story from *Time for Kids World Report*.

Crossing the Finish Line

The Olympic Games in Sydney came to a loud, colorful close at a giant party in Olympic Stadium. So ended two weeks of thrilling performances by star athletes, surprising upsets by underdogs and, of course, some disappointments. Olympic athletes broke records on land, in the air, and in the water! Memories of their triumphs will live on long after the Olympic flame has faded.

The splashiest action during the first week happened in the pool. Australian champ Ian Thorpe set three freestyle records. Both the Australian and American teams broke the world record in the freestyle relay. U.S. swimmer Megan Quann defeated world-record holder Penny Heyns of South Africa.

Success seemed even sweeter to athletes who overcame tough luck to compete. U.S. diver Laura Wilkinson thought her Olympic hopes were gone when she broke her foot last spring. She came back to win gold in the 10-meter platform diving.

Libraries provide indexes of local newspapers and some national newspapers. Newspapers from past years are often available on microfilm. You can view the film on special machines in the library. Also, many large newspapers have online indexes. You can now read many newspapers online.

Newspapers also include editorials, which are essays stating someone's opinion. They include columns by feature writers. Newspapers also have feature stories about people, books, entertainment, travel, and sports.

1) Write these verbs from the newspaper article: *broke, will live, has faded, defeated, seemed*. Next to each one, write the verb's tense and identify whether the verb is regular or irregular.

2) Find a recent newspaper article that you think is interesting. If the article is written in the past tense, rewrite one paragraph so that it is in the present tense.

Using Vivid Verbs

In this writing activity, you will practice using vivid verbs
in your writing.

Ordinary Verbs	Vivid Verbs
sing	serenade
laugh	chortle
dance	disco
hurry	dash
excite	energize
drop	plummet
cleanse	disinfect
break	eradicate

Follow these directions:

1) Think about an activity that you really like. It could be playing
   a sport, attending a family event, having a picnic, doing a
   craft, or reading a book.

2) Describe this activity for someone who has never had this
   experience. Perhaps this person is from another country. Use as
   many action verbs as possible.

3) Make a list of the reasons why you like this activity. They do
   not have to be in sentences. Your reasons will be different
   from anyone else's.

4) Now use the information you wrote and plan an essay. Write
   two paragraphs. The first paragraph will describe the activity.
   The second paragraph will tell why it is fun or important to
   you.

5) Read your paragraphs. Underline all of the verbs. If any of the
   verbs seem ordinary, replace them with vivid verbs.

WORD BANK

action verb

helping verb

infinitive

irregular verb

past participle

perfect tenses

present participle

progressive verb phrase

regular verb

simple tenses

tense

verb phrase

Part A On a sheet of paper, write the correct word or words from the Word Bank to complete each sentence.

1) A _____ is a verb whose past tense and past participle are formed by adding -ed or -d.

2) A _____ is the verb form used to form the perfect tenses.

3) An _____ is a word that tells what someone or something does, did, or will do.

4) A _____ is a main verb plus a helping verb.

5) A _____ is the form of a verb that ends in -ing and uses a form of be as a helping verb to show continuous action.

6) A _____ is a verb that combines with a main verb to form a verb phrase.

7) A verb _____ tells the time when an action takes place.

8) The three _____ are present perfect, past perfect, and future perfect.

9) An _____ is a verb whose past tense and past participle are formed in different ways.

10) Verbs can express three _____—present, past, and future.

11) A _____ is a verb form that shows continuing action.

12) An _____ is the word to plus the present tense of a verb.

Part B Write the verb or verb phrase in each sentence on your paper. Be sure to include the helping verbs.

13) Armando will have scored four points.

14) Nathan has been playing tennis for four years.

15) He plays on the varsity team.

16) Arnold Palmer won many major golf tournaments.

Part C On your paper, write the verb form that correctly completes each sentence.

17) Today (has been, have been) colder than usual.

18) The temperatures this winter (have breaked, have broken) many records.

19) Where has Neeru (went, gone)?

20) She (has took, has taken) the letter to the post office.

Part D On your paper, write the correct form of each verb.

21) Neeru _____ in the concert. (present progressive form of *sing*)

22) She _____ in many concerts. (present perfect tense of *sing*)

23) Emily _____ her clarinet. (past perfect tense of *play* with the helping verb *could*)

24) She _____ her music every day. (present tense of *practice* with the helping verb *does*)

25) Everyone _____ sorry she will miss the concert. (present tense of *be*)

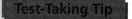
Test-Taking Tip Do you have vocabulary to learn? Make flash cards. Write a word on the front of each card. Write the definition on the back. Use the flash cards to test your skills.

CHAPTER 6

Using State-of-Being Verbs in Sentences

Some verbs do not express action. They express a state of being. A state of being is the way something is at the moment. A state of being can be the way someone looks or feels.

Look at the photograph on the opposite page. How would you describe the scene? You might say the mountains are high and the sky is blue. You could also say the air feels cool and smells clean. The verbs *are, is, feels,* and *smells* are state-of-being verbs. We use state-of-being verbs to express what we see, hear, taste, touch, or smell. We also use state-of-being verbs to express how we feel.

In Chapter 6, you will learn about state-of-being verbs. Each lesson tells about state-of-being verbs and how they are used in everyday speech and writing.

Goals for Learning

▶ To identify state-of-being verbs and verb phrases in sentences

▶ To distinguish between state-of-being and action verbs

▶ To use the correct form of state-of-being verbs in sentences

▶ To improve sentences with state-of-being verbs

State-of-being verb

A verb that tells something about the condition of the subject of a sentence

A state-of-being verb tells us something about the condition of the subject of the sentence.

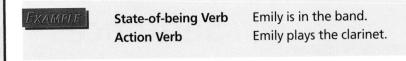

EXAMPLE		
State-of-being Verb	Emily is in the band.
Action Verb	Emily plays the clarinet.

The first sentence makes a statement about Emily. In the second sentence the verb *plays* tells an action that Emily does.

The most frequently used state-of-being verb is *to be*. Other forms of the verb include *am, is, are, was, were, being,* and *been. To be* means "to exist, to live, or to happen."

Verb Forms of *Be*		
Present	(singular)	(I) am, (he, she, it) is
	(plural)	are
Past	(singular)	was
	(plural)	were
Future		will be
Present perfect	(singular)	has been
	(plural)	have been
Past perfect		had been
Future perfect		will have been
Present progressive	(singular)	(I) am being, (he, she, it) is being
	(plural)	are being
Past progressive	(singular)	was being
	(plural)	were being
Future progressive		will be being

Activity A Write the verb or verb phrase in each sentence on your paper. Write the verb tense next to it.

Example   The weather is pleasant today.
           is—present

  1) Amanda and Emily have been at the mall.

  2) Neeru was at home.

  3) She goes to the mall once a week.

  4) Neeru is the lead soprano in the school choir.

  5) She will be the soloist this year.

Here are some other state-of-being verbs.

act	feel	keep	seem	stay
appear	get	look	smell	taste
become	grow	remain	sound	turn

The class stayed quiet during the video presentation.

The flowers still look fresh.

Activity B Write the verb or verb phrase in each sentence on your paper. Write the verb tense next to it.

Example   My best friend gets taller every year.   gets—present

  1) Emily's clarinet sounds out of tune.

  2) The art teacher remains Armando's strong supporter.

  3) The tea tastes bitter.

  4) Will everything turn out all right?

  5) Nathan appeared tired after his long trip.

Write the verb or verb phrase in each of these sentences on your paper.

1) The summer seems hotter than usual.

2) The sun gets warmer in the afternoon.

3) The family is staying cool inside.

4) Cool water would feel great.

5) The pool at the park looked very busy.

Complete each sentence with a state-of-being verb. Use the correct tense and try to use a different verb in each sentence. Write the sentences on your paper.

6) Nathan _____ like a friendly person.

7) Armando _____ an artist.

8) The sky _____ stormy.

9) That fresh bread _____ delicious.

10) We _____ friends for many years.

Using What You've Learned

Write an e-mail to a friend. Describe the sights and sounds of a recent school event. Use at least three state-of-being verbs. Underline them. If you don't have access to e-mail, write your message on a sheet of paper.

The verb *to be* expresses state of being when it is the main verb in a sentence.

> **EXAMPLE**   The sky is dark and stormy.
> The snow on the ground was deep.

Most state-of-being verbs can also be action verbs. To decide whether a verb expresses action or a state of being, think about the meaning of the sentence.

> **EXAMPLE**
>
> | | |
> |---|---|
> | **Action Verb** | Neeru feels the water to see if it is warm. |
> | **State-of-being Verb** | Neeru feels good today. |
> | **Action Verb** | Mrs. Choy grew roses in her yard. |
> | **State-of-being Verb** | Armando grew strong from exercise. |

Activity A Write the verb in each of these sentences on your paper. Next to each one, write *action* or *state of being* to tell how the verb is used. Ask yourself, "Is the subject doing something?" If it is, it is an action verb.

Example   The new neighbors look friendly.
              look—state of being

1) The weather today is cold and windy.

2) The temperature remains below freezing.

3) Angela tasted the hot chocolate.

4) The cold weather appeared out of nowhere.

5) The wind feels very cold.

Verbs often have more than one meaning. Some meanings express action and some express state of being.

EXAMPLE

appear	Action: to come into view; to become visible The storm appeared suddenly. State of being: to seem, to look The storm appears more dangerous than usual.
feel	Action: to touch; to think or believe Neeru felt the warmth of the fire. She felt that she would be safe. State of being: to be aware of a physical or mental sensation Neeru felt warm.
grow	Action: to cause to grow; to develop Mrs. Choy grows flowers. The roses grew all summer. State of being: to pass into a condition (become) The air grew colder.
smell	Action: to catch the scent or odor of something Jamar smelled the frying bacon. State of being: to have a certain scent or odor The bacon smells good.
look	Action: to use one's sense of sight Neeru looked out of the window at the storm. State of being: to appear a certain way Neeru looks cold.
taste	Action: to test the flavor of something Mrs. Choy tasted the tea. State of being: to have a certain flavor The tea tasted bitter.
get	Action: to fetch, to arrive at The package got to India on time. State of being: to be or to become or possess It gets cold after dark.

Activity B Decide whether the verb in bold expresses *action* or *state of being*.

1) Emily **felt** sick the night of the concert.

2) Her mother **felt** her forehead.

3) The fever **grew** worse by the hour.

4) Mrs. Wilson **grew** worried.

5) By evening Emily **appeared** better.

6) A coupon for free fries at Tony's **appeared** in the newspaper.

7) Jamar **tasted** the hot chocolate.

8) The marshmallow **tasted** very sweet.

9) The air **smelled** so clean and fresh.

10) Angela **smelled** the flowers.

The verb *seem* is always a state-of-being verb.

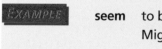

| EXAMPLE | **seem** to be, to appear |
| | Miguel seems lost. |

Activity C Write a description of something you think is beautiful. Use state-of-being verbs to describe it. Write five sentences. Use verbs other than *to be*. You may use past tense or any of the perfect tenses. Refer to the example box on page 158.

The mountain air smells clean and fresh.

1) Find nine verbs or verb phrases in the sentences in the paragraph. Write them on your paper. Write *action* or *state of being* next to each one.

> The American people love baseball. Many become fans of certain teams at an early age. Fans share trivia with each other. Who hit the first home run in Wrigley Field? It would have been in 1914. At the ballpark, hot dogs taste better. The air smells fresher. The children sound happier. Everyone appears happy and excited.

2) Write a paragraph about an activity or hobby that you enjoy. Use as many different state-of-being verbs as possible in your paragraph.

Vocabulary Builder

Building Words

Suffixes and prefixes are word parts that are added to root words. When suffixes and prefixes are added to root words, they make new words with new meanings. Sometimes a family of words can be built using one root word and different suffixes and prefixes.

The root word *port* means "to carry." The suffix *-able* means "able to be." So what does *portable* mean?

Root Word: *port*

export	import	transport
exporter	important	transportation
support	portable	reporter

Match each definition with one of the words above.

1) person who carries back the news
2) to send or carry goods out of the country
3) carrying great meaning or value

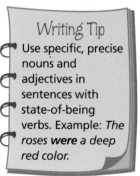

In a sentence, the verb must agree in number (singular or plural) with its subject. Subject-verb agreement for state-of-being verbs and action verbs is the same. We use one form with a singular subject and another form with a plural subject. Regular verbs and most irregular verbs add -*s* or -*es* to the present tense when the subject is singular.

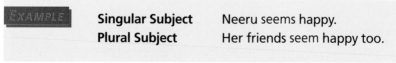

EXAMPLE		
Singular Subject	Neeru seems happy.
Plural Subject	Her friends seem happy too.

The past tense of the verb stays the same for singular and plural subjects.

EXAMPLE		
Singular Subject	Armando sounded excited about the game.
Plural Subject	His friends sounded excited too.

Activity A Write each sentence on your paper, using the proper form of the verb in parentheses. Be sure the subject and the verb agree.

Example   Emily's lemonade (taste) sweet.
Emily's lemonade tastes sweet.

  1) Armando (feel) sure that his answer is correct.

  2) The girls (appear) pleased with the results of the test.

  3) Emily (look) sad.

  4) The pasta sauce cooking on the stove (smell) delicious.

  5) The soup (taste) good.

The verb *to be* is an irregular verb. Its form depends on whether it is used with a singular or plural subject. It also depends on whether that subject is first, second, or third person.

Present and Past Forms of *Be*		
Singular	**Present**	**Past**
First person	I **am**	I **was**
Second person	you **are**	you **were**
Third person	he **is**	he **was**
	she **is**	she **was**
	it **is**	it **was**
Plural	**Present**	**Past**
First person	we **are**	we **were**
Second person	you **are**	you **were**
Third person	they **are**	they **were**

Use the same verb form with the pronoun *you*, whether it is singular or plural.

 EXAMPLE   You are a nice person.
You are nice people.

Activity B Complete each of these sentences with a form of the verb *to be*. Write the verb on your paper.

Example   Yesterday the weather _____ warmer.
             was

1) Emily _____ now a student at Wilson High School.

2) Emily's mother _____ a student there years ago.

3) Armando and Joe _____ in journalism class this year.

4) _____ you in the class too?

5) I _____ on the school newspaper staff.

State-of-being verbs have the same verb tenses as action verbs.

EXAMPLE	
Present	The water appears blue.
Past	The tea tasted sweet.
Future	The dog will smell better after a bath.
Present perfect	Miguel has been early every day.
Past perfect	Emily had seemed happy all week.
Future perfect	He will have been president for four years.

Activity C On your paper, write the state-of-being verb or verb phrase in each sentence. Write the verb tense next to each one.

Example   You look happy this evening.
        look—present

1) Mark Twain's real name was Samuel Clemens.

2) "The Celebrated Jumping Frog of Calaveras County" is a story by Mark Twain.

3) It became one of his most popular stories.

4) Mark Twain's story has remained popular.

5) The story will be fun for you to read.

Many critics think that Samuel Clemens, or Mark Twain, (1835–1910) was the greatest American humorist. As a young man, Twain was a riverboat pilot on the Mississippi River. The pen name *Mark Twain* comes from a riverboat term that means "12 feet deep."

Activity D Change the verb to the tense given and use it in a sentence as a state-of-being verb. Underline the verb or verb phrase.

Example   look—past
Armando <u>looked</u> tired after the game.

1) smell   present

2) appear   future

3) grow   present perfect

4) be   past perfect

5) feel   future perfect

Spelling Builder

Verb Tense

All of the verbs in a sentence should be consistent. Some sentences may include more than one main verb. Generally, all verbs should be in the same tense if the actions occur at the same time. However, different tenses can show that actions occur at different times.

> Armando hopes his team will win the match.
> (The verb *hopes* is present tense. The verb phrase *will win* is future tense. Right now, Armando hopes that his team will win in the future.)

Rewrite each sentence to make the verb tense consistent.

1) Pay attention to verb tense and your writing improved.

2) When the sun shines, the corn grew taller.

3) Nathan hoped his family will plan a trip to Boston.

Read each sentence. Choose the form of the verb that agrees with the subject. Write the sentence on your paper.

1) The survivor (was, were) cold and tired.

2) Frank (look, looks) restless.

3) The cats (appear, appears) uninterested.

4) Where (is, are) your jacket?

5) Armando and Joe (feel, feels) good about the game.

Write a sentence using each of the following verbs. Be sure the subject and verb agree.

6) am   **9)** was

7) is   **10)** have been

8) are

Find the verb or verb phrase in each sentence. Write it on your paper. Write the verb tense next to it.

11) In the last few years, personal computers have grown more popular.

12) For decades, computers have been important tools for engineers and scientists.

13) Today many people seem dependent on their laptop computers.

14) Many students have become expert computer users.

15) Computers will remain an important tool in schools, in businesses, and at home.

Where to Find It

Atlas

Suppose a friend took a trip to Reykjavik. Is this a city or a country? Where is it located? You could find this information in an **atlas**. An atlas is a book of maps. Libraries have many different kinds of atlases. There are world atlases and United States atlases.

You can look up names of cities and countries, as well as other mapped features, such as rivers and mountains, in the index of an atlas. The index shows the page on which to find each feature. It also shows the location of the feature on that page.

PLACE (Pronunciation)	PAGE	Lat. °	Long. °
Reyes, Point, c., Ca., U.S.	108	38.00°N	123.00°W
Reykjanes, c., Ice. (rā′kya-nes)	142	63.37°N	24.33°W
Reykjavik, Ice. (rā′kya-vēk)	142	64.09°N	21.39°W
Reynosa, Mex. (rā-ė-nō′sä)	112	26.05°N	98.21°W
Rezekne, Lat. (rā′zek-ne)	166	56.31°N	27.19°E
Rezh, Russia (rezh)	172a	57.22°N	61.23°E
Rezina, Mol. (ryezh′e-ni)	163	47.44°N	28.56°E
Rhaetian Alps, mts., Eur.	154	46.30°N	10.00°E
Rhaetien Alps, mts., Eur.	160	46.22°N	10.33°E
Rheinberg, Ger. (rīn′bergh)	157c	51.33°N	6.37°E

Find the answer to each of these questions in a world atlas. Answer each question with a complete sentence. Use a state-of-being verb in each sentence and underline it.

1) Is Reykjavik a city or a country? Write a sentence explaining where it is located.

2) In what country is the Yangtze River? What is one city on the river?

3) What countries surround Mont Blanc?

4) What is the capital of Montana? Is it closer to Billings or to Great Falls?

State-of-Being Verbs

State-of-being verbs are useful when you write descriptions of things that are not moving or doing anything.

Read these descriptions. See if you can identify each object. Write your answers on a sheet of paper.

1) This object is a piece of paper with boxes and numbers that hangs on the wall. What is it?

2) This object is made of hundreds of pieces of paper with lists of words. What is it?

3) This object is made of metal and has four legs and two arms. What is it?

4) This object is like a television set but runs programs instead of showing them. What is it?

Now write a description of an object in the classroom using at least one state-of-being verb. You can also use action verbs. After everyone has finished writing, take turns sharing the descriptions.

Here are some state-of-being verbs you might use:

is	looks	smells	feels	seems	sounds	acts

Part A Write the correct words to complete the sentence.

1) A _____ is a verb that tells about the condition of the subject of a sentence.

Part B Write the verb or verb phrase in each of these sentences on your paper.

2) The weather seems very threatening today.

3) The sky appears darker than usual.

4) The air even smells like snow.

5) Everyone gets excited.

6) The sleds are in the shed.

7) A ride down the hill seems like fun.

8) Neeru has never been in a snowstorm.

9) The weather in Calcutta is tropical.

10) The air is growing colder.

Part C Does the bold verb in each sentence express an action or a state of being? Write *action* or *state of being* on your paper.

11) The teacher **appeared** unexpectedly in the room.

12) The classroom **turned** quiet.

13) You **could feel** the tension in the air.

14) Everyone **felt** nervous.

15) "You **look** worried," Mr. Thomas said.

16) **Does** this test **seem** hard?

17) Nathan **remained** calm.

18) He **stayed** in his seat.

Part D Choose the verb form in each sentence that agrees with the subject. Write the answer on your paper. (Hint: Find the subject first and ask yourself if it is singular [one] or plural [more than one].)

19) Chandra (is, are) a cheerleader at Wilson High School.

20) This pie (smells, smell) fresh.

21) The cafeteria (is, are) noisy.

22) Every student there (was, were) talking.

23) Both of these juices (tastes, taste) tangy.

24) That movie (remains, remain) my favorite.

25) The computers (has been, have been) in the media center for a month.

26) Neeru (is being, are being) quiet today.

27) The students in my class (grow, grows) quiet as the movie begins.

Part E Use each verb or verb phrase correctly in a sentence. Write the sentences on your paper.

28) has been

29) have remained

30) is being

31) is practicing

32) was becoming

33) seemed

34) is getting

35) stayed

Test-Taking Tip

If you know you will be asked to label parts of a sentence on an English test, write sample sentences. Then practice identifying sentence parts.

Using Adverbs in Sentences

E very idea that we express has two parts. We talk about something, and that is the subject. We tell what the subject did, and that is the predicate. The main word in the predicate is the verb.

Verbs alone do not provide the best picture or description of what the subject is doing. What is happening in the photograph on the opposite page? Lightning strikes the ground. Dark clouds move across the sky. *Strikes* and *move* tell what is happening, but we want to know more. We want to know h*ow, when, where,* and *why.* Adverbs can answer those questions. Lightning strikes the ground suddenly. Dark clouds move rapidly across the sky.

In Chapter 7, you will learn about adverbs. You will learn how to use these words to make your ideas clearer to other people.

Goals for Learning

▶ To recognize adverbs in sentences
▶ To identify the verbs, adjectives, or other adverbs that the adverb answers questions about
▶ To use adverbs in comparisons
▶ To add adverbs to sentences
▶ To recognize double negatives

What Is an Adverb?

Adverb

A word that answers questions about a verb, an adjective, or another adverb in a sentence

An **adverb** is a word that can answer questions about a verb, an adjective, or another adverb in a sentence. Many adverbs tell about verbs. Verbs express action. An **adverb** answers the questions *how, when,* or *where* the action happened.

Adverbs that answer the question *how* are usually used with action verbs. They tell more about the way the action was done.

EXAMPLE

The flu hit suddenly.

The airplane banked sharply.

The family ate dinner quickly.

Activity A Find the adverb in each sentence and write it on your paper. The adverb will tell *how* the action happened.

1) Neeru sings beautifully.

2) Emily plays the clarinet well.

3) The librarian gladly helped Angela find a book.

4) I clumsily dropped the mug.

5) Angela swam her race fast.

Activity B Write these sentences on your paper. Look at the verb in bold. Add an adverb that answers the question *How was the action done?*

1) Nathan **studied.**

2) Mrs. Choy **cooked** dinner.

3) The actor **spoke** his lines.

4) Katie **juggles.**

5) The track team **runs.**

Adverbs can answer the question *when, how long,* or *how many times.* They tell more about the time of action or state of being.

Efran's father is leaving today on a business trip.
Neeru's aunt has owned the farm forever.
Emily worked twice last week.
Angela will be there tomorrow.

Adverbs can answer the question *where* or *in what direction.* They tell more about the place of the action or state of being.

The band room is there.
I left my clarinet outside.

Activity C Complete each sentence by writing an adverb that answers the question in parentheses.

1) Neeru will be home (when?).

2) Emily read that book (how often?).

3) Efran turned (in what direction?) at the next corner.

4) The school is (where?).

5) They have seen the movie (how many times?).

Activity D Write five sentences about a favorite activity such as swimming, walking, hiking, or playing a sport. Use adverbs that answer the question *when, how often, how long,* or *how many times.* Include some of the adverbs in the box or choose others.

Sometimes a noun can act as an adverb in a sentence. In the following sentence, the word *home* is an adverb that answers the question *where*.
   I am going **home**.

Adverbs			
again	next	previously	today
already	now	quickly	tomorrow
forever	once	shortly	usually
lately	presently	soon	yesterday

Write all the adverbs in these sentences on your paper. A sentence can have more than one adverb.

1) The students at Wilson High School are excitedly preparing for the winter party. They are having an indoor field day, as they do annually. For the winter theme, Emily and Nathan are carefully making snowflake decorations that they will hang in the gym today. Games and contests will be held tomorrow. Each class will play competitively. Usually the seniors win the games. Sometimes the juniors and sophomores win. In the "snowball" toss, teams will quickly toss beanbags into buckets. The next game is an obstacle course that each team will rapidly try to complete. Occasionally, the principal and assistant principal participate in the obstacle course.

Write an adverb that answers the question in parentheses about the verb in bold.

2) Neeru (how?) **wrote** a letter to her cousin.

3) She and her cousin **write** to each other (how often?).

4) Neeru sealed the letter and **walked** (where?) to mail it.

5) She hoped her cousin **would get** the letter (when?).

Using What You've Learned

Write a very short scary story. You may write about something that happened to you or make up an event. Use at least three adverbs that tell more about action verbs in the story. Read or tell your story aloud in a small group.

You have learned about adverbs that tell about verbs. Adverbs can also answer questions about adjectives and other adverbs. They answer the questions *how much, how little, how often,* and *to what degree.*

Writing Tip
Don't overuse the adverbs in the list when you write persuasively. Which of the following statements is more convincing?

This law is rather unfair.

This law is unfair.

Adverbs Used with Adjectives and Other Adverbs		
almost	extremely	rather
altogether	just	so
awfully	little	sometime
completely	nearly	too
entirely	partly	unusually
especially	quite	very

Adverbs that answer questions about adjectives usually are in front of the adjective.

Remember, adjectives describe nouns and pronouns. Adverbs tell more about verbs, adjectives, and other adverbs.

EXAMPLE

How hot?   The coffee was very hot.
How soft?   That puppy's ears are so soft.
How cold?   Today was extremely cold.

Activity A Find an adjective in each sentence. Then add an adverb that tells *how much, how little, how often,* or *to what degree.* If you add an adverb that begins with a vowel, be sure to change the article from *a* to *an.*

Example   Neeru's little sister is adorable.
Neeru's little sister is **quite** adorable.

1) Angela was fast in today's practice.

2) What a wonderful movie that was!

3) The sound of the rain on the roof is loud.

4) The chicken tastes spicy.

5) Emily is a careful reader.

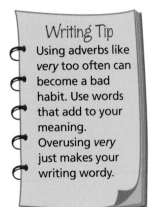

Writing Tip

Using adverbs like *very* too often can become a bad habit. Use words that add to your meaning. Overusing *very* just makes your writing wordy.

Adverbs that answer questions about other adverbs are usually in front of the adverb.

| EXAMPLE | How slowly? | The girls walked very slowly. |
| | How quickly? | Emily finished the test so quickly. |

Activity B Find the adverb in each sentence. Add an adverb that answers the question *how much, how little, how often,* or *to what degree.* Write the new sentences on your paper.

Example   Angela swam **fast** in today's practice.
Angela swam **extremely** fast in today's practice.

1) Angela swims the backstroke fast.

2) Neeru sings softly.

3) Mr. Thomas plans his lessons thoughtfully.

4) Katie worked diligently on her project.

5) Mrs. Benson clears her throat loudly to get the attention of the class.

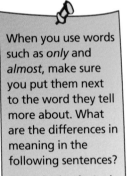

When you use words such as *only* and *almost*, make sure you put them next to the word they tell more about. What are the differences in meaning in the following sentences?

*She asked **only** Andy to take his sister.*
*She asked Andy to take **only** his sister.*
*She asked Andy to take his **only** sister.*

Katie worked diligently on her art project.

Find the adverbs that tell *how much, how little, how often,* or *to what degree* about adjectives or other adverbs in these sentences. Write them on your paper.

1) Emily almost always reads before going to bed.

2) Neeru was especially nervous before her voice recital.

3) I tripped rather clumsily while walking up the stairs.

4) Stacy was completely happy with her test scores.

5) Angela climbed the ladder extremely cautiously.

6) This summer has been unusually cool.

7) The forecast is for partly cloudy skies.

8) They live nearly 10 miles from here.

9) The turtle moved very slowly.

Write these sentences on your paper. The words in bold are either adverbs or adjectives. Add an adverb in front of each one. Use six different adverbs. If you add an adverb that begins with a vowel, be sure to change the article from *a* to *an*.

10)   Nathan woke up **late** and missed the bus. It was **silent** in the halls when he got to school. He **quietly** opened the door to the classroom and sat down.. **Suddenly,** he realized that he had forgotten to bring his notebook. This was turning out to be a **bad** day! Because he was **tired,** he fell asleep in class. Suddenly, his alarm clock went off and he woke up. He realized that it had all been a dream!

Adverbs of Negation

Adverb of negation

The adverbs never *and* not, *which tell that an action in a sentence will not happen or that a state of being is not present*

Never and *not* are **adverbs of negation.** A negative adverb means that the action will *not* happen or that the state of being is *not* present. The adverb *not* may be part of a contraction.

Remember that adverbs answer questions about a verb, an adjective, or another adverb.

> **EXAMPLE**
> Armando never misses his art class.
> Mrs. Choy is not home today.
> Angela can't wait for the party.

Activity A Write these sentences on your paper. Circle the adverbs of negation.

1) Neeru has never been to Niagara Falls.

2) Emily did not bring her extra reeds to band practice.

3) The snow was not deep, but it was heavy.

4) I never said this would be easy.

5) This is not Neeru's house.

Ain't as a contraction of *am not, is not,* or *are not* is not acceptable in most kinds of writing or speech.

Don't use double negatives.

> **EXAMPLE**
> **Incorrect** I don't have no paper.
> **Correct** I don't have any paper.

Activity B Rewrite the sentences to correct the double negatives.

1) Neeru does not know nothing about the game.

2) Emily didn't bring no music with her.

3) He is never not home.

4) I could not do nothing to fix my bike.

5) A picnic in the rain isn't no fun.

Adverbs of Negation in Contractions

You have learned that in a contraction, we make two words into one by replacing one or more letters with an apostrophe. Examples of contractions are *you'll* (*you will*) and *what's* (*what is*). A verb and the adverb *not* make up some contractions. In these contractions, the *o* in the adverb *not* is replaced by an apostrophe.

> **EXAMPLE**
> I haven't read that book yet. (have not)
> Emily can't finish her term paper today. (cannot)
> She won't finish her term paper today. (will not)

Most contractions are made up of two words. However, the word *cannot* is one word. The contraction of *cannot* is *can't*.

Activity C Find the contractions with adverbs of negation in these sentences. Write the contraction as two words.

Example   Efran isn't in class today. isn't—is not

1) Emily didn't watch the news last night.

2) Armando's mind wasn't on the game tonight.

3) Nathan couldn't wait to go fishing again.

4) You shouldn't have any trouble completing this assignment.

5) Angela wasn't at practice today.

Most contractions of verbs with *not* use the verb plus the shortened form of *not*. The contraction for *will not* is irregular, however. The contraction for *will not* is *won't*.

Activity D Rewrite these sentences on your paper. Add an adverb of negation to each sentence. You may use contractions. Be sure not to use double negatives.

Example   I have read *Great Expectations*.
                I have **not** read *Great Expectations*.

1) Angela has broken the school record in butterfly.

2) Mr. Thomas did give homework tonight.

3) I would be able to go to all the meetings.

4) It was Mike who scored the winning goal.

5) Emily had been to the store when I called her.

Write the adverbs of negation in these sentences on your paper. Some of them may be part of contractions.

1) I don't like waiting in line.

2) Emily couldn't see the movie because the person in front of her was too tall.

3) Mr. Thomas never assigns homework on weekends.

4) Adam would not stop talking in class.

5) Mrs. Langston didn't open the weight room after school yesterday.

Rewrite these sentences on your paper. Add an adverb of negation to each sentence.

6) There is extra paper if you need it.

7) I can go to the movies tonight.

8) Angela could find the right answer in her book.

9) Neeru has practiced for her voice lesson.

10) Chris is in my writing class.

Rewrite the sentences to correct the double negatives.

11) I didn't get no sleep last night.

12) Adam could not do nothing to stop the noise.

13) There isn't no more paper.

14) Angela won't never miss swim practice.

15) Chris did not find nothing in the closet.

Some words may be used as either adverbs or adjectives. The difference is in the way we use them in a sentence.

> EXAMPLE
>
> | **Adjective** | **Adverb** |
> |---|---|
> | Angela is a fast swimmer. | She swims fast. |
> | (What kind of swimmer is she?) | (How does she swim?) |

Activity A Read each sentence. Think about the word in bold. Decide whether it is an adjective or an adverb. Write your answer on your paper.

Example   The **first** game will be a snowball toss.
First is an adjective because it describes the noun *game.*

The freshman class will begin **first**.
First is an adverb because it tells about the verb *begin.*

1) The **next** game is an obstacle course.

2) The sophomore team will start that obstacle course **next**.

3) Students jumped **high** over the small wading pools.

4) Mrs. Benson won the **first** tricycle race.

5) She crossed the finish line **first**.

We can change many adjectives into adverbs by adding the ending *-ly.*

> EXAMPLE
>
> | **Adjectives** | **Adverbs** |
> |---|---|
> | That is her usual way. | She usually is late. |
> | Emily is a quiet person. | She speaks quietly. |
> | The ocean is calm. | The teacher spoke calmly. |

Activity B Write the words in bold on your paper. Decide if each word is an adjective or an adverb. Then write *adjective* or *adverb* next to the word.

1) Neeru was **happy** to see the good grades on her report card.

2) Armando finished his homework **quickly.**

3) Emily waited **excitedly** to buy tickets to see her favorite artist.

4) Mr. Choy likes **strong** coffee.

5) I **strongly** suggest you do your homework.

Not all words ending in *-ly* are adverbs. Many common adjectives end in *-ly*, too.

> **EXAMPLE** Mr. Wilson gave Nathan some fatherly advice.
> (*Fatherly* is an adjective describing the noun *advice*.)

Other words that end in *-ly* may be adjectives or adverbs.

> **EXAMPLE**
> **Adjective** He wrote a daily report.
> **Adverb** He wrote the report daily.

Activity C Write each word in bold on your paper. Next to each word, write *adjective* or *adverb*.

Example   Armando noticed a car going **dangerously** fast.
dangerously—adverb

Armando woke up **early** this morning so that he could do his **daily** exercises before school. He started with some stomach crunches and then went for a **lively** jog. Armando knew it was **dangerous** to jog on the road when it was still dark out. He was **careful** to stay on the sidewalk. Armando **quietly** went in the house to avoid waking anyone. He forgot to warm up this morning, and it proved to be a **costly** mistake. **Luckily,** his coach says his sore muscles only need rest.

Write the words in bold on your paper. Next to each word, write *adverb* or *adjective*.

1) This past summer, Nathan saw a **deadly** spider in Wyoming.

2) He and his family take a vacation **yearly.**

3) Nathan was on his **daily** hike when he saw the spider.

4) He woke up **early.**

5) He was whistling **happily** as he hiked.

6) **Lately,** he had been waking up to see the sunrise.

7) The sun had **partly** risen over the horizon.

8) Suddenly he saw the very **ugly** spider crawling on a branch.

9) He ran back to camp, breathing **hard.**

10) He breathed a sigh of relief when he reached the tent **safely!**

Vocabulary Builder

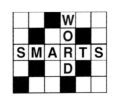

Words That Sound Alike

People often confuse pairs of words that sound almost alike. Read these examples aloud:

quiet (adjective)—lacking sound
quite (adverb)—almost

probable (adjective)—likely
probably (adverb)—likely

Write the word that correctly completes each sentence.

1) I thought the book was (quite, quiet) interesting.

2) Please be (quiet, quite) in the library.

3) Her team will (probable, probably) win the race.

4) It is (probable, probably) that Adam will play.

You can use adverbs to make comparisons. The three degrees of comparison are positive, comparative, and superlative.

EXAMPLE	Positive	Comparative	Superlative
	fast	faster	fastest
	slowly	more slowly	most slowly
	happily	less happily	least happily
	well	better	best

Activity A Write the adverbs in the sentences on your paper.

1) Armando is working harder this year.

2) He writes well.

3) Each week he writes his reports more clearly.

4) Joe contributes stories more regularly than Armando.

5) Joe writes faster than Armando.

Forming Comparisons

Rule 1 Most one-syllable adverbs form the comparative and superlative forms by adding -*er* and -*est*.

Rule 2 Most adverbs of more than one syllable use *more* and *most* or *less* and *least* to form the comparative and superlative.

Rule 3 A few adverbs, such as *well,* are irregular. The comparative and superlative of *well* are *better* and *best.*

The comparative form compares two people or things. The superlative form compares more than two people or things.

| Comparative | Miguel draws more quickly than Joe. |
| Superlative | Efran draws most quickly of them all. |

Activity B Write the form of the adverb that correctly completes each sentence. Then write *comparative* or *superlative*.

1) Neeru can sing (higher, highest) than anyone else in the choir.

2) Brittany writes for the school newspaper (more often, most often) than Armando.

3) Compared to the other employees, Emily works (harder, hardest).

4) Angela swam (faster, fastest) in the third event.

5) Some people like cassette tapes (better, best) than CDs.

Activity C Write a sentence using these adverbs in their comparative form. Write another sentence using these adverbs in their superlative form. Be sure that your adverb tells something about an action verb.

Example   loud   That band plays **louder** than the others.

1) quickly   **4)** brightly

2) wisely   **5)** early

3) late

The lead cyclist in the race rode much faster than the cyclist in second place.

Write the adverbs in these sentences on your paper. Next to each adverb, write its degree of comparison: *positive, comparative,* or *superlative.*

1) Nathan rapidly finished his report.

2) Armando's art magazine arrived late.

3) Of the three students, Angela swam fastest.

4) Who plays tennis better, Emily or Angela?

5) Can you paint a mural on the wall sooner than next month?

Write your own sentences using each of these adverbs or adverb phrases correctly.

6) more cheaply

7) most loudly

8) faster

9) more slowly

10) sadly

Spelling Builder

Suffixes That Begin with Consonants:
-ful, -less, -ly, -ness

When you add a suffix that begins with a consonant to a word, do you change the word's spelling? The answer depends on the word. Use these rules:

- If the word ends in any letter except *y,* just add the suffix: *sad—sadly.*
- If the word ends in *y,* change the *y* to *i* and add the suffix: *happy—happily.*

Add *-ly* to each of these words.

heavy   rapid   entire   busy

Adverbs often tell when the action in a sentence is taking place. *Ago* or *yesterday* indicates past time. *Later* or *tomorrow* tells us the action is in the future. The tense of the verb in the sentence and the adverb must agree.

We went there some time ago.	(past action)
Yesterday we went to school.	(past action)
They will go later.	(future action)
Tomorrow we will go to school.	(future action)

Activity A In these sentences, the adverbs are in bold. Write each sentence using the correct tense of the verb in parentheses.

1) I (order) the books a while **ago.**

2) The CD (be) on sale **weekly.**

3) Tomorrow Armando (go) fishing.

4) Neeru **always** (meet) us at the mall.

5) Yesterday Angela (look) at college applications.

Use an adverb, not an adjective, when you are telling about an action.

Armando worked carefully on the mural.
He slowly painted each section.

Remember to use an adjective in a sentence with a state-of-being verb. The adjective describes the subject of the sentence.

Armando was careful.
The mural looked beautiful.

Activity B On your paper, write the word that correctly completes the sentence. Check by reading the sentences aloud.

1) Neeru sang the song (perfect, perfectly).

2) Nathan liked to do his math (accurate, accurately).

3) Are these answers (correct, correctly)?

4) Efran's dessert tasted (delicious, deliciously).

5) Emily danced (graceful, gracefully).

Using *Good* and *Well*

Good is always an adjective and describes a noun. *Well* is usually an adverb. *Well* means "in a good or proper manner."

> The juice tastes good. (*Good* describes juice.)
> They worked well together. (*Well* describes the action *worked*.)

Well is an adjective when it describes someone's health. Either *good* or *well* will work in this sentence.

> Emily feels well today.
> Emily feels good today.

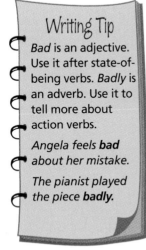

Writing Tip

Bad is an adjective. Use it after state-of-being verbs. *Badly* is an adverb. Use it to tell more about action verbs.

*Angela feels **bad** about her mistake.*

*The pianist played the piece **badly.***

Activity C Decide whether to complete each sentence with *good* or *well*. Write your answers on your paper.

1) Neeru is (good, well) at singing.

2) No one plays the clarinet as (good, well) as Emily.

3) Miguel says that he cleans his room (good, well) every week.

4) Mrs. Choy's tea tasted especially (good, well).

5) No one can play soccer as (good, well) as Armando.

On your paper, write the word that correctly completes each sentence. Then say the sentences aloud. Try to "hear" the correct sentence.

1) Mrs. Benson said she needed the story (quick, quickly).

2) The river water smelled (bad, badly).

3) Everyone knows that Emily speaks (soft, softly).

4) Angela is a (graceful, gracefully) swimmer.

5) Efran can draw anything (perfect, perfectly).

Decide whether *good* or *well* correctly completes each sentence. Write your answers on your paper.

6) Efran mixed the batter really (good, well).

7) Everyone thought the winter games were a (good, well) idea.

8) I thought the sweet potatoes tasted (good, well).

9) Yesterday I could not see (good, well) because of the fog.

10) Everyone worked (good, well) together at the winter games.

Write each sentence using the correct tense of the verb in parentheses. Be sure that the verb tense and the adverb agree.

11) Joe (deliver) newspapers in his neighborhood daily.

12) Emily and Meg (play) a duet shortly.

13) Yesterday we (go) to a basketball game.

14) He is excited that he (graduate) soon.

15) She (go) regularly to yoga classes.

Telephone Book

Suppose you want to find the phone number of a friend or your family dentist. Of course, you go straight to your local telephone book. The white pages of the phone book list people alphabetically by their last names. But sometimes you may want to find a person or a company for a specific product or service. For example, you want to order flowers for Mother's Day. To find a florist, you turn to the yellow pages of the phone book.

The yellow pages are arranged alphabetically by category. You can find categories from AUTOMOBILE REPAIRS to MAGICIANS to YOGA INSTRUCTION. Under each category is an alphabetical list of the businesses that offer that product or service. Each listing provides the company's or individual's address and phone number.

The yellow pages also contain paid advertisements for some of the companies that are listed. Some companies pay for ads to attract readers' attention. If you were looking for flowers, you might be attracted to the following ad.

Beautiful Bloom Flowers
We arrange flowers creatively and uniquely.
We deliver bouquets on time to meet your needs.
We use the most freshly cut flowers.
BLOOM'S FLOWERS
(878)555-2398

Yellow page ads can be informative. But be aware that they are ads like those in newspapers and magazines. You may want to call several businesses for additional information before choosing a particular company.

1) On your paper, write the adverbs that appear in the text of the ad above.
2) Look through your yellow pages. Find an ad that includes at least two adverbs. Write the phrases or sentences that include the adverbs on your paper.
3) Create your own yellow page ad for a business that you invent. Use at least three adverbs in your ad and underline them.

Using Adverbs

Write five to seven sentences about one of the topics listed here. Use adverbs in your sentences to make your ideas clearer. You may use adverbs from the box below or any others you choose. Try not to use the same adverb twice.

Topics to Write About

- A camping experience
- A frightening event
- A recent school activity
- Learning to use a computer

Common Adverbs		
absolutely	extremely	so
almost	fairly	sometime
altogether	just	somewhat
approximately	little	too
awfully	moderately	totally
chiefly	nearly	unusually
completely	partly	very
entirely	quite	wonderfully
especially	rather	

Part A On a sheet of paper, write the correct word or words from the Word Bank to complete each sentence.

1) An _____ answers questions about verbs, adjectives, or other adverbs.

2) An _____ means that an action will not happen or that a state of being is not present.

Part B On your paper, write the word that correctly completes each sentence. Then say the sentences aloud.

3) Emily learned to use a computer (easy, easily).

4) She can keyboard (fast, faster) than Katie.

5) Of all the students, Emily keyboards (better, best).

6) She uses a very (good, well) word processing program.

7) Angela felt (bad, badly) because she had never used a word processor.

8) She is hoping to learn to use the word processing program (quick, quickly).

9) Of all of her friends, Angela learns (rapid, most rapidly).

10) Angela feels (good, well) about learning a new skill.

Part C Find the adverb or adverbs in these sentences. Write them on your paper.

11) Emily doesn't know how she could ever complete her schoolwork without her computer. She thinks her laptop is extremely useful. She often takes it downtown with her to her part-time job at the music store. She can type very rapidly.

Part D Rewrite these sentences on your paper. Add an adverb of negation to each sentence.

12) Angela has bought a new computer.

13) She was happy to throw away her typewriter.

14) She says she will go back to it.

15) Her new computer is portable.

Part E Rewrite these sentences on your paper. Correct the double negatives.

16) Nathan does not have no interest in computers.

17) He never said he was no computer expert.

18) His friends couldn't teach him nothing about computers.

19) He won't never listen to what they say.

Part F Find the adverbs in these sentences. List them in order on your paper. A sentence may have more than one adverb.

20)   In the past, people carefully used a pen to do all their writing. Fortunately, C. L. Sholes, an American journalist, invented the typewriter in 1868. Soon, typewriters were essential almost everywhere. Students often took typing classes in high school. Recently, in the 1980s, computers began to replace typewriters. Now students work hard at a new skill called keyboarding.

Test-Taking Tip When you are reading a test question, pay attention to words that are emphasized in bold type or in capital letters. Those words will help you decide how best to answer the question.

Using Prepositional Phrases

A preposition is a word that shows a relationship between a noun or pronoun and the rest of a sentence. A preposition is always part of a phrase.

Study the photograph on the opposite page. Where is the diver? The diver is in the water. The diver is above the reef. The prepositional phrases *in the water* and *above the reef* describe the diver's location in relation to the water and the reef.

In Chapter 8, you will learn to use prepositional phrases. Prepositional phrases will help you express ideas more clearly and in a more exciting way.

Goals for Learning

▶ To identify prepositional phrases in sentences

▶ To distinguish between prepositions and adverbs

▶ To identify the form of pronouns used in prepositional phrases

▶ To write sentences with prepositional phrases

Preposition

A word that shows a relationship between a noun or pronoun and other words in a sentence

A **preposition** shows a relationship between a noun or pronoun and other words in a sentence. A preposition is always a part of a **prepositional phrase**. A prepositional phrase is a group of words that includes a preposition and the **object of a preposition.** The object of a preposition is the noun or pronoun that follows the preposition in a prepositional phrase.

Prepositional phrase

A group of words made up of a preposition, an object, and adjectives and adverbs that describe the object

> EXAMPLE
> The computer is on the desk.
> (*On the desk* is a prepositional phrase.
> *On* is the preposition. *Desk* is the object
> of the preposition.)

In this sentence, the prepositional phrase tells *where* the computer is in relation to the desk. Each preposition has a specific meaning.

Object of a preposition

The noun or pronoun that follows the preposition in a prepositional phrase

> EXAMPLE
> The computer could be beside the desk.
> The computer could be under the desk.

Activity A Write five sentences telling other ways that the computer could be related to the desk. Use these prepositions: *by, near, beneath, behind,* and *above.*

Activity B The preposition is missing from the sentence by each picture. Write the sentence on your paper. Add a preposition that expresses the relationship that you see in the picture. (Hint: Use the preposition list on page 198.)

1) Emily is sitting _____ a field of wildflowers.

2) The pelican soars _____ the water looking for fish.

3) The green apple is sandwiched _____ the two red apples.

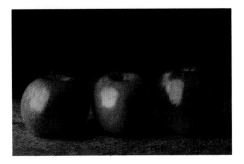

4) Armando holds his pen _____ the notebook.

5) The players are _____ the field.

Activity C Here is a list of prepositions. Choose five and use each one in a sentence. Then underline the prepositional phrases in your sentences.

Example The soda spilled <u>on the desk</u>.

Prepositions				
about	at	by	near	through
above	before	down	of	to
across	behind	during	off	toward
after	below	except	on	under
against	beneath	for	out	until
among	beside	from	over	with
around	between	in	past	within
as	but	into	regarding	without

Parts of a Prepositional Phrase

Every preposition has an object. A preposition plus an object make up a prepositional phrase. The object is a noun or pronoun. There may be adjectives in front of the object.

> EXAMPLE
>
> on the desk
>
> on his sloppy desk
>
> beside his new car
>
> to me

A prepositional phrase can also have an adverb.

 after the very long meeting
near an extremely busy highway

Activity D Use each of these prepositional phrases in a complete sentence. Write the sentences on your paper and underline the prepositional phrase in each one.

Example   after the very long meeting
             We went home <u>after the very long meeting.</u>

1) around the corner

2) during the very cold night

3) in the dark, star-filled sky

4) in my right hand

5) through the wide doorway

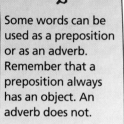

Some words can be used as a preposition or as an adverb. Remember that a preposition always has an object. An adverb does not.

*Tom fell **down**.* (adverb)

*Tom fell **down the hill**.* (preposition)

The object of a preposition may be a proper noun.

 Armando wrote a letter to Aunt Edna.
He wrote a letter to his dear Aunt Edna.

Activity E Find the prepositional phrases in these sentences and write them on your paper.

1) Joe did not arrive until 6:00 P.M.

2) The family took a trip to Colorado.

3) Nathan read a book by Daniel Defoe.

4) This gift is for your cousin Henry.

5) President James Polk was born in North Carolina.

The object of the preposition can be a pronoun. Usually when the object is a pronoun, the phrase will be only two words—the preposition and the object.

Give that book to him.

Please sit here by me.

Did you vote for her?

Activity F Find the prepositional phrases in these sentences and write them on your paper.

1) Everyone stayed late except her.

2) Jennifer waited outside with them.

3) Please sit beside him.

4) To me, writing letters is fun.

5) What did she say about you?

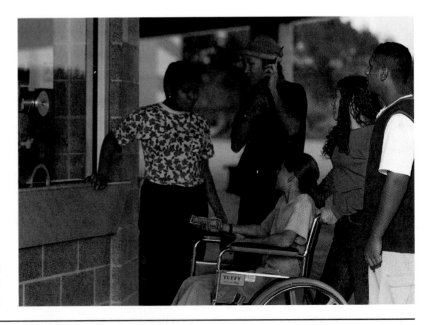

Jennifer bought movie tickets and popcorn for them.

1) Find 10 prepositional phrases in this paragraph. Write them on your paper. A sentence may have more than one prepositional phrase.

The telephone is one of the most important inventions ever. Using the telephone, we can communicate better with each other. In 1830, Michael Faraday proved that people could change vibrations of metal to electrical impulses. Alexander Graham Bell and Elisha Gray both invented a practical telephone. Both men filed for a patent on their inventions on the same day. These two events happened on February 14, 1876. Bell beat Gray by only two hours.

2) Write a paragraph about the telephones of today. Underline the prepositional phrases you used.

Vocabulary Builder

Compound Prepositions

Compound prepositions are prepositions that are made up of two or more words.
    Nathan sat down next to Emily.
Here are some compound prepositions:

according to	due to	next to
along with	in addition to	instead of
because of	in place of	out of

Choose the compound preposition that best completes each sentence. Write the sentence on your paper.

1) Angela became a swimmer _____ Janet Evans.
2) Would you like tea _____ coffee?
3) The flight was delayed _____ bad weather.
4) _____ the review, the play was a success.

The Object of a Preposition

Remember, the object of a preposition may be a noun or pronoun.

> **EXAMPLE**
>
> Armando kicked the ball into the net.
> (*Net* is a noun.)
>
> The crowd cheered for him.
> (*Him* is a pronoun.)

Activity A Write the object of the preposition on your paper. Identify it as a noun or a pronoun.

Example   They played basketball on the playground.
            playground—noun

1) Emily plays the clarinet in the orchestra.

2) She sometimes practices scales on it.

3) Nathan looked at his stamp collection.

4) His father bought a new stamp for him.

5) Is Angela attending the concert with you?

In Chapter 3, you learned that personal pronouns can have three forms: subject, object, possessive. The object of a preposition must be in the object form.

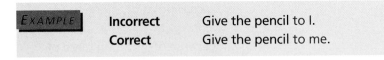

> **EXAMPLE**   **Incorrect**   Give the pencil to I.
>   **Correct**   Give the pencil to me.

Use *I* for subjects. Use *me* for objects.

Personal Pronouns			
	Subject	**Object**	**Possessive**
Singular			
First Person	I	me	my, mine
Second Person	you	you	your, yours
Third Person	he, she, it	him, her, it	his, her, hers, its
Plural			
First Person	we	us	our, ours
Second Person	you	you	your, yours
Third Person	they	them	their, theirs

Activity B Write the pronoun that correctly completes each sentence. Then identify the form: *subject* or *object*.

Example   Why did (she, her) do that?   she—subject
                He studied with Emily and (I, me).   me—object

1) In the journalism class, Brittany sat between Joe and (I, me).

2) I found the pen that (he, him) had lost.

3) (She, Her) and Deb sat in the back.

4) Emily gave the notebook to (he, him).

5) I tried not to look at (they, them).

Careful writers choose a preposition with the exact meaning they need. Use *between* when you are discussing two people or things. Use *among* when you are discussing three or more people or things.

EXAMPLE   Brittany is sitting between Nathan and Joe.

                They could not see Brittany among the students in the crowded corridor.

Activity C On your paper, write the preposition that correctly completes each sentence.

1) (Between, Among) the swimmers, Angela is the fastest in the backstroke.

2) "Let's split the work (between, among) all the family members," suggested Nathan.

3) The three boys decided to divide the pizza (between, among) them.

4) Emily and Angela eat lunch (between, among) third and fourth periods.

5) (Between, Among) the two of them, they got the job done.

Spelling Builder

Suffixes That Begin with Vowels:
-ous, -able, -ible, -y, -ance, -ence

When you add a suffix that begins with a vowel to a word, do you change the word's spelling? The answer depends on the word. These rules can help you add most suffixes that begin with vowels to words.

- If the word ends in any letter except *y* or *e*, you just add the suffix: *honor—honorable.*
- If the word ends in a consonant and a *y*, you change the *y* to *i* and add the suffix: *envy—envious.*
- If the word ends in *e*, you usually drop the *e* and add the suffix: *use—usable.*

To be sure you have added a suffix to a word correctly, check the spelling in the dictionary.

Add *-able* to each of these words.

value   reason   vary   enjoy

LESSON 2	**Review**

On your paper, write the pronoun that correctly completes each sentence. Then identify the form: *subject* or *object*.

1) Nathan studied with Emily and (I, me).

2) (Her, She) walked to school with him.

3) Have you been around (they, them) before?

Write the preposition that correctly completes each sentence.

4) Can you see Neeru (between, among) the people in the theater?

5) She sat (between, among) Emily and Angela at lunch.

6) The family members divided the pie (between, among) themselves.

7) Angela has history (between, among) her English and science classes.

Word Bank

about
across
around
beneath
beside
between
during
into
near
over
through
to
under
with

Fill in the blank with an appropriate preposition from the Word Bank. Write the complete sentence on your paper. Use a different preposition in each sentence.

8) Joe lives _____ the river.

9) We talked _____ classes.

10) The flag hung _____ the door.

11) Angela joined the team _____ her.

12) I am going to walk _____ Nathan's house.

13) We lost a tree _____ the storm.

14) The family had a picnic _____ the trees.

15) Armando read a book _____ school.

A prepositional phrase begins with a preposition and ends with a noun or pronoun. You can use a prepositional phrase as an adjective phrase or an adverb phrase.

> **EXAMPLE**
>
> **Adjective**   The middle book is mine.
> **Prepositional Phrase**   The book in the middle is mine.

Adjective phrase

A group of words that tells which one, what kind, *or* how many *about a noun*

An adjective is a word that describes a noun or pronoun. The prepositional phrase *in the middle* is an **adjective phrase.** A prepositional phrase used as an adjective describes *which one, what kind,* or *how many* about a noun. Notice in the example above that the adjective comes before the noun. The prepositional phrase comes after the noun.

Activity A Find the prepositional phrase in each sentence and write it on your paper. Then write the word each phrase describes.

1) We read a book about China.

2) The story by Ji-Li Jiang was exciting.

3) The invention by Alexander Graham Bell changed the world.

4) The book with the blue cover caught Joe's eye.

5) The computer on the teacher's desk had the vocabulary list.

An adjective phrase can describe the object of another preposition.

> **EXAMPLE**   A team from a school in upstate New York arrived.
> (The adjective phrase *from a school* describes the noun *team.* The adjective phrase *in upstate New York* describes the noun *school.*)

Activity B Look at the prepositional phrases in bold and write them on your paper. Write the noun they describe.

Example   The trees **beside the lake in the park** are pines.
                beside the lake—trees
                in the park—lake

1) Emily shopped at the store **in the center of the city.**

2) Angela swam in the pool **at school.**

3) Nathan liked the car **on the cover of the magazine.**

4) Angela used the weights **in the gym at the YMCA.**

5) Nathan visited campgrounds **in national parks in the West.**

The writer decides whether to use an adjective or an adjective phrase.

EXAMPLE

Adjective	Our school's swim team won.
Adjective Phrase	The swim team from our school won.

Activity C Write each of these sentences on your paper. Change the words in bold to a prepositional phrase.

Example   That **poetry** book is my favorite.
                That book of poetry is my favorite.

1) **White cotton** curtains hung in the kitchen.

2) Angela lives in a **brick** house.

3) **Edgar Allan Poe's** story was popular with the students.

4) We bought a **six-room** house.

5) The **roller coaster** ride thrilled Neeru.

Writing Tip

Using too many prepositional phrases can make your writing wordy. Try changing some prepositional phrases to adjectives. Too wordy: *I wore a shirt of red cotton with long sleeves and a skirt of blue denim with silver buttons.*

Better: *I wore a long-sleeved red cotton shirt and a blue denim skirt with silver buttons.*

Find the prepositional phrases in these sentences. Write them on your paper. After each phrase, write the noun or pronoun that the phrase describes.

1) The girl from India enjoyed life in the United States.

2) Angela brought him with her.

3) The water in the pool was warm.

4) Some friends of ours had a party at the pool.

5) The girl with Neeru is her cousin from Calcutta.

Write these sentences on your paper. Add a prepositional phrase after each noun or pronoun in bold. Be sure your phrase tells something about the noun or pronoun.

6) **Everyone** enjoyed the winter games.

7) The student liked the **movie**.

8) The **others** are on their way here.

9) The horse was standing in the **shade**.

10) Efran's **room** was painted.

Write each sentence on your paper. Change the words in bold to a prepositional phrase.

11) I sat on a **park** bench.

12) The **gold foil** crown looked real.

13) The teacher read aloud **Emily's** poem.

14) The author's name is on the **book's** cover.

15) The **pool** party began at 2:00 P.M.

Adverb phrase

A group of words that answers the question how, when, where, how much, or how long about the verb in a sentence

You can use a prepositional phrase as an **adverb phrase.** An adverb is a word that answers questions about a verb. An adverb answers the question *how, when, where, how much,* or *how long.*

EXAMPLE

Adverb	Neeru sang the song enthusiastically.
Adverb Phrase	She sang with enthusiasm.

An adverb phrase may be in different places in the sentence. Read the two sentences below aloud. Are their meanings different? No, in both sentences the adverb phrase *after dinner* answers the question *when.*

After dinner we went **to a movie**.

We went **to a movie** after dinner.

Activity A Write the adverb phrase in bold on your paper. Next to each phrase, write the question that the adverb phrase answers about the verb. Write *how, when, where, how much,* or *how long.*

Example The choir sang **for three hours**.

for three hours—how long

1) The wrestling season began each year **in December.**

2) The coach held the tryouts **for three weeks.**

3) "Sign your name **on this sheet** of paper," said the coach.

4) Armando stayed **for about two hours.**

5) He played **with great skill.**

An adverb phrase can also answer the question *why.*

EXAMPLE

They were tired because of their hard work. (Why were they tired? Because of their hard work.)

Activity B Write the adverb phrase that answers the question
why in each of the sentences.

Example   Mrs. Choy was late due to traffic.
              due to traffic

1) The road flooded due to the heavy rain.

2) They were tired because of their hard work.

3) Armando tried out for the team because of his dad's
encouragement.

4) Emily was thirsty from her long walk.

5) Because of the drought, the price of wheat was high.

An adverb phrase can tell about an adjective or another adverb.

 EXAMPLE   Jason was late by 15 minutes.
              (*By 15 minutes* answers the question
              how late. *By 15 minutes* tells more about the
              adjective *late*.)

Activity C Write the adverb phrases in these sentences. Next to
each one, write the question that the phrase answers. A sentence
can have more than one prepositional phrase.

Example   They fished in the stream.
              in the stream—where

1) In the race, Angela swam faster than her opponent by four
seconds.

2) The ball was in the air for several seconds.

3) The sun had not shone for days.

4) Neeru has lived in America for several months now.

5) Angela walks every day for two miles.

Write the adverb phrases in these sentences on your paper.

1) The school newspaper published the results on Friday.

2) He wrote the article on his computer.

3) The time passed quickly because of his concentration.

4) Armando has been writing for several years.

5) He has been a reporter for two years.

Add an adverb phrase to each sentence. The phrase must answer a question about the verb, an adjective, or another adverb. Write each new sentence on your paper. Underline the adverb phrase or phrases that you added. You may need to change the tense of the verb.

6) Mrs. Langston coaches the swimming team.

7) The students reported early.

8) Mr. Thomas has taught history.

9) The students brought their books.

10) The history class began.

Using What You've Learned

Write a report about a meeting you have attended recently. Describe who spoke and the subjects that were discussed. Underline each prepositional phrase in your report.

Where to Find It

Index

Books are a good source of information for studying and for writing reports. But how do you find the facts you need in a lengthy book? An index helps you find the information you are looking for.

A book's index appears at the end of the book. The index lists the topics in the book alphabetically. Suppose you need information about using commas. You might find a listing such as the following in the index of a grammar book.

Colon, 132–136	
with appositives	134
in business letters	133
misuse of	135
with quotations	134
Comma, 120–124	
in addresses	120
for clarity	121
between clauses	122
in dates	120

The page numbers that follow each main heading and subheading tell you where to find the information. The index lists the subheadings alphabetically. Small words such as *a, the,* and prepositions do not count in alphabetizing. Sometimes you cannot find a topic in an index right away. It is not where you expect it to be listed. Try looking under a different topic. It may be a subheading under another main topic. For example, *comma* may be a subheading under *punctuation* in some indexes.

Some books are indexes. The *Readers' Guide to Periodical Literature* lists magazine articles on many topics. As in other indexes, the topics are listed alphabetically.

1) Write the prepositional phrases included under the topic *colon* in the index above. Underline each preposition. Circle each object of the preposition.

2) Think of a topic you are currently studying in history. Use the library catalog and book indexes to find a book that includes your topic. Write the title and author of the book and the page numbers that discuss your topic.

Writing Project

Writing Directions

Prepositions are especially helpful when you write directions. Choose one of the following and write directions in sentences. Use some of the prepositions from the box below or any others you choose. Underline all of the prepositional phrases you use.

- From your home to the mall

- From your school to your home

- From your home to a friend's home

- From your home to your grandparents' home

Here is an example.

Directions from Wilson High School to Emily's home:

Turn left <u>on Rt. 450</u> and drive <u>for one block</u>. <u>At the light</u>, turn left <u>on Moylan Drive</u>. <u>After about a mile</u>, turn right <u>on Chapel Forge Drive</u>. Continue <u>to the end</u> <u>of the street</u>. Go <u>through the first intersection</u>. <u>After the church</u> <u>on the left</u>, you will see a stand <u>of tall trees</u>. Turn right <u>on Woodhaven Lane.</u> Stop <u>at the two-story house with a white front porch</u>.

Common Prepositions					
about	around	below	for	into	past
across	at	by	from	on	through
after	behind	down	in	over	toward

WORD BANK

adjective phrase

adverb phrase

object of a
  preposition

preposition

prepositional
  phrase

Part A On a sheet of paper, write the correct word or words from the Word Bank to complete each sentence.

1) A _____ is a word that shows a relationship between a noun or pronoun and other words in a sentence.

2) The noun or pronoun that follows the preposition in a prepositional phrase is the _____.

3) A group of words that tells *which one, what kind,* or *how many* about a noun is an _____.

4) A _____ is a group of words made up of a preposition, an object, and adjectives or adverbs that describe the object.

5) A group of words that tells *how, when, where, how much,* or *how long* about the verb in a sentence is an _____.

Part B Write the prepositional phrase in bold on your paper. Next to each one, write whether it is an *adjective phrase* or an *adverb phrase.*

6) **During the storm,** the wind blew our old maple tree down.

7) Mrs. Hernandez made pizza **with a delicious sauce.**

8) Armando invited his friends **to his house.**

9) Every one **of his guests** had left by 10:00 P.M.

10) The house **by the ocean** is built on stilts.

11) Emily waited at the bus stop **for 20 minutes.**

Part C Write these sentences on your paper. Add at least one prepositional phrase to each one to make the sentence more colorful.

12) Mrs. Hernandez invited them.

13) The pizza smelled so good.

14) Armando's friends helped clean up.

15) Armando will have another party.

Part D Write these sentences on your paper. Correct any mistakes.

16) In the school election, Armando voted for he.

17) He had to choose among Jason Sirowitz and Keefe Harvey.

18) Between you and I, there has always been an understanding.

19) In journalism class, Armando sat behind Nathan and she.

Part E Find the prepositional phrases in this paragraph and write them on your paper.

20) Toni Morrison is one of America's most famous writers. Her work about African Americans makes her one of the most important writers of the twentieth century. She received the National Book Critics Circle Award for *Song of Solomon*. Her picture appeared on the cover of a national weekly news magazine. She received the Pulitzer Prize for *Beloved*. Her most important achievement is the 1993 Nobel Prize for literature. Only eight women have won this prize in 100 years!

Test-Taking Tip When taking a matching test, match all the items that you know go together for sure. Cross these items out. Then try to match the items that are left.

Using Conjunctions and Interjections

Conjunctions are words that connect parts of sentences. The words *and, but, or,* and *so* are conjunctions. Look at the photograph on the opposite page. What do you see? Two people are shaking hands. Their clasped hands make a connection. In the same way, we use conjunctions to make connections in sentences.

Interjections are words that express strong feelings. They are words such as *Oh no! My goodness!* and *Ouch!* Interjections add interest to our writing.

In Chapter 9, you will learn about conjunctions and interjections and how to use them in sentences.

Goals for Learning

▶ To identify conjunctions in sentences

▶ To write compound sentences using coordinating conjunctions

▶ To write complex sentences using subordinating conjunctions

▶ To write sentences using correlative conjunctions

▶ To punctuate sentences with conjunctions

▶ To use interjections in sentences

▶ To write and punctuate sentences that contain interjections

Conjunction

A word that connects parts of a sentence

Clause

A group of words with a subject and a verb

Coordinating conjunction

A word that connects two or more equal parts of a sentence

A **conjunction** is a word that connects parts of a sentence. A conjunction can connect words, phrases, or clauses. A **clause** is a group of words with a subject and a verb.

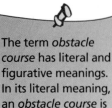

The term *obstacle course* has literal and figurative meanings. In its literal meaning, an *obstacle course* is an area in which barriers such as hurdles, walls, and water must be crossed by athletes running through it. In its figurative meaning, an *obstacle course* is any group of difficulties that must be overcome. For example, detours or rough roads under construction may be called an obstacle course.

EXAMPLE

Conjunctions connect words	Armando is a good hitter and fielder.
Conjunctions connect phrases	Give the book to me or to her.
Conjunctions connect clauses	Mr. Young would play golf today, but it is raining.

A **coordinating conjunction** connects two or more parts of a sentence that are equal such as two subjects, two verbs, or two adjectives.

Coordinating Conjunctions			
and	but	or	nor
for	so	yet	as well as

Activity A On your paper, write the words that the coordinating conjunction connects in these sentences. Circle the conjunction.

Example   Three and three add up to six.   Three (and) three

1) The winter games were fun but tiring.

2) Armando pedaled the tricycle, and Nathan stood on the back.

3) Armando won the obstacle course race as well as the tricycle race.

4) These obstacles were in the middle and on the side.

5) Emily did not enter the tricycle race, nor did she enter the broad jump.

Series

A group of more than two words, phrases, or clauses

Comma

A punctuation mark (,) used to separate words, phrases, or clauses in a series

Coordinating conjunctions can connect words, phrases, or clauses in a **series.** When there are more than two items that are similar in a series, put a **comma** after each item except the last one.

EXAMPLE

Words in a series	Armando, Nathan, and Joe entered the beanbag toss.
Phrases in a series	They got in line, warmed up, and threw beanbags.
Clauses in a series	Armando made decorations, Michelle cut them out, and Efran hung them in the gym.

Activity B Write these sentences on your paper. Add the missing commas.

1) Have you seen Emily Angela or Neeru?

2) I am entering the tricycle race the beanbag toss and the broad jump event.

3) I plan to win first second third fourth or fifth prize.

4) They held the games in the gym the hall and the cafeteria.

5) I saw Nathan eating popcorn candy and ice cream.

Rule 1 Use *and* to connect two items when both are true.
Armando and Nathan entered the race.
(Both of them entered.)

Rule 2 Use *but* to point out a difference between two ideas.
Armando entered the tricycle race, but Emily did not.
(Only Armando entered.)

Rule 3 Use *or* to connect ideas that are choices or differences.
Armando or Nathan will enter the race.
(One of them will enter. We don't know which one yet.)

Rule 4 Use *nor* to point out that *neither* of the subjects did the action.
Emily did not enter the snowball contest, nor did Angela.
(Emily did not enter. Angela did not enter.)

Activity C Write the conjunction that correctly completes each sentence.

1) Emily dug through the sand in the treasure hunt, (and, but) she didn't find anything.

2) Nathan ate popcorn (and, but) ice cream.

3) Emily is with Nathan (but, or) Efran.

4) Angela was not in the gym that day, (or, nor) was Neeru.

5) I don't know who won the race, (and, but) Joe might.

A coordinating conjunction can connect two or more complete ideas. Do not repeat the words that are the same in both sentences (or ideas).

> EXAMPLE
>
> **We can say** Armando doesn't like tea.
>   Armando doesn't like coffee.
>
> **Or, we can say**
> Armando doesn't like tea or coffee.

Activity D Use a coordinating conjunction to combine each pair of sentences. Write the new sentence on your paper.

1) Emily saw Nathan.

   Emily saw Armando.

2) Angela ate popcorn.

   Emily ate ice cream.

3) He is not at home.

   He is not at school.

4) Nathan likes to play baseball.

   Nathan does not like to play football.

5) I watched the tricycle race.

   I watched the broad jump.

When we combine two subjects, we may need to change the verb form. In the first two sentences, both subjects are singular, so the verb ends in *s*. The combined sentence has a plural subject, so the verb does not end in *s*.

EXAMPLE	Singular Subjects	Mary plays tennis. Rebecca plays tennis.
	Plural Subject	Both girls play tennis.

Writing Tip

Use a comma to separate two independent clauses joined by a coordinating conjunction. For example, *Angela gave a party, and her friends came.* When you connect two predicates with a conjunction, do not use a comma to separate the predicates. For example, *At her party, Angela played CDs and served pizza.*

Activity E Use a conjunction to join these sentences together into one sentence. You may need to change the verb form.

1) A baby pool was part of the obstacle course. A sandbox was part of the obstacle course.

2) One contest was the obstacle course. Another contest was the treasure hunt.

3) Students jumped over the baby pool. They dug in the sandbox for treasure.

4) The student council sold ice cream. The student council sold popcorn.

5) The council made money selling popcorn. The council did not make money selling ice cream.

6) Emily helped clean up after the games. Armando did not help.

7) Maybe Neeru won the beanbag contest. Maybe Emily did. One of them won.

8) Armando did not win the beanbag contest. Nathan did not win.

9) Did Joe find a treasure in the sandbox? Did Emily find a treasure in the sandbox?

10) Finally, Neeru arrived at the games. Finally, Angela arrived too.

On your paper, write the words that the coordinating conjunction connects in these sentences. Circle the coordinating conjunction.

1) The boys rode the tricycle down the runway and across the finish line.

2) Angela and Neeru arrived late to the winter party.

3) Emily entered the treasure hunt but not the tricycle race.

4) Some teachers entered the games, but others did not.

5) I think I will have lemonade or a root beer.

Use a coordinating conjunction to join these sentences together into one sentence. You may need to change the verb form and add commas.

6) Nathan likes root beer. Armando likes root beer. Joe likes root beer.

7) Armando entered the tricycle race. He did not enter the beanbag toss.

8) Angela made paper snowflakes. She made paper snowmen.

9) In the sand were polished stones. In the sand were coins.

10) One contest was the beanbag toss. One contest was the tricycle race. One contest was the treasure hunt.

Subordinating conjunction

A word that connects a dependent clause to an independent clause in a sentence

A **subordinating conjunction** is a word that connects a dependent clause to an independent clause.

 We were in school when it started to rain.
We went home before the storm began.
(*When* and *before* are subordinating conjunctions.)

Subordinating Conjunctions		
after	before	until
although	even though	when
as	if	whenever
as if	since	where
as though	so that	wherever
because	unless	while

Dependent clause

A clause that does not express a complete thought

A **dependent clause** does not express a complete thought. Dependent clauses may be at the beginning or end of a sentence.

An **independent clause** expresses a complete thought. An independent clause is a sentence.

Independent clause

A clause that expresses a complete thought

EXAMPLE

Dependent Clause
After the party was over,

Independent Clause
we went home.

Independent Clause
We went home

Dependent Clause
after the party was over.

Activity A Write the dependent clause in each sentence on your paper. Circle the subordinating conjunction.

Example   The golfers came home when the sun went down.
           (when) the sun went down

1) Michelle read a magazine until she saw the dentist.

2) Mrs. Choy likes a cup of tea while she is having dinner.

3) After she became engaged, Julie sent an announcement to the newspaper.

4) Since the season is winter, the weather is cold.

5) When January arrived, the temperature dropped below freezing.

Activity B Write each sentence on your paper. Underline the dependent clause once. Underline the independent clause twice. Circle the subordinating conjunction.

Example   <u>I sang a song</u> (while) <u>Julie played the piano.</u>

1) After Nathan ate the popcorn, he was very thirsty.

2) Because everyone had fun, the party was a success.

3) The contest judges had to look at the rules before they could declare a winner.

4) I couldn't leave the party unless Emily left too.

5) Although they all like root beer, they ordered lemonade instead.

Notice that there is a comma after a dependent clause when it is at the beginning of a sentence. There is no comma when we add a dependent clause to the end of a sentence.

<table>
<tr><td>EXAMPLE</td><td>**No comma**</td><td>The game was canceled because it rained.</td></tr>
<tr><td></td><td>**Comma**</td><td>Because it rained, the game was canceled.</td></tr>
</table>

Activity C Write these sentences on your paper. Add a comma after the dependent clause if one is needed.

1) Because she sprained her ankle Mrs. Choy was unable to go bowling.

2) Mrs. Choy will get a substitute until her ankle is well.

3) If she feels up to it Mrs. Choy will go to the bowling alley with her husband.

4) Although she cannot bowl she can support the team.

5) "I will keep score while you bowl," she said.

Dependent clauses do not express a complete thought by themselves. They need an independent clause to finish the thought.

<table>
<tr><td>EXAMPLE</td><td>**Incomplete thought**</td><td>Because he was late</td></tr>
<tr><td></td><td>**Complete thought**</td><td>Because he was late, he missed dinner.</td></tr>
</table>

Activity D Add an independent clause (a sentence) to each of these dependent clauses. Be sure to add a comma if one is needed.

1) whenever he goes home

2) since March arrived

3) unless you finish your book

4) although Emily enjoys music

5) as time goes by

We use some words as subordinating conjunctions or as prepositions. The conjunction introduces a clause. A clause has a subject and a verb. A prepositional phrase has an object.

EXAMPLE		
Conjunction	They halted the game until the rain stopped.
Preposition	They halted the game until the next day.
Conjunction	After the game ended, Armando went home.
Preposition	He went home after the game.

Activity E Write on your paper whether the word in bold is a *conjunction* or a *preposition*.

1) Neeru has art class **before** lunch.

2) Armando went to the gym for practice **before** he went home.

3) **Because** Armando pedaled so fast, he and Nathan won the tricycle race.

4) In his opinion they won **because of** Nathan.

5) **Until** the rain stops, no one can play outside.

Write the dependent clause in each sentence on your paper. Circle the subordinating conjunction.

1) After the principal made a speech, the winter games began.

2) If you hurry, you won't miss the race.

3) They enjoyed the games even though it was cold.

Add an independent clause (a sentence) to each dependent clause. Be sure to add a comma if one is needed.

4) before she left

5) unless he studies

6) after the games were over

On your paper, write whether the word in bold is a *conjunction* or a *preposition*.

7) Armando left the gym **before** Nathan did.

8) **After** his last class, Joe went home.

9) They talked together **before** class.

10) **After** I called Neeru, we met at Tony's.

Vocabulary Builder

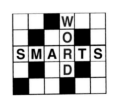

Clipped Words

Sometimes people drop one or more syllables from long words to make shorter words. These are called clipped words.

    Examination = exam   Gymnasium = gym

Write the clipped word for each of these words: *advertisement, automobile, telephone, photograph, dormitory.*

| **Correlative conjunction** |
| A pair of conjunctions that expresses a shared relationship |

Correlative conjunctions express a shared relationship. Use correlative conjunctions in pairs.

EXAMPLE

Neither Angela nor Neeru was on time.

Both Angela and Neeru were late.

Either Miguel or Armando will win the next poster contest.

Not only are they talented, but they also work hard.

Whether they win or they lose, they enjoy designing posters.

Correlative Conjunctions		
both … and	neither … nor	whether … or
either … or	not only … but also	

Activity A Write the correlative conjunctions in each of these sentences on your paper.

1) Jackson plays neither soccer nor baseball.

2) Whether Emily Watson performs or not, the concert will begin at 8:00 P.M.

3) Not only will Neeru Peri sing, but she will also give a short talk.

4) Emily has either the flu or a bad cold.

5) Both Armando and Nathan received prizes.

Compound subject

Two or more subjects connected by a conjunction

In a **compound subject** with two singular subjects joined by *or* or *nor,* use the singular verb form. A compound subject is two or more subjects connected by a conjunction.

> Neither Neeru nor Angela has signed up for that event.

When one of the subjects joined by *or* or *nor* is singular and one is plural, the verb must agree with the subject near the verb.

> Neither Neeru nor her friends were on time.
> (*Friends* is plural.)
>
> Either the students or their teacher is lost.
> (*Teacher* is singular.)

A compound subject connected with *and* uses the plural verb form. A compound subject with the correlative conjunctions *both … and* also uses the plural verb form.

> Neeru and Angela are in the event.
> Both Armando and Nathan are winners.

Activity B Decide which sentence in each pair is correct and write it on your paper.

1) Neither Neeru nor Angela are on the committee.
Neither Neeru nor Angela is on the committee.

2) Both Angela and Julie are looking forward to the wedding.
Both Angela and Julie is looking forward to the wedding.

3) Either the children or their mother walk the dog.
Either the children or their mother walks the dog.

4) Either you or he need a watch.
Either you or he needs a watch.

5) Not only Angela but also Neeru were late.
Not only Angela but also Neeru was late.

Write the correlative conjunctions in each of these sentences on your paper.

1) Both Angela and Emily like flowers.

2) Not only do they like flowers, but they also prefer roses.

3) She had to decide whether to go to a play or to a movie.

4) Neither Emily nor Michelle has seen that movie.

5) I'd like to see either a movie or a play.

Decide which sentence in each pair is correct and write it on your paper.

6) Emily and Julie play the clarinet.

Emily and Julie plays the clarinet.

7) Either the coach or the players has to make that decision.

Either the coach or the players have to make that decision.

8) Neither Neeru nor Angela are helping with the party.

Neither Neeru nor Angela is helping with the party.

9) The race will begin, whether you or she is ready.

The race will begin, whether you or she are ready.

10) Not only Armando but also Nathan were a winner.

Not only Armando but also Nathan was a winner.

Interjection

A word or phrase that expresses a feeling and is not related to other parts of a sentence

An **interjection** is a word or phrase that expresses a feeling. Interjections are not related to other parts of a sentence. They are independent words. They are not part of the subject or the predicate.

Punctuation separates an interjection from the rest of the sentence. The punctuation can be a period, a comma, a question mark, or an exclamation mark. It depends on the feeling that the interjection expresses.

Writing Tip

Interjections usually appear at the beginning of a sentence. You can also use them at the end of a sentence. You use a comma or end punctuation to separate the interjection from the rest of the sentence.

Ah, a dip in the lake feels good on such a hot day.

We just made it. Whew!

> EXAMPLE
>
> No kidding. I like spinach.
> So what? It's not important.
> Say, could you help me?

When you use end punctuation after an interjection, capitalize the first word that follows. If you use a comma, do not capitalize the next word unless it is a proper noun.

> EXAMPLE
>
> Hey, don't ask me again.
> Yes, indeed! That's really nice.

Interjections			
ah	hurrah	ouch	stop
alas	hurry	please	terrific
fine	hush	quick	thanks
gosh	listen	quiet	well
great	look out	really	what
ha	my goodness	so	whew
hello	oh	so what	wow
hey	oh, boy	sorry	yes

Activity A Write the sentences on your paper. Add punctuation after an interjection and at the end of each sentence. Capitalize a word if it is the first word in a sentence.

Example   quick hide someone is coming
              Quick, hide! Someone is coming.

1) ouch that hurt my foot

2) wow do I have good news for you

3) yum that chocolate cake is delicious

4) oh no I missed the bus again

5) no I don't need any help now

Activity B Add an interjection to each sentence. Use the list of interjections on page 231. Punctuate each sentence. Remember to capitalize the first word in a sentence.

1) That is beautiful.

2) Would you like a break?

3) The test was difficult.

4) The party was fun.

5) I really needed that rest.

<aside>

Using What You've Learned

Think about an event at your school. It could be a dance, a sports event, an academic debate, or a fair. Write a description of the event. Use sentences with conjunctions in your description. Also use one or more interjections in the description.

</aside>

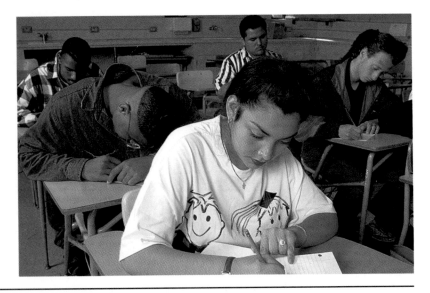

Quiet! The students are taking a test.

Write these sentences on your paper. Add punctuation after the interjections and at the end of the sentences. Capitalize the first word in the sentence after any end punctuation.

1) my goodness you are right

2) what I didn't hear that

3) ouch you stepped on my foot

4) whew it is hot today

5) ah that is just what I needed

Write these sentences on your paper. Add an interjection and any needed punctuation to each sentence. Remember to capitalize the first word in each sentence.

6) Is that you?

7) I don't agree with you.

8) That is fantastic.

9) He finally arrived home.

10) The storm worsened.

Spelling Builder

Words with ie *or* ei

Does knowing whether to use *ie* or *ei* when spelling give you *grief*? If so, use this simple rhyme:

- Write *i* before *e*, except after *c* or when sounded like *a* as in *neighbor* and *weigh*.

With this rule, you can spell many words with *ei* or *ie*. Yet, every rule has its exceptions. You must memorize the exceptions such as *either, height, seize,* and *science.* Confirm word spellings by checking a dictionary.

Write *ie* or *ei* to complete each word: *rec___ve a gift, a br___f report, a f___ld of grass, the number ___ght.*

Where to Find It

Almanac

What do you do when you need to find a fact quickly? For example, what is the current population of the United States? How many hurricanes were there in 2000? Who won the U.S. Masters Golf Tournament in 1998? An **almanac** can help you answer these questions.

An almanac contains information on many different topics, including geography, history, sports, and entertainment. Much of the information appears in graphic form: in lists, tables, charts, and graphs. For example, here is part of a list of the best movies of all time, as chosen in a poll, from *The World Almanac and Book of Facts, 2001:*

1)	*Citizen Kane* (1941)	**4)**	*Gone With the Wind* (1939)
2)	*Casablanca* (1942)	**5)**	*Lawrence of Arabia* (1962)
3)	*The Godfather* (1972)		

Short summaries of information also appear in an almanac. You can find general information, such as an explanation of the weather phenomenon El Niño. You can also find current information that may not be available in an encyclopedia. *The World Almanac* is published each year. It summarizes the most important news events of that year. Information is organized by general topic. For example, you would find information about the Olympics in the Sports section. These sections are listed in the table of contents at the front of the book. A detailed index also appears at the front of the book.

1) Read the following paragraph from *The World Almanac and Book of Facts, 2001.* Then write the conjunctions in the paragraph on your paper.

   In a dramatic Election Night, Nov. 7–8, 2000, Texas Gov. **George Bush** (R) and his Democratic opponent, Vice Pres. **Al Gore,** battled for electoral votes, but neither gained a majority. The presidency hinged on the outcome in Florida, where the voting was so close—and so crucial—that it led to a recount.

2) Look through an almanac. Find a topic that interests you and take notes. Present the information orally to a small group of classmates.

Using Conjunctions to Combine Ideas

Read the following paragraph about forest fires. Look for conjunctions and make a list of them on your paper. Choose a sentence and rewrite it using a different conjunction.

Fire Ravages Western States

In May 2000, forest rangers fought fires in New Mexico, Idaho, and other western states. Winds of 50 miles an hour whipped the fires out of control, while tinder-dry weather contributed to the fires' spread. The fires destroyed 45,000 acres of forests and more than 400 houses. Although the damage was widespread, Idaho had the most damage, losing almost 470 square miles of forest. Neither the firefighters nor the forest rangers were able to stop the flames from spreading.

Write a paragraph that describes a recent event that has been in the news. Use conjunctions to combine ideas. When you finish your paragraph, read it to check your spelling and punctuation. Then go through it and underline the conjunctions you used.

WORD BANK

clause

comma

compound subject

conjunction

coordinating
    conjunction

correlative
    conjunction

dependent clause

independent
    clause

interjection

series

subordinating
    conjunction

Part A On a sheet of paper, write the correct word or words from the Word Bank to complete each sentence.

1) A _____ is a word that connects parts of a sentence.

2) An _____ is a word or phrase that expresses a feeling.

3) A _____ connects two or more equal parts of a sentence.

4) Three or more items connected with a conjunction are a _____.

5) A group of words with a subject and a verb is a _____.

6) An _____ expresses a complete thought.

7) A _____ is a pair of conjunctions that expresses a shared relationship.

8) A _____ connects a dependent clause to an independent clause.

9) A _____ does not express a complete thought.

10) A punctuation mark used to separate words, phrases, or clauses in a sentence is a _____.

11) A _____ is two or more subjects connected by a conjunction.

Part B Find the conjunctions in these sentences and write them on your paper.

12) Is the Valentine's Day dance on Friday or Saturday?

13) Neither Armando nor Nathan has asked anyone to the dance.

14) Let's decorate the gym with streamers and flowers.

15) Neeru is very excited because this is her first dance in the United States.

16) Both Emily and Angela bought new dresses for the dance.

17) Nathan will either rent a tuxedo or wear a suit.

Part C Write these sentences on your paper. Use a conjunction to connect the ideas.

18) To make the decorations, Armando needs construction paper. He needs scissors. He needs streamers.

19) Miguel will help him. Efran will help him.

20) Angela has decided to have fruit punch. She has decided to have heart-shaped cookies. She has decided to have a huge heart-shaped cake.

Part D Add a dependent clause to each sentence to tell when, where, how, or why something happened.

21) Neeru has a rose corsage.

22) The weather will be cold.

23) Angela will go to the dance with Armando.

Part E Write these sentences on your paper, adding punctuation and capital letters where they are needed.

24) ah what a wonderful party this is

25) because the committee had planned so carefully the dance was a success

Test-Taking Tip

If you do not know the meaning of a word in a question, read the question to yourself and leave out the word. Then see if you can figure out the meaning of the word from its use in the sentence.

Chapter 10

Recognizing Sentence Patterns

Look at the photograph on the opposite page. It shows part of a quilt. The quilt has a pattern, or an arrangement of forms and colors. Can you see the pattern? The dark blue square in the middle is attached to four light blue squares; they are attached to eight medium blue squares; and so on.

If you have done any woodworking or sewing, you know that a pattern can also be a model or guide for something you are making. The pattern shows you how to put the pieces together to make the whole item.

Languages have patterns too. For example, English has six main sentence patterns. By learning these patterns, you can recognize how words are arranged to make sentences. You will also better understand how to arrange words to make your own sentences.

In Chapter 10, you will learn the six basic sentence patterns in English.

Goals for Learning

▶ To identify and write simple and compound sentences

▶ To recognize direct and indirect objects in sentences

▶ To identify object complements in sentences

▶ To identify predicate nouns and predicate adjectives

▶ To write sentences using the six basic sentence patterns

Pattern 1 sentences are the simplest kind of sentence. These sentences express a complete thought with a subject and a verb or verb phrase.

Pattern 1 Sentence: Subject + Verb

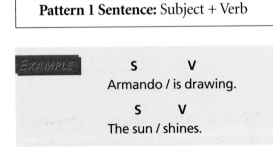

EXAMPLE

         S   **V**
Armando / is drawing.

       S   **V**
The sun / shines.

Activity A Write each of the Pattern 1 sentences on your paper. Draw a line between the subject and the verb as in the example above.

1) Nathan is studying.

2) Neeru sings beautifully.

3) My class went bowling.

4) Everyone laughed.

5) My little brother fell.

Pattern 1 sentences may have adjectives and adverbs. An adjective describes a noun or pronoun. An adverb tells more about a verb. In a Pattern 1 sentence, an adverb may come at the beginning of a sentence. It may come between the helping verb and the main verb.

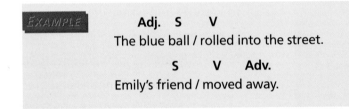

EXAMPLE

      Adj. **S**   **V**
The blue ball / rolled into the street.

         S   **V**   **Adv.**
Emily's friend / moved away.

Activity B Write these sentences on your paper. Write *S* above the subject, *V* above the verb or verb phrase, *Adj.* above any adjectives, and *Adv.* above any adverbs.

	S	V	Adv.

Example   The stars were shining brightly.

1) The old mower runs.

2) Nathan runs fast.

3) The little girl is laughing.

4) Emily practices often.

5) Today it rained hard.

A Pattern 1 sentence may have a prepositional phrase. The prepositional phrase may be an adjective phrase that describes the subject. It may be an adverb phrase that tells more about the verb.

> EXAMPLE
>
>   S   **Adj. Phrase**   V
>
> The girl behind me screamed.
> (Which girl? the one behind me)
>
>   S   V   **Adv. Phrase**
>
> Amanda is jogging to the park.
> (Where is Amanda jogging? to the park)

Activity C Write each of these Pattern 1 sentences on your paper. Draw a line between the subject and the verb. Underline the prepositional phrases in the sentences.

Example   Some of the team members arrived by car.
     Some of the team members / arrived by car.

1) No one in our family laughs at Uncle Mike's jokes.

2) My neighbor on the left has gone to the store.

3) My friend from California is visiting this week.

4) Everyone on our block is at work.

5) All of us are thinking about a vacation.

A Pattern 1 sentence may have a compound subject or a **compound verb**. A compound verb is two or more verbs connected by a conjunction.

> **EXAMPLE**
>
> **Compound Subject**   Armando and Nathan left for school.
>
> **Compound Verb**   They walked to the corner and talked.

You may join two Pattern 1 sentences with a conjunction to form a compound sentence. Add a comma before the conjunction.

> **EXAMPLE**
>
> Neeru was shopping on Presidents' Day.
> Angela went with her.
>
> Neeru was shopping on Presidents' Day, and
> Angela went with her.

Activity D Some of these sentences have a compound subject or verb. Some are compound sentences. Write each sentence on your paper. Underline the compound part.

1) Neeru and Efran went to the Valentine's Day Dance.

2) Both students and faculty attended the party.

3) We danced or talked all evening.

4) The band played, and everyone applauded.

5) Ann came with friends and danced with them.

A Pattern 1 sentence may give a command or make a request. The subject *you* is understood. The entire sentence in a command or a request is the predicate.

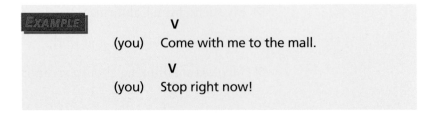

> **EXAMPLE**
>
>   **V**
> (you)   Come with me to the mall.
>
>   **V**
> (you)   Stop right now!

Activity E Each of these sentences has only a predicate. The subject *you* is understood. Write the verb or verb phrase in each sentence.

1) Stay at home today.   **4)** Listen to the question.

2) Please do not run.   **5)** Please leave for school now.

3) Go to the store and shop for groceries.

A Pattern 1 sentence can ask a question. Part of the verb phrase may help form the question. It will come before the subject.

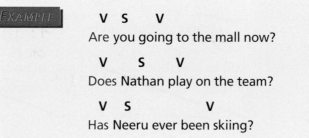

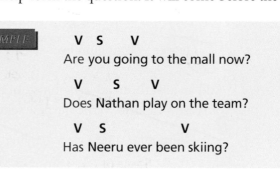

```
EXAMPLE        V  S    V
               Are you going to the mall now?

               V    S     V
               Does Nathan play on the team?

               V    S            V
               Has Neeru ever been skiing?
```

We often begin questions with an interrogative adverb or an interrogative pronoun.

```
EXAMPLE                              V        S
Interrogative Adverb      Where are my keys?

                                S    V
Interrogative Pronoun     Who is running to the park?
```

Activity F Write these sentences on your paper. Write *S* above the subject and *V* above the verb or verb phrase.

1) Where is Nathan going now?

2) Is there a sale at the mall?

3) Have you heard about Presidents' Day?

4) Do you know about the sales?

5) Why is Neeru leaving early?

Write each of these sentences on your paper. Draw a line between the subject and the verb. Underline the prepositional phrase in each sentence.

1) We went to the mall.

2) Emily and I often jog in the park.

3) Neeru and Efran are eating at their favorite restaurant.

4) They will look for a good movie.

5) George Washington lived at Mount Vernon.

Add an adverb, an adverb phrase, or an adjective phrase to each of these sentences. Write the new sentences on your paper.

6) Neeru and Angela were giggling.

7) Armando listens.

8) Some people arrived.

9) Her friend is visiting.

10) They are talking.

Write these sentences on your paper. Write *S* above the subject and *V* above the verb or verb phrase. In some sentences, the subject *you* is understood.

11) Who is coming for dinner?

12) Please leave your bags at the door.

13) Why is Emily smiling?

14) Do not play with matches.

15) Has Joe arrived yet?

Direct object

A noun or pronoun that receives the action of a verb

Pattern 2 sentences have a subject and an action verb. The action of the verb is transferred to another person or thing. The person or thing that receives the action is the **direct object.** The direct object is a noun or pronoun.

Pattern 2 Sentence: Subject + Verb + Direct Object

The direct object answers the question *what* or *whom* after the verb.

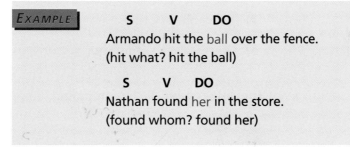

EXAMPLE

　　　　　　S　　V　　DO
Armando hit the ball over the fence.
(hit what? hit the ball)

　　　　　　S　　V　　DO
Nathan found her in the store.
(found whom? found her)

Activity A Write *S, V,* and *DO* to identify the subject, verb, and direct object in these sentences.

1) Armando plays baseball in the spring.

2) The coach chose Armando for the team.

3) He still likes art.

4) Nathan took pictures at the game.

5) He gave them to the school newspaper staff.

Activity B Write the direct object in each sentence on your paper. The verb is in bold.

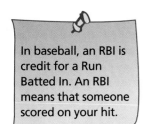

In baseball, an RBI is credit for a Run Batted In. An RBI means that someone scored on your hit.

1) Armando **caught** the ball.　**4)** No one **caught** it.

2) He **tagged** the runner.　　**5)** He **got** credit for an RBI.

3) Armando **hit** a double.

When the direct object is a pronoun, it is in the object form.

                   S   V   DO
                   Nathan's father drove him to school.

Activity C On your paper, write the pronoun that correctly completes each sentence. (See page 63 if you need help.)

1) Have you seen (she, her)?

2) Nathan saw (she, her) at the library.

3) Angela made posters and Joe hung (they, them) in the gym.

4) Terry called (I, me) at home.

5) Don't wake (he, him) up.

The direct object can be compound.

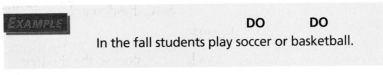   DO   DO
                   In the fall students play soccer or basketball.

If the sentence has a compound verb, each verb can have a direct object.

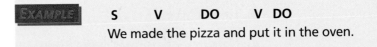   S   V   DO   V DO
                   We made the pizza and put it in the oven.

Activity D Write these sentences on your paper. Underline the direct objects. Underline the direct object twice if it is compound.

1) Emily plays the clarinet and the flute.

2) Do you prefer that song or this one?

3) She lost her homework and her book in one day.

4) We enjoyed the party and the company.

5) The friends made popcorn and ate it.

A command or request can have a direct object.

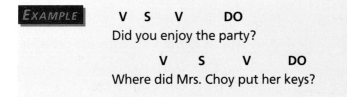

    V   DO

Get the pizza out of the oven.

    V   DO   V DO

Complete the test and bring it to me.

A question can have a direct object.

  V S V   DO

Did you enjoy the party?

    V   S   V   DO

Where did Mrs. Choy put her keys?

Direct objects are never part of a prepositional phrase.

Activity E Write the direct object or objects in each sentence on your paper.

1) Angela read a story to the children.

2) She teaches them at the YMCA.

3) She is performing community service.

4) Finish your paper and give it to me.

5) Did you send an e-mail to me?

Activity F Write these sentences on your paper. Cross out the prepositional phrases. Circle the direct object.

1) Rain forests cover a very small part of the earth.

2) Julie is saving her money for a new computer.

3) On Valentine's Day, Mr. Choy brought flowers to his wife.

4) Can you change this flat tire?

5) Pour a glass of juice for me.

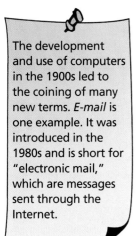

The development and use of computers in the 1900s led to the coining of many new terms. *E-mail* is one example. It was introduced in the 1980s and is short for "electronic mail," which are messages sent through the Internet.

Write each sentence on your paper. Write *S* above the subject,
V above the verb or verb phrase, and *DO* above the direct object.

1) Put this computer on my desk.

2) She gave a certificate to him.

3) He made sandwiches and put them in the picnic basket.

4) Julie is saving her money.

5) Angela found a bridesmaid's dress and shoes.

6) The store had a sale.

7) Patrice enjoys the beach in the summer.

8) Have you ever seen the Statue of Liberty?

9) Do you want this CD or that one?

10) Take the clarinet out of the case.

On your paper, write the pronoun that correctly completes the
sentence. Some pronouns are subjects and some are direct
objects.

11) Where did (she, her) go?

12) Armando saw (she, her) at the mall.

13) The usher escorted (we, us) to our seats.

14) Please drive (I, me) to the store.

15) Nathan returned (they, them) to the library.

Indirect object

A noun or pronoun that receives the direct object of an action verb

Some sentences have both a direct object and an **indirect object.** The indirect object receives the direct object of the action verb. It is a noun or a pronoun. Pattern 3 sentences have a subject, an action verb, a direct object, and an indirect object.

Pattern 3 Sentence:
Subject + Verb + Indirect Object + Direct Object

An indirect object answers the question *to whom, to what, for whom,* or *for what* about the verb. It comes before the direct object.

EXAMPLE
      S   V   IO   DO
     Miguel bought her some paint.
(Miguel bought paint for whom? He bought it for her.)

      S   V   IO   DO
    Julie sent her friends invitations to her wedding.
(Julie sent invitations to whom? She sent them to her friends.)

You can cross out the indirect object and the sentence will still make sense. If you cross out the direct object, you will change the meaning of the sentence.

EXAMPLE
      S   V   IO   DO
    Armando sold Miguel his old bike.

      S   V   DO
    Armando sold his old bike.
(The sentence still makes sense. You just do not know to whom Armando sold the bike.)

      S   V   IO
    Armando sold Miguel.
(Leaving out the direct object changes the meaning, and the sentence no longer makes sense.)

Activity A Write the indirect object in each sentence on your paper. Find the verb. To find the indirect object, ask the question *to whom, to what, for whom,* or *for what* about the verb.

1) Emily bought her dog a toy.

2) Michelle brought them a snack.

3) The YMCA gave the swimming students certificates.

4) Angela gave them the certificates.

5) She handed the children their diplomas.

When an indirect object is a pronoun, it is always in the object form.

EXAMPLE			
	S	V	IO	DO
	Mrs. Choy offered him some pizza.		

Activity B Write the indirect object in each sentence on your paper.

1) The bank teller gave him his money.

2) She showed her the CD.

3) Julie mailed me an invitation.

4) Emily gave the class a description.

5) They awarded them the prize.

Sarah showed Michelle the band's latest CD.

An indirect object can be compound.

V   IO   IO   DO
Give him and me a slice of pizza.

Activity C On your paper, write the indirect object in each sentence.

1) Angela lent Neeru and Emily a book.

2) Tell him and me the truth.

3) Are you giving Emily and me a straight answer?

4) Yes, I am telling you the total truth.

5) Show me the pictures.

A command can have an indirect object.

V   IO   DO
Give me a chance.
(The subject *you* is understood.)

A question can have an indirect object.

V   S   V   IO   DO
Would you give Emily this letter?

Activity D On your paper, write the indirect object in each sentence.

1) Will Emily tell Neeru an interesting fact?

2) Will the chamber of commerce offer students a scholarship?

3) Should Neeru ask her a question?

4) Bring me an application.

5) Give the Student Council the forms.

You can change the indirect object into a prepositional phrase.

> **EXAMPLE**
>
>   **IO   DO**
> Armando gave his mother a gift.
>
>   **DO   Prep. Phrase**
> Armando gave a gift to his mother.

Activity E Write each sentence on your paper. Change the indirect object to a prepositional phrase using the preposition *to.*

1) The judges awarded Armando a prize.

2) Mr. Thomas gave every student an A.

3) Mrs. Choy taught Angela Chinese.

4) Patrice showed me her new CD.

5) They offered the contestants money.

Vocabulary Builder

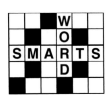

Words from Literature

Sometimes characters in books become so well known that their names, or words based on their names, become part of the English language. For example, in his book *A Christmas Carol,* Charles Dickens wrote about Ebenezer Scrooge. Scrooge was a mean person who was very stingy with money. So if someone calls you a scrooge, he or she is *not* giving you a compliment!

Look up the words *quixotic* and *sherlock.* Copy this chart on your paper and fill in the information.

	quixotic	sherlock
Meaning		
Character		
Book(s)		
Author		

Write each sentence on your paper. Write *S* above the subject and *V* above the verb or verb phrase. Then write *IO* above the indirect object and *DO* above the direct object. In a command, the subject *you* is understood.

1) Angela gave her friend another clue.

2) Give me your opinion about this issue.

3) Emily offered Michelle her ideas.

4) Who bought Efran the CD?

5) Allow yourself some time.

6) Did the store manager give Patrice her receipt?

7) I handed her the book.

8) Will you tell me the time?

9) She gave me an answer to my question.

10) He sold me the same shoes in a different color.

Add an indirect object to each sentence. Write each new sentence on your paper.

11) My friends and I gave a birthday party.

12) Please pass the bread.

13) Will you read the story?

14) Nathan handed the telephone.

15) She showed the video.

Object complement

A noun or an adjective that follows and refers to the direct object

Pattern 4 sentences have a subject, an action verb, a direct object, and an **object complement.** An object complement adds meaning to the direct object. It is always a noun or an adjective. In a sentence, the object complement follows the direct object.

> **Pattern 4 Sentence:**
> Subject + Verb + Direct Object + Object Complement

The object complement either renames or describes the direct object.

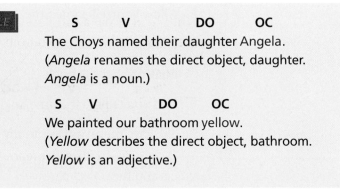

EXAMPLE

| | S | V | DO | OC |

The Choys named their daughter Angela.
(*Angela* renames the direct object, daughter. *Angela* is a noun.)

The words *complement* and *compliment* sound alike. *Complement* is something that completes something else. *Compliment* is praise. When you write, be sure to choose the correct word. For example: *The noun* **complements** *the direct object. The boy gave his friend a* **compliment.**

We painted our bathroom yellow.
(*Yellow* describes the direct object, bathroom. *Yellow* is an adjective.)

Activity A Find the object complements in these sentences and write them on your paper.

1) The umpire called the hit foul.

2) The team made Armando captain.

3) He made the game exciting.

4) The exercise made the players thirsty.

5) The fans declared Armando their hero.

The object complement can be compound.

    S   V   DO   OC   OC

They painted the house blue and white.

If the sentence has a compound direct object, each direct object can have an object complement.

    S   V   DO   OC   DO

They elected Efran president and Brittany

    OC

treasurer.

If the sentence has a compound verb, each verb can have a direct object, and each direct object can have an object complement.

    V   DO OC   V   DO OC

Don't make the soup spicy and don't serve it cold.

Activity B Write these sentences on your paper. Find the direct objects and the object complements. Write *DO* over each direct object and *OC* over each object complement.

Example   **DO OC   DO OC**

    Efran painted the walls blue and the ceiling white.

1) The exercise made the players hot and tired.

2) Many students find computer studies interesting and keyboarding class helpful.

3) The team named Armando the most valuable player and elected him captain.

4) The fall weather turned the leaves gold and orange.

5) The flight delay made her anxious and other passengers angry.

A command can have a direct object and an object complement.

          V   DO   OC
        Make Joe the leader.

A question can have a direct object and an object complement.

      V   S   V DO OC
    Will that dark room make you sleepy?

Activity C Write the object complements on your paper.

1) Will you make the cake chocolate?

2) Did the polls name him the winner?

3) Has Emily found the instructions helpful?

4) Make the tacos spicier please.

5) The heat in the oven turned the rolls brown.

Activity D Find the object complements in the paragraphs below. List them on your paper in order. Not every sentence will have an object complement.

      The friends were involved in a debate. Emily considered *Titanic* the best film of all time. Nathan found that movie boring. Armando named *Star Wars* the greatest. That film made its producer rich. Everyone considers Harrison Ford a great actor. Angela argued for Leonardo DiCaprio. Break the tie, Neeru.

      "I judge them equal," she said diplomatically.

Write each sentence on your paper. Write *S* above the subject and *V* above the verb or verb phrase. Then write *DO* above the direct object and *OC* above the object complement. Some sentences will not have an object complement.

1) Nathan found the history class fascinating.

2) The people elected Franklin Roosevelt president in four elections.

3) Some historians consider Franklin Roosevelt the greatest president.

4) Other presidential scholars judge Abraham Lincoln best.

5) Everyone calls George Washington a great leader.

6) Don't close the doors yet!

7) Does that loud noise bother you?

8) She painted the garage red and black.

9) The students voted Armando king and Emily queen.

Complete these sentences by adding an object complement. Write the completed sentence on your paper.

10) Mrs. Hernandez made the chili too _____.

11) The storm turned the air _____ and _____.

12) Neeru painted her bedroom _____.

13) They elected Emily _____ of the band.

14) The art teacher considered Miguel _____.

15) The frost turned the grass _____.

Linking verb

A state-of-being verb that joins the subject with an adjective, a noun, or a pronoun in the predicate

Predicate noun

A noun or pronoun that follows a linking verb and renames the subject

Pattern 5 sentences have a subject, a **linking verb,** and a **predicate noun.** In some sentences, a linking verb joins the subject to a word in the predicate. A linking verb is always a state-of-being verb. *Feel, look, become, remain,* and *be* are some linking verbs.

EXAMPLE

Action Verb	Armando plays baseball.
Linking Verb	Armando is a baseball player.

A linking verb joins the subject to a predicate noun. A predicate noun is a word or words in the predicate that rename the subject. The predicate noun can be a noun or a pronoun.

> **Pattern 5 Sentence:**
> Subject + Linking Verb + Predicate Noun

A predicate noun helps the sentence express a complete thought.

EXAMPLE

The clarinet is. (incomplete sentence)

    S   LV   PN
The clarinet is a musical instrument.

    S   LV PN
Armando is an artist.

    S   LV PN
The book is a novel.

Activity A On your paper, write the predicate nouns in these sentences.

1) Abraham Lincoln was our sixteenth president.

2) Babe Ruth was a home run hitter.

3) Janet Evans was an Olympic winner.

4) Lassie and Wishbone were dogs in television programs.

5) "The New Colossus" is a famous poem.

A predicate noun is never part of a prepositional phrase.

Activity B Write these sentences on your paper. Cross out the prepositional phrases. Label the subjects, linking verbs, and predicate nouns.

Example   S   LV   PN
                Nathan is my choice ~~for class president~~.

1) Ellis Island was the gateway to America for many immigrants.

2) The Empire State Building was the tallest structure.

3) A woman from Utah became the president of the company.

4) My best friend from school is the secretary of the Student Council.

5) Angela and Emily remained friends in high school.

The predicate noun can be a pronoun. Because the pronoun renames the subject, it must be in the subject form.

> EXAMPLE   Who is it? It is I.

Writing Tip

Read your sentences out loud to see how they sound. You can catch many mistakes that way.

Activity C On your paper, write the pronoun that correctly completes each sentence. Read the sentence out loud.

1) Who is (she, her)?

2) That is (she, her).

3) I see (he, him).

4) Which one is (she, her)?

5) Give that book to (I, me).

The predicate noun can be compound.

> EXAMPLE
>
>   S   LV   PN   PN
> Joyce Carol Oates is a novelist and a poet.

Pattern 5 sentences can have adverbs and prepositional phrases that answer questions about the linking verb.

> EXAMPLE
>
>   S   S   LV   PN
> Nathan and Armando have been friends for a long time.
> (How long have they been friends? for a long time)

A command or question can have a predicate noun or pronoun.

> EXAMPLE
>
> LV   PN
> Be my valentine. (The subject *you* is understood.)
> LV S   PN
> Is that your house?

Activity D Add a predicate noun to each sentence that renames the subject.

1) Bolivia is a _____ in South America.

2) Are those people your _____?

3) Please stay my _____ always.

4) Emily is a _____ to Angela and a _____ to Kaylie.

5) Ted was the _____ on the team.

Write each sentence on your paper. Write *S* above the subject, *LV* above the verb, and *PN* above the predicate noun.

1) Be a kind person!

2) Picasso is a famous Spanish artist.

3) Is Angela's swim team the state champion?

4) Angela is a great swimmer.

5) Florida is a southeastern state.

6) She is a soprano with a very strong voice.

7) Is Emily's father a musician?

8) Emily and her mother are the musicians in their family.

9) He and Jennifer are my classmates.

Write this paragraph on your paper. Identify the subject, linking verb, and predicate noun. Cross out the prepositional phrases.

10)   Thomas Jefferson was our first secretary of state. He was our second vice president. This statesman was our third president. He was the purchaser of the Louisiana Territory. The Louisiana Territory was the land across the Mississippi River. Jefferson's home was Monticello. He was a Virginian. Throughout his life Jefferson remained a picture of good health. He was an early advocate of the benefits of daily walks. Jefferson was a remarkable person.

Pattern 6 sentences have a subject, a linking verb, and a predicate adjective. The predicate adjective follows a linking verb and describes the subject.

> **Pattern 6 Sentence:**
> Subject + Linking Verb + Predicate Adjective

Predicate adjectives are used with linking verbs such as *be, look, seem, taste, smell,* and *feel.* A predicate adjective helps the sentence with a linking verb express a complete thought.

EXAMPLE

The new computer is. (incomplete sentence)

           S   LV PA
The new computer is fast.

The predicate adjective describes the subject of the sentence. The subject is a noun or pronoun.

EXAMPLE

     S   LV   PA
Everyone seems tired.

     S   LV   PA
That book is suspenseful.

A predicate adjective is in the predicate, not the subject.

EXAMPLE

      Adj. Adj. S   V
The adorable little puppy barked.

     S   LV   PA
The puppy is adorable.

Activity A Write the predicate adjectives in these sentences on your paper.

1) Yesterday the weather was warm.

2) The apple pie looks delicious.

3) The velvet jacket feels soft.

4) The new car is shiny.

5) Neeru seems cheerful today.

The predicate adjective is not part of a prepositional phrase.

> EXAMPLE
>   **S   LV PA Prep. Phrase**
> The air feels warm in June.

Activity B Write these sentences on your paper. Cross out the prepositional phrases. Label the subjects, linking verbs, and predicate adjectives.

Example   S LV PA
          Emily is happy.

1) Armando's Aunt Edna from St. Mary's, Kansas, keeps active.

2) His aunt seems quite healthy in mind and body.

3) This 85-year-old woman feels great.

4) She is always cheerful.

5) Aunt Edna looks very young for her age.

The predicate adjective can be compound.

> EXAMPLE
>   **S LV PA   PA**
> He was hot and thirsty after the game.

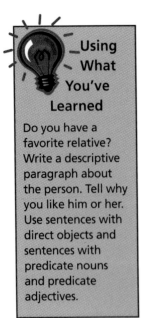
If the sentence has a compound linking verb, both verbs can have predicate adjectives.

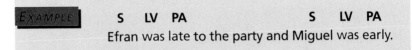

EXAMPLE

S LV PA   S LV PA

Efran was late to the party and Miguel was early.

Activity C Write the predicate adjectives in these sentences on your paper.

1) Everyone feels happy and cheerful today.

2) The spring weather is sunny and mild.

3) Yesterday everyone seemed gloomy and downcast.

4) The weather was cold and rainy.

5) It was cold today but it was hot yesterday.

A command or question can have a predicate adjective.

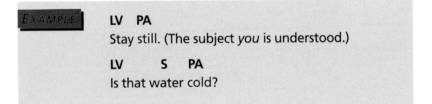

EXAMPLE

LV PA

Stay still. (The subject *you* is understood.)

LV   S   PA

Is that water cold?

Activity D Write the predicate adjective in each sentence on your paper. Some sentences may have a compound predicate adjective.

1) Will the movie be good or bad?

2) The optimistic weather report was welcome.

3) Remain calm please.

4) Are you feeling okay today?

5) Is the stew too salty or spicy for you?

Add a predicate adjective to each sentence. Use a different adjective in each sentence. Write the new sentence on your paper.

1) Was Angela's speech too _____?

2) No, her speech was just _____.

3) Her speech seemed _____.

4) Has she always been so _____ at speeches?

Write these sentences on your paper. Find each verb. If it is a linking verb, find the predicate adjective and underline it.

5)   Be careful around that pool. The water is deep at that end. Angela warned her students about the danger of drowning. All of the children in her class seemed happy. They enjoyed their swimming lessons. Angela is friendly to them. She is also patient with them.

Spelling Builder

Homophones

Homophones are words that sound alike but have different spellings and meanings. You need to know the meanings of homophones to be sure you choose and spell the right ones.

Use these homophones to complete the sentences:
    here   hear   sale   sail

1) You _____ with your ears.

2) Can you run from _____ to there?

3) The store had a _____ on shoes.

4) The wind blew the boat's _____.

Encyclopedia

Suppose someone asked, "When was the first manned space flight?" Now suppose you have this assignment: Write about an important person or event in the history of space exploration. A good place to look in both of these situations is an encyclopedia. You can find facts and a general history of space exploration. An encyclopedia is an excellent place to look first for many kinds of information.

If you looked up "space exploration" in the *World Book Encyclopedia,* you would find several pages that include photos, graphs, lists, and diagrams. You would find the following paragraph at the beginning of the article:

> The space age began on Oct. 4, 1957. On that day, the Soviet Union launched Sputnik (later referred to as Sputnik 1), the first artificial satellite to orbit the earth. The first manned space flight was made on April 12, 1961, when Yuri A. Gagarin, a Soviet cosmonaut, orbited the earth in the spaceship Vostok (later called Vostok 1).

After reading this paragraph, you might decide to find out more about Sputnik or Gagarin. You could answer the question, "When was the first manned space flight?"

Most encyclopedias arrange their articles in alphabetical order. One whole volume of the encyclopedia may be devoted to topics beginning with *A.* You can find several different encyclopedias in the library. You can also find many encyclopedias online.

1) Identify the sentence pattern of each sentence in this paragraph from the article "Dinosaur" in the *World Book Encyclopedia.*

> During the second half of the Mesozoic Era, the first flowering plants appeared.
>   **a)** Pattern 1   **b)** Pattern 2   **c)** Pattern 3
> Forest trees included the first modern conifers as well as primitive magnolias, oaks, palms, and willows.
>   **a)** Pattern 3   **b)** Pattern 4   **c)** Pattern 5
> Birds had evolved from small meat-eating dinosaurs.
>   **a)** Pattern 1   **b)** Pattern 2   **c)** Pattern 3

2) Find an article in an encyclopedia on an animal that interests you. Write five facts about the animal.

Writing Project

Writing a Review

When you write a review, you use critical thinking skills.
Choose one of the following items to review:

- Your favorite television program
- A book you have read recently and enjoyed
- A movie you have seen and liked
- A new CD you have listened to and enjoyed

Follow these steps to write your review:

1) Begin by writing a description of the program, book, movie, or CD. Tell about it as if your reader had never heard of it before. Write at least five sentences.

2) In your next paragraph, tell your reader why you enjoyed this program, book, movie, or CD. Explain why it is better than others. Convince the reader that he or she will like it as much as you did. Ask yourself:

   - What makes the program, book, movie, or CD likable?

   - Is there anything about it that you did not like? Anything that you would change? Explain how you would make it better.

3) Edit your first draft and copy it on another piece of paper.

4) Check for vivid verbs. Look for and fix grammar and spelling errors. Use a dictionary if you need to.

5) Prepare your final draft by copying your edited review on another piece of paper. Make any additional edits.

WORD BANK

compound verb

direct object

indirect object

linking verb

object
  complement

predicate noun

Part A On a sheet of paper, write the correct word or words from the Word Bank to complete each sentence.

1) The noun or pronoun that receives the action of a verb is a _____.

2) The noun or pronoun that receives the direct object of an action verb is the _____.

3) A noun or an adjective that follows and refers to the direct object is an _____.

4) A state-of-being verb that joins the subject with a word in the predicate is called a _____.

5) A noun or pronoun that follows a linking verb and renames the subject is a _____.

6) A _____ is two or more verbs connected by a conjunction.

Part B Write a sentence using each sentence pattern you learned in this chapter.

7) Pattern 1 Sentence: Subject + Verb

8) Pattern 2 Sentence: Subject + Verb + Direct Object

9) Pattern 3 Sentence:
Subject + Verb + Indirect Object + Direct Object

10) Pattern 4 Sentence:
Subject + Verb + Direct Object + Object Complement

11) Pattern 5 Sentence:
Subject + Linking Verb + Predicate Noun

12) Pattern 6 Sentence:
Subject + Linking Verb + Predicate Adjective

Part C Write these sentences on your paper. Identify each as a statement, command, or question. Label the subject, verb, and any objects or complements. Not all sentences will have an object or a complement. Use these labels:

S = Subject   **V** = Verb
DO = Direct object   **IO** = Indirect object
OC = Object complement   **PN** = Predicate noun
PA = Predicate adjective

13) Why do we celebrate Presidents' Day in February?

14) Give me a hint.

15) Efran smiled.

16) His birthday is the same day as Abraham Lincoln's birthday.

17) Is he happy about this?

18) He considers Lincoln a true hero.

19) Lincoln was president during the Civil War.

Part D Find the mistakes with verbs and pronouns in these sentences. Write the sentences on your paper correctly.

20) "Is that Angela? Who is at the door? Is it her?"
    "No, it is she."
    "Is Angela with they?"
    "Who is they?"
    "They is Armando and Nathan."

Test-Taking Tip   Look over a test before you begin answering questions. See how many parts there are. Think about what you are being asked to do in each part.

Identifying Verbals and Verbal Phrases

We often use verbs in sentences to do things other than express action or state of being. When we use verbs as other parts of speech, they are called *verbals.* We use verbals as nouns, adjectives, and adverbs in sentences.

Look at the photograph on the opposite page. We can use verbals in sentences about the picture. Here is a verbal used as a noun— *Flying is fun.* (*Flying* is the subject of the sentence.) Here is a verbal used as an adjective—*Watch the flying squirrel!* (*Flying* describes the noun *squirrel.*) Here is a verbal used as an adverb— *It is ready to fly.* (*To fly* describes the adjective *ready.*)

In Chapter 11, you will learn about three kinds of verbals:
- Gerund—a verb ending in *-ing* that we use as a noun.
- Participle—a verb that we use as an adjective.
- Infinitive—the word *to* plus a verb that we use as a noun, an adjective, or an adverb.

Goals for Learning

▶ To identify and use infinitives and infinitive phrases in sentences

▶ To identify and use gerunds and gerund phrases in sentences

▶ To identify and use participles and participle phrases in sentences

Verbal

A verb used as another part of speech

A **verbal** is a verb that you use as another part of speech. The three kinds of verbals are *infinitives, gerunds,* and *participles.*

An infinitive is *to* plus a verb. Usually you use it as a noun, but it may also be an adverb or an adjective.

EXAMPLE		
Noun	I like to swim.	
	(*To swim* is the object of the verb.)	
Adverb	He practices to win.	
	(*To win* tells us why he practices.)	
Adjective	We had lots of food to eat.	
	(*To eat* describes the noun *food.*)	

Gerund

A verb ending in -ing that is used as a noun

A **gerund** is a verb that ends in -*ing*. We use it as a noun.

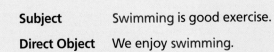

EXAMPLE		
Subject	Swimming is good exercise.
Direct Object	We enjoy swimming.

Participle

A verb that can be used as an adjective

A **participle** is a verb that you use as an adjective. All verbs have present and past participles.

EXAMPLE	
Past Participle	The toy is broken.
	(*Broken* is an adjective that follows the linking verb and describes *toy.*)
Present Participle	The barking dog scared the stranger.
	(*Barking* is an adjective that describes *dog.*)

Activity A Find the verbals in these sentences. Write them on your paper. Identify each one as *infinitive, gerund,* or *participle.*

1) Angela likes to swim.

2) Drawing is one of Armando's favorite activities.

3) "I have several books to read," said Nathan.

4) Emily's dog is lost.

5) Her friends looked for the missing dog.

Complement

A word or phrase that completes the meaning of a verbal

Verbals often have **complements.** A complement is a word or phrase that completes the meaning of a verbal. There may also be adverbs and adverb phrases that answer the questions *where, how, when,* and *why.*

Infinitive Phrase	He hoped to win the contest. (*Contest* is the direct object of the infinitive *to win.*)
Gerund Phrase	Cooking dinner is fun. (*Dinner* is the direct object of the gerund *cooking.*)
Participle Phrase	We saw Nathan jumping the fence. (*Fence* is the direct object of the participle *jumping.*)

A sentence can have more than one verbal or verbal phrase.

Jesse offered to take his brother on a camping trip.
(The infinitive *to take* is the direct object of the verb *offered.*
The participle *camping* is an adjective describing *trip.*)

Activity B Find the verbal phrases in these sentences. Write them on your paper. Identify the kind of verbal each phrase is.

Example Nathan plans to leave early.
            to leave early—infinitive phrase

1) Neeru hoped to find a job after school.

2) Working at the mall would be fun.

3) To be a good salesperson would not be easy.

4) Neeru saw Emily working in the music store.

5) She walked over to say hello.

Activity C Identify the kind of verbal phrase in each sentence. Then identify the complements and write them on your paper.

1) "I want to put in an application," Neeru said.

2) Is there an opening here?

3) If you are willing to work hard, there is a job.

4) The smiling Neeru filled out the application.

5) "I will enjoy earning money," she thought.

Vocabulary Builder

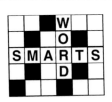

Internet Words

Many new words have entered the English language so that we can talk about the Internet. You cannot find these words in older dictionaries. Some are not even listed in new dictionaries. What do you think each word means? Write a definition for each one on your paper. Then check the definitions in a dictionary.

1) dot.com company
2) e-commerce
3) e-mail
4) Internet
5) keyboard (verb)
6) Web cast
7) Web site
8) download
9) bookmark
10) online

Write the verbals on your paper. Label each one as a gerund, a participle, or an infinitive. Remember, a sentence can have more than one verbal.

1) At the circus, we saw a dancing bear.

2) Neeru enjoys singing in the chorus.

3) Planning a vacation takes a lot of time.

4) Where do you want to go on vacation?

5) Armando wants to try out as a running back for the team.

On your paper, write the verbal phrases in these sentences. Underline the complements that complete each verbal.

6) Julie and her cousin, Angela, plan on taking a winter trip.

7) They have chosen to visit Hawaii.

8) They want to surf in the ocean.

9) Julie finds out about hotels in Hawaii by using the Internet.

10) She calls a travel agent to make airline reservations.

Find the verbal phrases in these sentences. Write them on your paper. Identify the kind of verbal each phrase is—*infinitive, gerund,* or *participle.* Remember, a sentence can have more than one verbal.

11) Playing in a band can be hard work.

12) Speaking quietly, the girl strumming the guitar introduced the song.

13) We saw Gabriela entering the media center.

14) She went there to use a computer.

15) She has to type a report written for history class.

The infinitive is *to* plus a verb. The infinitive is usually the same as the present tense. Only the infinitive *to be* is irregular.

> **EXAMPLE**
>
> Armando and Joe decided to go to the lake.
> Their plan is to leave early.
> They hoped to catch several trout.

An infinitive is usually in the present tense. It can also be in the present perfect tense.

> **EXAMPLE**
>
> They are pleased to have caught several fish.
> (They caught the fish before they were pleased.)

Activity A Write the infinitives in these sentences on your paper.

1) A committee met to plan the band's annual picnic.

2) Emily agreed to be the committee chairperson.

3) What do you want me to bring?

4) Would you like to get the hot dogs?

5) Emily is happy to have served as the chairperson.

Sometimes *to* is missing from the infinitive. It is "understood" to be part of the sentence.

> **EXAMPLE**
>
> Don't make me (to) laugh.
> Help me (to) reel in the fish.

Activity B Write the infinitives in these sentences on your paper.

1) We heard the audience cheer for the band.

2) Let me hear the sound of that music.

3) They watched Emily play her clarinet.

4) Their applause made Emily feel proud.

5) Will you let me thank everyone?

Do not mix up infinitives and prepositional phrases. An infinitive is *to* plus a verb. A prepositional phrase is *to* plus a noun or pronoun.

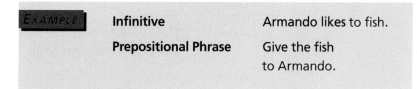

| EXAMPLE | **Infinitive** | Armando likes to fish. |
| | **Prepositional Phrase** | Give the fish to Armando. |

Activity C Write the words in bold on your paper. Next to each phrase, write whether it is an *infinitive* or a *prepositional phrase*.

1) Will you walk with me **to school?**

2) I am going **to paint** now.

3) It is important **to get** there on time.

4) They planned **to begin** the picnic at 6:00 P.M.

5) Everyone went **to the park.**

Infinitive phrase

An infinitive, its complements, and any words that describe it

We often use an infinitive as a noun. An **infinitive phrase** includes the infinitive, its complements, and any words that describe it. Words that describe infinitives include adjectives, adverbs, adjective phrases, and adverb phrases.

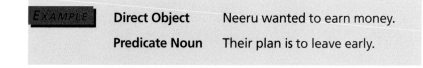

| EXAMPLE | **Direct Object** | Neeru wanted to earn money. |
| | **Predicate Noun** | Their plan is to leave early. |

Activity D Find the infinitives in these sentence. Underline them and try to figure out what part of the sentence they are.

1) They planned to get together after school.

2) Their wish was to have a picnic.

3) The cold rain made the students feel cold.

4) The rain caused them to cancel the picnic.

5) To gather their things took time.

An infinitive can be an adverb or an adjective.

EXAMPLE

Adverb	Neeru will need a new dress to work in. (Why does she need a new dress?)
Adjective	She has plenty of clothes to wear. (What kind of clothes does she have?)

Activity E Write these sentences on your paper. Underline the infinitives. Tell whether each infinitive is used as a *noun*, an *adverb*, or an *adjective*.

Example   Neeru is eager <u>to work</u>.
              adverb

1) Neeru's goal is to get a job.

2) She has time to work on weekends.

3) She decided to look for a job at the mall.

4) A job will be fun to have.

5) She will work to earn money.

Write the infinitive in each sentence on your paper. If the sentence does not have an infinitive, write *None.*

1) Can you help me find a ride?

2) I'm going to the movies.

3) I want to see the newest blockbuster film.

4) Jeff is sure to have seen it already.

5) I don't have the courage to watch scary movies.

Write the infinitive or infinitive phrase in each sentence on your paper. Tell whether it is used as a subject, a direct object, a predicate noun, an adjective, or an adverb. There may be more than one infinitive in a sentence.

6) To describe an interesting person was the assignment.

7) "I need to think about this," Emily said to herself.

8) Finally, she decided to tell about her cousin Bobby.

9) His goal was to be a performer.

10) He had the talent to sing, to dance, and to tell jokes.

Use each of these infinitives in a sentence. Underline the entire infinitive phrase. Think about the role the infinitive takes in the sentence.

11) to find

12) to have opened

13) to write

14) to look

15) to be

A gerund is a verb ending in *-ing* that we use as a noun. In sentences, gerunds act like nouns.

EXAMPLE

Subject	Surfing is popular at the ocean.
Direct Object	Armando likes playing tennis.
Object of Preposition	Vincent Van Gogh is famous for his painting.
Predicate Noun	Angela's favorite sport is swimming.

Activity A Write the gerunds in these sentences on your paper. Tell how each gerund is used in the sentence.

Example   Tanya loves riding her bike.
              riding—direct object

1) Tanya's family returned to the United States after living in Switzerland.

2) Tanya enjoyed living in Switzerland.

3) While there, the family learned about clock making.

4) Hiking and skiing became their favorite activities.

5) Cooking is one of Tanya's favorite things to do.

The progressive forms of a verb and a gerund end in *-ing*. Do not confuse progressive verb phrases and gerunds.

EXAMPLE

Verb Phrase	Angela is swimming in the pool today.
Gerund	Angela likes swimming every day.

Gerund phrase

A gerund and its complements

Not all words that end in *-ing* are gerunds. Some adjectives, nouns, and prepositions also end in *-ing*. To be a gerund, the word must be a verb used as a noun. These words are not gerunds: *during, interesting, king, morning, clothing, exciting, according, including, thing,* and *something.*

Activity B Write these sentences on your paper. Decide whether the word in bold is part of a verb phrase or a gerund. Write *gerund* or *verb phrase*.

Example Josh practiced **passing** the ball.
passing—gerund

1) Angela was **enjoying** the television program.

2) It was about deep-sea **diving.**

3) **Seeing** the unusual fish interested her.

4) Angela thought about **becoming** a deep-sea diver someday.

5) She is **planning** to learn more about the ocean.

A **gerund phrase** is a gerund plus any adjectives, adverbs, prepositional phrases, or other complements. A gerund acts like a noun in a sentence. As a result, it may have an adjective that describes it.

> EXAMPLE   Armando helps win games through strong hitting.
> (*Hitting* is the object of the preposition *through*. *Strong* is an adjective that describes *hitting*.)

A gerund can also have an adverb or a prepositional phrase.

> EXAMPLE   Neeru enjoys singing in the school chorus.
> (*Singing* is the direct object of the verb *enjoys*. The prepositional phrase *in the school chorus* tells where Neeru likes *singing*.)

If the gerund expresses action, it can have a direct object.

> EXAMPLE   Playing baseball is fun.
> (*Baseball* is the direct object of *playing*.)

If the gerund is a linking verb, it can have a predicate noun or adjective.

She liked being the oldest child.
(*Child* is the predicate noun of *being*.)

Activity C The gerund in each sentence is in bold. Identify how the gerund is used in the sentence.

Example Angela likes **swimming.**
swimming—direct object

1) Efran likes **playing** volleyball.

2) **Playing** volleyball is Efran's favorite leisure activity.

3) **Serving** and **passing** are part of the game.

4) Efran is thinking about **organizing** a volleyball club.

5) He likes **playing** with his friends.

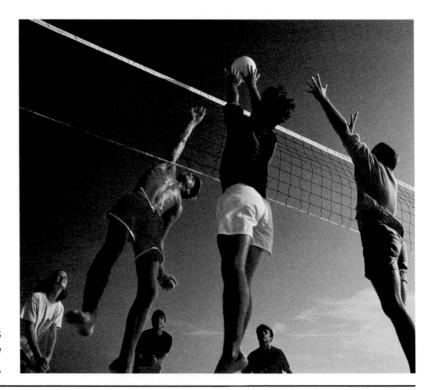

Efran and his friends enjoy playing volleyball.

Write these sentences on your paper. Underline the gerund phrases.

1) Saving money for college was Emily's goal.

2) She had thought about going to college long ago.

3) Emily thinks about studying music.

4) Teaching music in high school would be great.

5) Becoming a music teacher is her ambition.

Write the gerund in each sentence on your paper. Tell whether it is used as a subject, a direct object, a predicate noun, or an object of a preposition.

6) When she was very young, Emily began taking lessons.

7) Now one of her favorite activities is playing her clarinet.

8) She also enjoys writing short tunes.

9) Learning new musical pieces is easy for her.

10) She learns about music by listening to it too.

Spelling Builder

Cede or Ceed?

Do you *procede* or *proceed* to an exit? You *proceed* to an exit. Some verbs have parts spelled *ceed* or *cede*.

- Three common verbs in English use the *ceed* spelling: *proceed, succeed, exceed.*
- Most other (sēd) verbs use *cede: precede, recede.*

Write sentences using these *ceed* and *cede* words: *succeed, exceed, precede.* Use a dictionary to check the definitions.

A participle is a verb form. We use participles to form the perfect tenses and the progressive forms.

> **EXAMPLE**
>
> | **Present Perfect** | Mrs. Young has baked cookies. |
> | **Progressive** | Mrs. Young is baking cookies. |

We also use participles as adjectives.

> **EXAMPLE**
>
> We smelled the baking cookies.
> (*Baking* describes *cookies*.)
>
> We ate the baked cookies.
> (*Baked* describes *cookies*.)

Activity A Find the participles in these sentences. Write the participle and the noun that the participle describes on your paper. Look for verb forms that are adjectives in these sentences.

Example Workers cut the fallen tree apart.
fallen—tree

1) Efran enjoys cooked carrots.

2) The howling wind kept us awake.

3) The movie was frightening.

4) The setting sun colored the sky orange.

5) We visited the Painted Desert in New Mexico.

A participle may be an adjective or it may be part of a verb phrase.

Writing Tip

Some verbs have irregular past participles. They do not end in *-ed*. For example, *taught* is the past participle of *teach* and *broken* is the past participle of *break*. If you are unsure of the past participle of a verb, look up the present tense in the dictionary. If the verb has an irregular past participle, the entry will include it.

EXAMPLE

Participle as an Adjective
Mr. Choy likes to wear a starched shirt.

Participle as Part of a Verb Phrase
Mrs. Choy has starched his shirts for years.

Activity B Decide whether the word in bold is a participle used as an adjective or as a verb. Write your answer on your paper.

1) We **steamed** the vegetables.

2) She likes **steamed** vegetables.

3) Mark Twain wrote a famous story about a **jumping** frog.

4) The frog is **jumping** across the pond.

5) We **locked** the door as we left the car.

Participle phrase
*A participle plus
any words that
complement or
describe it*

A **participle phrase** is a participle plus any words that complement or describe it. A participle comes right before or right after the noun or pronoun that it describes.

EXAMPLE

Jumping high, she cleared the fence.
(The participle phrase *jumping high* describes *she*.)

The keys locked inside the car were of no use.
(The phrase *locked inside the car* describes *keys*.)

Activity C Write these sentences on your paper. Underline each participle phrase. Draw a line to the noun or pronoun it describes.

1) Emily mailed a letter of application addressed to the college.

2) Concentrating on his book, he didn't hear his mother.

3) Pizza made by Mrs. Hernandez was a special treat.

4) The picture hanging on the wall was attractive.

5) Emily made a phone call to a girl waiting at the store.

Like other verbals, a participle can have a direct object, a predicate noun or adjective, adverbs, and prepositional phrases.

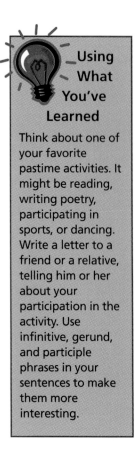

Using What You've Learned

Think about one of your favorite pastime activities. It might be reading, writing poetry, participating in sports, or dancing. Write a letter to a friend or a relative, telling him or her about your participation in the activity. Use infinitive, gerund, and participle phrases in your sentences to make them more interesting.

Activity D Write these sentences on your paper. Underline the participle phrase in each sentence. Draw two lines under the noun or pronoun it describes.

1) Reaching the high notes easily, Neeru performed for the school.

2) The team, hoping for victory, ran out onto the field.

3) I wondered about the boy seeming so shy.

4) The young girl looking so happy won the race.

5) Did you see the woman standing by the side of the road?

Write these sentences on your paper. Underline each participle. Draw a line from the participle to the noun or pronoun it describes.

1) Mrs. Choy likes microwaved potatoes.

2) She uses stewed tomatoes in many recipes.

3) The aroma of the cooking onions filled the air.

4) The simmering stew is on the stove.

5) Angela prefers frozen desserts.

Write these sentences on your paper. Underline each participle phrase. Draw a line from the phrase to the noun or pronoun it describes.

6) The zipper invented in 1893 changed our clothing forever.

7) Radio waves discovered in 1895 made telephones possible.

8) The fax machine sitting in our office is out of paper.

9) Vacuum bottles, also called thermos bottles, keep hot drinks warm.

10) In 1925, scientists invented the technology we use in fax machines operating in offices today.

Write sentences using these participle phrases. Be sure to use the participle as an adjective.

11) addressed to her aunt

12) sitting on the floor

13) being brave

14) watching the movie

15) volunteering for duty

Where to Find It

Table of Contents

You can find books on just about every subject, from astronomy to zoology, in the library. To use a book, you must be able to locate the information you need. One way to find information in a book is by looking up topics in the book's index. Another way is by reading the table of contents at the beginning of the book.

The table of contents lists the book's chapter titles and page numbers. You can turn to a chapter and scan it to find information on your topic. Suppose you locate a book on outdoor activities in the West. Here is part of the table of contents from the book.

If you wanted information on fishing in Idaho, you could turn to Chapter 6, which starts on page 71. You could scan the chapter to find facts on fishing in Idaho.

Reading a table of contents helps you quickly find out whether a book contains the information you are looking for.

1) Suppose you are interested in the following topics. Use the table of contents above. Write the chapter and page number that you would refer to for facts on each topic.

    a) Equipment for white-water rafting

    b) The most challenging ski slopes in Colorado

    c) Types of fish in Montana lakes and rivers

2) Write one infinitive phrase and two gerund phrases from the table of contents above.

3) Locate a book on a topic that interests you. On your paper, write the title of the book. Then write the chapter titles and page numbers that contain the information you need.

Writing E-Mail

Sending e-mail to family and friends is a popular way
of communicating.

New Message

Geneva	12	**B** *I* U	

To...   jgeinberg@zip.com

Cc...

Subject: School

Dear Mom and Dad,

I am enjoying college very much. Yesterday I started my new classes.
I have English, Math, and History on Monday, Wednesday, and Friday.
I have PE and Biology on Tuesday and Thursday. So far everything is
going well. I have my first test on Friday though.

My roommate and I are getting along very well. He is from Idaho so it is
tough getting used to living in a big city like Chicago.

Love, Benjamin

If you have access to a computer, do this activity on your computer. If not, write
the activity on your paper. Write SEND TO: followed by an e-mail address. Write
the word SUBJECT. Write a short phrase that tells the subject of the e-mail.
Then write your message. Check your grammar and spelling. Fix any mistakes,
then send the message to a friend.

CHAPTER 11 Review

WORD BANK

complement

gerund

gerund phrase

infinitive phrase

participle

participle phrase

verbal

Part A On your paper, write the correct word or words from the Word Bank to complete each sentence.

1) A _____ is a verb used as another part of speech.

2) A _____ is a verb that we use as a noun. It ends in *-ing*.

3) A participle and its complements are called a _____.

4) A _____ is a word or phrase that completes the meaning of a verbal.

5) *To earn money* is an example of an _____.

6) A _____ is a verb that we use as an adjective.

7) A _____ is a gerund and its complements.

Part B On your paper, write the infinitive or infinitive phrase in each sentence.

8) Nathan has decided to buy a new CD.

9) His parents used to listen to records.

10) In 1979, the compact disc began to take over the music industry.

11) Records began to disappear from music stores.

12) Some people now visit flea markets and thrift shops to look for records.

13) Some search the Internet to find sellers of record albums.

14) Nathan might start to collect record albums.

Part C Write the gerund or gerund phrase in these sentences on your paper.

15) People began traveling into space in 1957.

16) The United States played a major role in exploring space.

17) In the 1960s, President Kennedy made traveling to the moon a national goal.

18) Achieving that objective happened in 1969.

19) In 1969 Americans and the world celebrated Neil Armstrong's walking on the moon.

20) Space shuttles began making trips into space in 1986.

21) Building an international space station is a major goal today.

Part D Write the participle or participle phrase in these sentences on your paper. Identify the noun the participle is describing.

22) Working in groups or individually, many scientists contributed to motion picture technology.

23) The motion picture projector created by Thomas Edison also made movies possible.

24) The first movie shown in New York City was a major event.

25) Movies showing in theaters became a major form of worldwide entertainment.

Test-Taking Tip Read test questions carefully to identify questions that require more than one answer.

Writing Compound and Complex Sentences

The photograph on the opposite page shows several musical instruments. Played alone, each instrument can make music. But played together, the instruments can make music that has more variety. It is more entertaining to listen to. In the same way, if you use different kinds of sentences in your writing, you can create something that is more exciting to read.

When you talk, you use all kinds of sentences. Your listener can ask you to explain anything that is unclear. When you write, it is important to write sentences that make your meaning clear. After all, your reader cannot ask you to explain your ideas.

You have already learned about independent and dependent clauses and compound sentences. In Chapter 12, you will learn more about these and other kinds of clauses and sentences. You will also learn how to use them to make your writing clearer.

Goals for Learning

▶ To distinguish between phrases and clauses

▶ To write and punctuate compound and complex sentences

▶ To identify different types of dependent clauses and their uses in sentences

▶ To write different types of sentences

Phrase

A group of words that work together

Words can be organized into **phrases** and clauses. A phrase is a group of words that work together. A phrase does not have both a subject and a predicate.

EXAMPLE

Prepositional Phrase	near the road
Verb Phrase	has gone
Infinitive Phrase	to build a fire
Gerund Phrase	swimming in the pool
Participle Phrase	watched him from the window
Subject	the youngest girl in the family
Predicate	took her vitamins

A clause is a group of words with both a subject and a predicate.

EXAMPLE   Sheryl did research on the Internet.

Activity A Read each group of words. Tell whether they are a phrase or a clause. Write *phrase* or *clause* on your paper.

1) Tanya went to Switzerland.

2) For three years.

3) To be with her family.

4) Her family moved there.

5) Because her father worked for a Swiss company.

Simple sentence
A sentence with one subject and one predicate

An independent clause expresses a complete thought. A **simple sentence** is an independent clause. It has one subject and one predicate and expresses a complete thought. A clause that does not express a complete idea is a dependent clause.

EXAMPLE	**Independent Clause**	Emily likes television. (simple sentence)
	Dependent Clause	If she likes television. (not a sentence)

Activity B Decide whether these clauses are independent or dependent clauses. Write *independent* or *dependent* on your paper.

1) Because skiing is a popular sport.

2) Switzerland attracts many visitors in winter.

3) Since Tanya returned to the United States in late January.

4) She has been going to Wilson High School since February.

5) Whoever knew Tanya before.

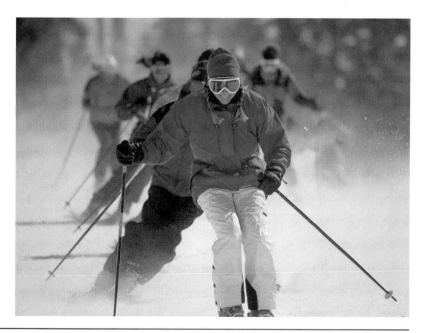

Skiing is a popular winter sport.

Identify each group of words as a phrase or a clause. Write *phrase* or *clause* on your paper.

1) Until she moved back from Switzerland.

2) Although the poem has four verses.

3) Tanya was unable to see the movie.

4) When it was written.

5) She rented it and took it home.

Identify each group of words as an independent or a dependent clause. Write *independent* or *dependent* on your paper.

6) Because she enjoyed *Star Wars.*

7) Tanya went home to watch the movie.

8) She had watched all three films in the series.

9) When it was released.

10) Tanya saw a movie about the FBI.

Vocabulary Builder

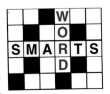

Interesting Acronyms

FBI is an acronym—a word formed from the first letter or letters of a series of words. The word *acronym* first appeared in the English language in 1943.

Write the words these acronyms stand for: *RBI, ASAP, NASA, www, UFO.* Use a dictionary if necessary. Remember to check your dictionary to see if it has an Abbreviations section at the back. Then list five more acronyms and their meanings.

Compound

Two or more sentences or parts of a sentence that are connected with a conjunction

Compound sentence

Two or more related clauses that are connected with a conjunction

A **compound** is two or more sentences or parts of a sentence connected with a conjunction. Any part of a sentence can be compound—subjects, predicates, objects, phrases.

A **compound sentence** is two or more related clauses connected with a conjunction. Each clause has its own subject and verb. Use a comma in front of the conjunction in a compound sentence.

> EXAMPLE
>
> We decided to go out for pizza, and the movie began at 8:00 P.M. (These two clauses are not clearly related.)
>
> The wind blew from the north, and the air grew chilly. (These two clauses are related.)

Coordinating Conjunctions				
and	but	for	or	so

Activity A Use a conjunction to connect each pair of sentences. Write the compound sentences on your paper.

1) Your assignment is to write a paper. You could draw a poster.

2) Angela does not have a test on Monday. She does have a paper due.

3) The order was late. It was lost in the mail.

4) We needed milk. We went to the grocery store.

5) The coach suggested entering only one event. Angela agreed.

Use commas to separate the clauses in a series of three or more.

EXAMPLE Josh is on the debate team, Caren is in the science club, and Michelle belongs to the chess club.

Activity B Write these sentences on your paper. Punctuate the items in each series correctly.

1) Tom went to soccer practice Steve went to tennis practice and Hanna went to exercise.

2) The English test is on Monday the grammar part is on Tuesday but the essay section will be on Wednesday.

3) Don brought a salad Judy made sandwiches and Gary fixed lemonade.

4) The cat meowed the dog barked but the fish didn't make a sound.

5) One doctor said yes another said no and a third said maybe.

Use a semicolon (;) to punctuate two clauses joined with these conjunctions. Use a comma after the conjunction.

More Conjunctions		
accordingly	furthermore	nevertheless
also	however	otherwise
besides	instead	therefore
consequently	moreover	

EXAMPLE Nathan enjoys wrestling; however, he likes baseball more.

Emily practiced for hours; nevertheless, she was nervous before the concert.

Activity C Combine these sentences using one of the conjunctions in the box on page 298. Punctuate the new sentence using a semicolon.

1) Jesse went to the library to use the computers. Students filled all of the carrels.

2) He hoped to use the Internet. He used reference books in the library.

3) Jesse got a B on the test. He needs this report to raise his final grade.

4) The report has to be typed. It has to include at least two graphics.

5) Armando helped with the graphics. Jesse wouldn't get the report finished in time.

Activity D Write five sentences that include conjunctions. Punctuate the sentences correctly.

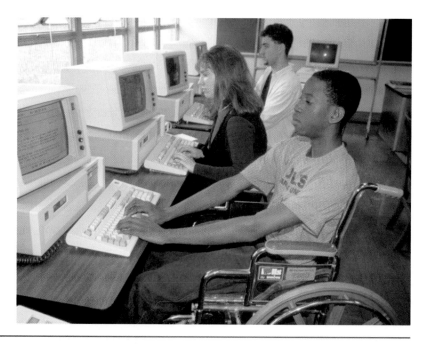

Jesse worked hard on his report; consequently, he received an A in the class.

Change each pair of simple sentences into a compound sentence. Use a conjunction to connect each pair of sentences. Write your sentences on your paper.

1) Francis Scott Key wrote the words to "The Star-Spangled Banner." Katherine Lee Bates wrote the words to "America the Beautiful."

2) In 1893, Bates wrote "America the Beautiful" as a poem. It was later set to music.

3) Bates was a poet. She was a college professor.

4) "America the Beautiful" is a well-known song. People often sing it on the Fourth of July.

5) In 1882, Samuel Augustus wrote "Materna." Today it is better known as the music for "America the Beautiful."

Write a paragraph describing your favorite television program and the characters. Use at least two compound sentences in your description.

Some sentences have both independent and dependent clauses. Dependent clauses may be adverb clauses, adjective clauses, or noun clauses.

Adverb clause

A dependent clause that works like an adverb in a sentence

An **adverb clause** is a dependent clause that works exactly like an adverb in a sentence. An adverb clause has a subject and a verb. It tells something about the verb, an adjective, or another adverb.

> EXAMPLE   **Adverb Clause**   The snow started before the sun was up.

Like adverbs, adverb clauses answer questions such as *where, when, why, how much, how often,* and *how soon.*

> EXAMPLE   Armando waited to use the computer after other students left. (tells when)
>
> He waited because all the computers were in use. (tells why)
>
> This winter the weather was colder than it has been in any other year. (tells how much)

An adverb clause begins with a subordinating conjunction. A subordinating conjunction is a word that begins a dependent clause. If an adverb clause begins a sentence, use a comma after it.

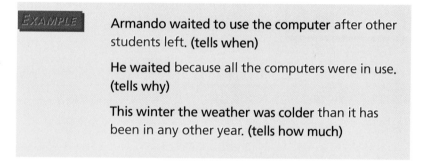

Common Subordinating Conjunctions			
after	if	unless	wherever
although	in order that	until	whether
as	since	when	while
because	so that	whenever	
before	than	where	

Activity A Write the adverb clause in each sentence on your paper.

1) Tanya received a new computer when she returned to the United States.

2) Because the computer came with a disk for the Internet, Tanya is setting up an e-mail account.

3) If it is available, she wants the e-mail address "tanyasmail."

4) Her parents gave her the computer because she needed it for school.

5) Her computer is faster than most older computers are.

Noun clause

A dependent clause that works like a noun in a sentence

A **noun clause** is a dependent clause that works exactly like a noun in a sentence. A noun clause often begins with a relative pronoun. The relative pronouns are *that, what, which, who, whom, whose, whatever, whichever, whoever,* and *whenever.* Other words that introduce noun clauses include *if, whether,* and *why.*

EXAMPLE

Subject	Whoever wins the race gets the prize.
Predicate Noun	She is who she seems to be.
Direct Object	Armando believed what I told him.
Indirect Object	Give whoever wants it my coat.
Object Complement	You can name the boat whatever you like.
Object of Preposition	Armando gave a ride to whoever needed one.

Activity B On your paper, write the noun clause in each sentence. Identify how the writer used the clause.

1) Order what you want.

2) What you should do is request the school's catalog.

3) The small laptop will do whatever we need.

4) Whoever wants to go to the college should send in an application.

5) Neeru sold a CD to the lady who wanted one.

An **appositive** renames or explains a noun in the same sentence. An appositive may be a word, a phrase, or a clause.

Appositive

A noun, phrase, or clause that is placed next to a noun to rename or explain it

> **EXAMPLE**
>
> My friend Tanya has a laptop computer. (noun)
>
> Her computer, a small portable, is easy to carry. (noun plus adjectives)
>
> Tanya's computer, a birthday present from her parents, is lightweight. (noun plus adjectives and an adjective phrase)
>
> She showed me the laptop, a machine that can do many tasks. (noun plus an adjective and a clause)

Tanya's laptop computer is fun and easy to use.

Usually you use a comma to separate an appositive from the rest of the sentence. If the appositive is in the middle of the sentence, you use commas before and after it.

If an appositive is needed for the meaning of the sentence, you do not use commas.

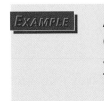 Armando's friend Josh plays soccer too. (Armando has more than one friend. The appositive *Josh* is needed to know which friend. Therefore, a comma is not used.)

You can also use dashes to separate the appositive from the rest of the sentence.

 Judy Garland—an extremely talented performer—starred in many movies including *The Wizard of Oz.*

Activity C On your paper, write the word that the appositive renames or explains in each of these sentences. Then write the appositive and tell whether it is a word, a phrase, or a clause.

Example   Gabriela's cousin Miguel is visiting her.
               cousin, Miguel—word

1) Nathan had a secret wish—that he would someday be a scientist.

2) Eleanor of Aquitaine, a lady from the 12th century, inherited part of France from her father.

3) Neeru's lovely voice, one that can reach very high notes, will win her a music scholarship.

4) Angela, the best swimmer at Wilson High School, could be an Olympic champion.

5) Ben Franklin, an important person in colonial America, experimented with electricity.

Writing Tip

To decide whether commas are needed with an appositive, ask yourself, "Is there more than one possibility?" If there is, then you do not need commas. For example, if you have two brothers, the name used as an appositive does not need commas.

My brother Paul came with me.

Adjective clause
A dependent clause that describes a noun or pronoun

An adjective describes a noun or pronoun. We use an **adjective clause** in a sentence exactly like an adjective. An adjective clause is a dependent clause that describes a noun or pronoun.

EXAMPLE		
Adjective	Neeru is talented.
Adjective Phrase	She is a girl with many talents.
Adjective Clause	Neeru is a girl who is very talented.

The relative pronouns (*who, whom, that, whose, which, what*) can introduce adjective clauses. The relative pronoun is often the subject of the clause. The words *where* and *when* can also introduce adjective clauses. An adjective phrase and an adjective clause usually follow the noun they describe.

Activity D Identify the words in bold as adjective, adjective phrase, or adjective clause. Write *adjective, adjective phrase,* or *adjective clause* on your paper.

1) Armando is **artistic.**

2) Armando is a student **with artistic talent.**

3) He is a student **who is artistic.**

4) The painting **that decorates the wall** is a landscape.

5) The landscape **on the wall** is lovely.

Activity E Write the adjective clause in each sentence on your paper.

1) Armando had dinner with Andrea who is an old friend.

2) Josh was accepted by the college that he wanted to attend.

3) The music store where Emily works is open on Sundays.

4) Nathan was the actor whom the director wanted as a star.

5) The book that Neeru gave me has a surprise ending.

Activity F Use each of these adjective clauses in a sentence. Be sure the clause tells about a noun in the sentence.

1) who won first prize

2) that sits on the top shelf

3) where my friend lives

4) when we went to New York

5) which Shantal bought

6) that is very short

7) whom Emily admires

8) whose house they visited

9) which Nathan read

10) who sings in the chorus

Spelling Builder

Pronunciation and Spelling

Are you meeting someone at the *libary* or the *library?* Sometimes we say a word without saying a letter or a syllable. To help you spell such words correctly,

- say the word aloud and exaggerate the pronunciation of the letters and syllables.
- write the word.
- check the word in the dictionary.

Work with a partner. Say each word and have your partner write it: *February, different, Wednesday, probably.*

On your paper, write the dependent clause in each sentence.

1) Patrice is quieter today than she usually is.

2) The restaurant where they often meet is open until 10:00 P.M.

3) You will need snow tires if you plan to drive anywhere today.

4) Michelle waved when she saw Jackson.

5) Did you see the video that won three awards?

On your paper, write the dependent clauses in the sentences. Identify each clause as an adverb clause, a noun clause, an adjective clause, or an appositive.

6) Those who live in the mountains have had almost a foot of snow.

7) The cold front moved more quickly than it ever had before.

8) Whoever made those predictions did not get them right!

9) Will it take long to plow the roads after the storm is over?

10) The storm—one forecast by the weather service—arrived as predicted.

Using What You've Learned

Write a paragraph identifying an artist—painter, sculptor, author, or musician—whose work you like. Tell why you like the artist. Try to use a variety of sentences in your paragraph. Using simple, compound, and complex sentences can help make your paragraph more interesting.

<table>
<tr><td>

Complex sentence

A sentence with one independent clause and one or more dependent clauses

</td></tr>
</table>

A **complex sentence** has one independent clause and one or more dependent clauses. The dependent clause may be an adverb, a noun, or an adjective clause.

> EXAMPLE

Independent Clause   **Dependent Clause**
I will rent a DVD today if you will watch it with me.

Activity A Write the sentences on your paper. Underline the independent clauses. Underline the dependent clauses twice.

1) The well-wishers who attended the party thought that Armando deserved the prize.

2) Armando's portrait of the school principal that is now hanging in the front lobby is amazingly accurate.

3) The portrait that he painted won first prize in the contest.

4) After he won the contest, Armando and his friends celebrated at Tony's restaurant.

5) Nathan suggested that Armando's friends go to Tony's.

Activity B Decide what kind of sentence each of these sentences is. Write *simple, compound,* or *complex* on your paper.

1) Armando's favorite artist is Edouard Manet.

2) Manet, who was a French artist in the mid-1800s, painted many works that showed everyday life.

3) Manet went to art school in Paris where he learned from Thomas Couture, a well-known artist of the time.

4) Manet exhibited his work at art shows that were sponsored by the government.

5) Armando has seen many of Manet's paintings in books, and he saw one of the actual paintings in a museum.

Write each dependent clause on your paper. Identify each one as an adverb, adjective, or noun clause.

1) Because they are a rich source of vitamin A, many people eat carrots.

2) The part of the carrot plant that people eat is the root.

3) Do you know what weed is a close relative of carrots?

4) Queen Anne's lace, which has a cluster of small white flowers, is a wild carrot.

5) The root of the wild carrot cannot be eaten since it is tough and woody.

Identify each sentence as a simple, complex, or compound sentence. Write *simple, complex,* or *compound* on your paper.

6) Parsley and carrots belong to the same family of vegetables.

7) The top of the carrot, the part that is above ground, looks like parsley.

8) Although people eat the roots of carrots, it is the leaves of parsley that they eat.

9) Some people say that the flavor is too strong.

10) Parsley is often used as decoration.

Where to Find It

Biographical Reference Book

Where would you go to find information about Albert Einstein, Sandra Day O'Connor, or Louis Armstrong? Facts about well-known people, both living and dead, are available in biographical reference books. In the library's reference section, you will find many types of biographical references.

One biographical reference is *Merriam-Webster Biographical Dictionary.* It has brief listings on well-known people, living and dead, from all walks of life. Each listing gives important dates in a person's life and a brief description of his or her accomplishments. Other biographical references, such as the *Encyclopedia of World Biography,* have more detailed listings. Like other encyclopedias, these books have several volumes.

Still other biographical references provide information about people in a particular field. You can find reference books on artists, writers, musicians, explorers, political figures, and many other categories. Following is part of a listing on Ludwig van Beethoven. It is from *The Harvard Biographical Dictionary of Music.*

> **Beethoven, Ludwig van** (b. Bonn, 15 or 16 Dec., bapt. 17 Dec. 1770; d. Vienna, 26 Mar. 1827). Composer. He was born into a family of musicians who had served at the Bonn court of the Elector of Cologne since 1733. That year his grandfather, Ludwig van Beethoven (1712–73), had come from Mechelen, Belgium, as a bass singer for the court. His son Johann van Beethoven (ca. 1740–92), the composer's father, became a tenor and music teacher at the court.

1) Suppose you needed each of the following. Decide whether you would refer to a biographical dictionary, a biographical encyclopedia, or a book about people in a particular field.

    a) A detailed article on the artist Claude Monet

    b) Information about John Lennon

    c) Facts about the 19th-century businessman Andrew Carnegie

2) Use a biographical reference book to find facts about an artist, writer, or musician you admire. Write an oral report using the facts.

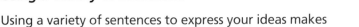

Writing Project

Using a Variety of Sentences

Using a variety of sentences to express your ideas makes
your writing more enjoyable to read. When you write, decide what type of sentence
best expresses each of your ideas. You can express the same idea in several ways.

Simple Sentence	At the age of six, Josh finally learned to ride a bike.
Compound Sentence	Josh was six years old, and he finally learned to ride a bike.
Complex Sentence	Josh finally learned to ride a bike when he was six years old.

Write five to seven sentences about one of the following topics. Begin by writing
your ideas. Then decide what kinds of sentences will help make your writing more
interesting. Use different kinds of sentences to group your ideas or relate them to
one another. Use conjunctions and semicolons in some of your compound sentences.
When you are finished writing, underline the independent clauses in each of your
sentences and circle the dependent clauses.

Choose One of These Topics or One of Your Own

- Going out with your friends
- Why a healthy diet is important
- The many uses of a laptop computer
- The benefits of exercise
- Why people enjoy watching sports

Writing Tip
Have a friend read your paragraph aloud to you. Listen for awkward wording
and mistakes.

WORD BANK

adjective clause

adverb clause

appositive

complex sentence

compound

compound
   sentence

noun clause

phrase

simple sentence

Part A On your paper, write the correct word or words from the Word Bank to complete each sentence.

1) A _____ is a group of words that work together.

2) A _____ is a sentence with one subject and one predicate.

3) An _____ is a noun, phrase, or clause placed next to a noun to rename or explain it.

4) A _____ is two or more sentences or parts of a sentence connected with a conjunction.

5) A _____ is two or more related clauses connected with a conjunction.

6) A _____ is a dependent clause that acts like a noun.

7) An _____ is a dependent clause that describes a noun or pronoun.

8) An _____ is a dependent clause that acts like an adverb.

9) A _____ is a sentence with one independent clause and one or more dependent clauses.

Part B On your paper, write whether each group of words is a phrase or a clause. Find the appositive in one of the phrases or clauses and write it on your paper.

10) Emily, an employee at the music store, purchased a new CD.

11) With the soundtrack from the latest blockbuster movie.

12) Because the movie score has new songs and old hits.

13) Sung by the original artists.

14) The CD is very popular.

Part C Write the subject and verb in each of these independent clauses on your paper.

15) In his math class, Nathan learned about the stock market.

16) People buy and sell stocks.

17) Stocks are shares of companies.

18) The owner of the stock owns a part of the company.

19) The prices of stocks go up and down.

Part D Write the dependent clause in each sentence on your paper. Then write what kind of clause it is: *adverb clause, noun clause,* or *adjective clause.*

20) Very few people know what proper breathing is.

21) You can release a lot of tension if you take a few deep breaths.

22) When you feel tense, breathe in and out slowly.

23) The nervousness that you may feel during a test will go away.

24) Think about your lungs as two balloons that are located inside your chest cavity.

25) Write five sentences about your favorite hobby. Use simple, compound, and complex sentences to describe the hobby. When you are finished, share your description with a classmate.

When a teacher announces a test, listen carefully. Write down the topics that might be included. Write down the names of any specific readings the teacher says to review.

Repairing Sentence Problems

What do we use to fix a leaky faucet? Repair a sagging bookshelf? Make a chair stop squeaking? We use tools. Look at the photograph on the opposite page. What tools do you see? How might you use the hammer, wrench, and pliers? Tools are useful things to have and to know how to use when there are repairs to make in a house or an apartment.

Sometimes we need to repair sentences. A hammer, wrench, and pliers won't help us, but there are other tools we can use. We can use conjunctions and punctuation to repair run-on sentence problems. We can use subjects, predicates, and independent clauses to repair sentence fragments. We can edit and proofread to improve our writing and to fix any mistakes.

In Chapter 13, you will learn about common writing mistakes. You will also learn about tools you can use to correct those mistakes.

Goals for Learning

▶ To recognize and correct run-on sentences

▶ To recognize and correct common writing mistakes

▶ To identify editing and proofreading steps

What Is a Run-on Sentence?

Run-on sentence

Two or more ideas written as one without proper punctuation or conjunctions

Sometimes people run sentences together without using end punctuation or conjunctions. This kind of sentence is a **run-on sentence.** The ideas in a run-on sentence need to be separated with proper punctuation.

> EXAMPLE   Just before spring came, there was a big snowstorm school was closed for two days then the weekend came school opened again on Monday.

How to fix a run-on sentence problem

- Separate the ideas into individual sentences.
- Capitalize the first word in each sentence.
- End each sentence with a period, a question mark, or an exclamation mark.

> EXAMPLE   Just before the spring came, there was a big snowstorm. School was closed for two days. Then the weekend came. School opened again on Monday.

The snowstorm caused major delays.

Activity A Rewrite the following groups of words on your paper so that they are not run-on sentences.

1) The storm lasted for two days the snow was more than one foot deep the drifts were at least four feet high.

2) We put on our winter coats and walked out to the barn the horses needed to be fed we had to pour hot water in their water trough to melt the ice.

3) Because of the deep snow, the police closed our road no one could come or go for two days.

4) Luckily we had enough food and water we always have emergency supplies in case of bad weather.

5) The snowplow finally reached our neighborhood two days after the storm started we were relieved to see it coming.

It is correct to use conjunctions to connect related ideas. Sometimes, however, people write one very long sentence using *and* to connect too many ideas. These long sentences are difficult to understand.

Our dog is going to have puppies so we took her to the veterinarian for a checkup and Dr. Cook said that she probably will have three puppies and they will arrive by March 26.

You can fix this type of run-on sentence by separating it into separate sentences.

Our dog is going to have puppies! We took her to the veterinarian for a checkup. Dr. Cook said that she probably will have three puppies, and they will arrive by March 26.

Activity B Rewrite the following groups of words so that they are not run-on sentences. Add commas and conjunctions or make separate sentences.

1) Yesterday I had to reinstall my Internet browser and something happened and the program did not save any of my incoming messages.

2) Did you send me an e-mail in the last week if so, I didn't get it and I would like to hear from you and I wish you would write me soon.

3) I am so busy here in college and I have more homework than I ever imagined and there are also all of my activities that take so much of my time.

4) I need to do my laundry and my friends and I want to go to a concert and I need to buy several books for class and I really need money and could you send me some?

5) Winter break is just a month away and some of my friends are going skiing and I want to go with them.

<table>
<tr><td>

Comma fault

The use of commas rather than end punctuation to separate sentences

</td><td>

Sometimes a run-on sentence is the result of a **comma fault.** A comma fault happens when a writer uses a comma to separate sentences instead of end punctuation.

</td></tr>
</table>

EXAMPLE
> The winter storm started on a Wednesday morning, students were already in class, the superintendent of schools decided to close school, all of the buses left school two hours early.

You can fix this problem by changing commas to periods or by adding a conjunction to connect related ideas. The solution you choose depends on the way you interpret the ideas in the sentences. Look at the example on page 319.

The winter storm started on a Wednesday morning. Students were already in class when the superintendent of schools decided to close school. All of the buses left two hours early.

(We changed the comma after *morning* to a period. We used the conjunction *when* to connect two related sentences. We changed the comma after *school* to a period.)

Activity C Here is an e-mail that Armando sent to Nathan. Rewrite it, fixing the comma faults.

Nathan,

Meet me after school at Tony's restaurant, we can grab some dinner, then we can go to the meeting at the library, there is going to be information about local colleges.

Armando

Vocabulary Builder

Idioms

An idiom is a phrase or an expression that means something different from what the words actually say.

The bright red cardinal caught his eye.
Caught his eye means "got his attention."

Look up each idiom or idiomatic expression below in a dictionary. Rewrite it, restating the idea without the idiom.

1) After jumping the fence, he stopped to catch his breath.

2) You could tell by his tone that the coach meant business.

3) She gave her answer in a nutshell.

Fix the run-on sentence problems in these sentences. Write the revised sentences on your paper.

1) Do you know a Web site that has information about colleges can you tell me how to get an application and also could you suggest colleges that would be best for me?

2) The game was about to begin, the crowd cheered, the referee blew his whistle.

3) Patrice tutors a younger student after school she helps him with his homework she enjoys working with the student because of this experience she is thinking of becoming a teacher.

4) Nathan thought he did not like classical music Emily pointed out that some of Ludwig van Beethoven's music is on his favorite CD.

5) Despite its name, the inchworm is not a worm, it is a caterpillar, this caterpillar is the larva of a moth.

Spelling Builder

Words with Apostrophes

We use apostrophes in contractions to replace one or more letters and in possessive nouns to show ownership.

- For singular possessives, add apostrophe -s: *car—car's.*
- For plural possessive nouns that end in -s, only add an apostrophe: *cars—cars'.*
- For plurals that do not end in -s, add apostrophe -s: *children—children's.*

Write the following sentences on your paper. Add apostrophes where they are needed. *The childrens toys are in the closet. You shouldnt arrive before noon. My cars oil needs changing.*

A fragment is a part of something. Sometimes we think of fragments as small, broken pieces. A sentence fragment is a piece of a sentence. You can also think of a sentence fragment as a broken sentence.

A sentence is a group of words with a subject and a verb that expresses a complete thought. A group of words that does not express a complete thought is a sentence fragment.

One type of sentence fragment has a subject but no predicate. We know who or what is doing something, but we do not know what they are doing. The predicate tells us what the subject is doing or what is happening to the subject.

> **EXAMPLE**   **Fragment**   The cold winter weather.
>
>   **Sentence**   The cold winter weather made us grumpy.

Activity A On your paper, create a complete sentence by adding a predicate to each of these subjects.

1) Mail-order catalogs on the desk.

2) A cool fresh taste of a sports drink.

3) The noise in the bowling alley from the falling pins.

4) The cloudless, blue sky.

5) The cold winter day.

The cold winter day was perfect for sledding.

Another type of sentence fragment has a predicate but no subject. We know what is happening, but we don't know who is doing the action. The subject tells us who or what is doing something.

 Fragment   Fell gently on the ground.

Sentence   The soft rain fell gently on the ground.

Activity B On your paper, create a complete sentence by adding a subject to each of these predicates.

1) arrived in the mail.

2) found a coin on the street.

3) came in first in the poster contest.

4) completed a report on frogs in record time.

5) sent in an application to a community college.

Activity C On your paper, rewrite the following paragraph. Make sentence fragments into complete sentences by adding subjects or predicates. Use your imagination to fill in the missing information.

All of the students at Wilson High School, especially Emily and Angela. They were happy that spring finally had arrived. Their favorite sport, tennis. Were warming up on the court. They planned to enter a tournament. As doubles partners.

A dependent clause has a subject and a predicate but does not express a complete idea.

 Fragment   Because it was Saturday.

Sentence   Because it was Saturday, we went shopping.

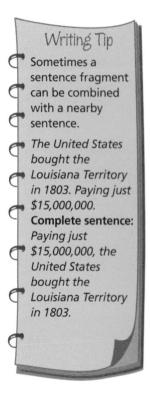

Writing Tip

Sometimes a sentence fragment can be combined with a nearby sentence.

The United States bought the Louisiana Territory in 1803. Paying just $15,000,000.

Complete sentence: *Paying just $15,000,000, the United States bought the Louisiana Territory in 1803.*

Activity D Make each sentence fragment into a complete sentence by adding an independent clause. Write your sentence on your paper.

1) Since the family returned from vacation.

2) Because Emily wants to be a music teacher.

3) After they finished playing tennis.

4) Until spring arrived.

5) If you don't mind.

Speakers often use sentence fragments to answer questions. The person who asks the question usually understands the fragment answer. Compare the fragment answer with the sentence answer in the example below.

EXAMPLE

Question	When is your birthday?
Fragment Answer	July 17
Sentence Answer	My birthday is July 17.

An answer that is a sentence fragment doesn't make sense unless the reader knows the question.

Activity E Answer these questions in complete sentences. The answers should make sense to a reader who does not know the question. Remember not to use a pronoun without a clear antecedent.

1) What is your name?

2) Where do you go to school?

3) What is the name of your community?

4) How old are you?

5) How far do you live from school?

Read each group of words carefully. Decide whether each group expresses a complete idea. Write *S* for sentence or *F* for fragment on your paper.

1) Cal Ripken Jr., a baseball player known as the Iron Man.

2) Ripken played in more consecutive games than any other player.

3) Given a most valuable player award.

4) His brother Billy also a baseball player.

5) Ripken played his entire career for the Baltimore Orioles.

Add words to each sentence fragment to make it a complete sentence. Write your sentences on your paper.

6) because the temperature is only 20°.

7) when she was standing at the bus stop.

8) gave the award to Bradley.

9) at the concert, the chorus.

10) because it is raining.

Write a paragraph about your first day of school. You may have been in kindergarten or first grade. Write five sentences about that experience. Tell how you felt. Write everything you remember about that day. When you are finished, check your work to be sure you do not have any sentence fragments or run-on sentences.

First draft

The rough, unedited copy of a written work

Edit

To revise, improve, and correct a written work

When you write, your first attempt is the **first draft.** Even the very best writers look for ways to improve their writing. After you finish the first draft, your next task is to **edit** it. *Edit* means "to revise and correct." *Revise* means "to change."

When you edit, follow these steps.

- Make sure each sentence begins with a capital letter and ends with an end punctuation mark.

- Think about your main idea. Make sure you have a strong topic sentence that expresses that idea and your point of view.

- Take out sentences that do not support, describe, or explain the main idea.

- Combine short sentences into compound and complex sentences.

- Move sentences around to make your ideas "flow" better.

- Add additional sentences if you need more facts, examples, or details to support your idea.

- Read the draft aloud and fix awkward passages or mistakes you hear.

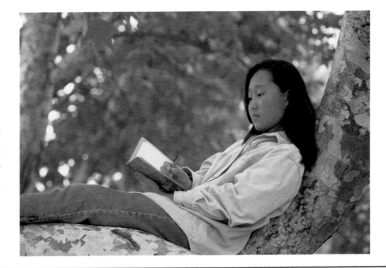

A good writer looks for ways to improve her writing.

Activity A Write this paragraph on your paper. Edit the paragraph, using the steps on page 325.

Jobs for Dogs
by Emily Watson

Dogs work as gard dogs and patrol dogs. Some dogs track birds and other game Some dogs herd geese sheeps or cattle. Cats can't do that. These jobs use dogs keen senses of sight, hearing, and smell. Think of Lassie, benji, and wishbone. Dogs preform on television in the movies and on stage. Labrador retrievers and German shepherdes work as guide dogs for blind. malamutes and huskies pull sleds across the snow. What do dogs do best. They make great pets and companion. Greyhounds race swiftly around tracks.

Proofread

To read a paper for mistakes in spelling, grammar, and punctuation

After you edit your draft, you must **proofread** it. When you proofread, you look for mistakes in spelling, grammar, and punctuation.

Follow these steps when you proofread.

- Correct any run-on sentences or sentence fragments.

- Check all the punctuation including commas, periods, question marks, and exclamation marks.

- Look carefully at every word with an apostrophe ('). Possessive pronouns do not have apostrophes. Plural nouns do not have apostrophes. Possessive nouns and contractions do have apostrophes.

- Fix spelling mistakes. If necessary, use a dictionary to check the spelling of a word.

- Check the verbs. If they are irregular, be sure that you spelled them correctly. See pages 128–132 of this book for lists of irregular verbs.

- Be sure each sentence begins with a capital letter.

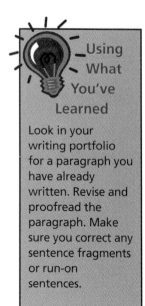

Using What You've Learned

Look in your writing portfolio for a paragraph you have already written. Revise and proofread the paragraph. Make sure you correct any sentence fragments or run-on sentences.

Here is a list of proofreading symbols to use when you edit your papers. After you edit your paper, copy it over with the corrections.

Proofreading Symbols

⟋	Delete or take out	⩗	Insert an apostrophe
(sp)	Spell out	⩗⩗	Insert quotation marks
∧	Insert	*lc*	Change to lowercase
#	Insert # or more space	≡	Change to capital letter
⊙	Insert a period	⊂	Close up; take out space
⌃	Insert a comma	¶	Begin a paragraph
⌃;	Insert a semicolon	*tr*	Transpose letters or words

Activity B Write this paragraph on your paper. Write on every other line of your notebook paper. Angela's essay has run-on sentences, sentence fragments, and mistakes in spelling and punctuation for you to correct. Look for other kinds of usage mistakes such as incorrect comparative adjectives and adverbs. Look for mistakes with pronouns. Look at the title. Use proofreading symbols to mark the errors.

Does Anyone Know a Psychiatrist for Dog's?
by Angela Choy

When I was a little girl. I had a Labrador retriever. Named Bear. This dog was not as fierce as a bear, he were the most sweetest dog I ever had and everyone loved him. Bear had a strange problem he liked to eat socks. No one's socks were safe. He also liked to eat bread along with the bag that it was wrapped in. "What does he think he is? A goat?" asked my mother.

When you revise and proofread, use a checklist to help you know that you have reviewed everything. You can create your own checklist or use one that is similar to this one.

Checklist for Revising
and Proofreading a Paragraph

- **Check your title.** The reader's first clue to what your essay is about comes from the title. Ask yourself if your title expresses the main idea.
- **Start your paragraph on a different line.** Your first paragraph should start on a different line from your title.
- **Indent the first line.** You should indent the first line of every paragraph.
- **Examine the topic sentence.** Include a topic sentence in every paragraph. The topic sentence expresses the main idea of your paragraph. You may put the topic sentence anywhere in the paragraph, but it often is the first sentence.
- **Review the details in your paragraph.** Do they support the main idea? Have you included facts, explanations, reasons, examples, or illustrations?
- **Take out sentences not related to the main idea.** Use them in a different paragraph or throw them away.
- **Improve your sentences.** Add specific and powerful adjectives. Replace ordinary verbs with vivid verbs. Combine short, related sentences into compound or complex sentences.

Don't forget to check for—
- spelling
- punctuation
- capitalization of proper nouns and adjectives
- subject-verb agreement
- agreement of pronouns and antecedents
- consistent use of verb tense
- sentence fragments or run-on sentences.

Proofread each sentence. Correct spelling, grammar, punctuation, and capitalization errors. Write the corrected sentence on your paper.

1) Do you work here.

2) That book belongs to emily.

3) Many short stories by that author has surprise endings.

4) Sharyls brother will pick us up after the game.

5) Josh said that he would bring her camera.

Write the paragraph by Raoul Rizik on your paper. Use the checklist on page 328 to revise and proofread this paragraph. Then write the corrected paragraph on your paper.

The Writer's Group
by Raoul Rizik

Danny is a high school student, he belongs to my writer's group. That met every Tuesday. Another member of the group are Charlene, she is Danny's former girlfriend. She does not like Danny's writing stories about her she tells him to write about something else. The other people in the group. They think the whole situation is funny and they look forward to what Danny will write next and what Charlene will say about it to him.

Write a paragraph about a funny experience you have had. Use the checklist on page 328 to revise your first draft. Then write a final draft of the revised paragraph.

Software for Checking Spelling

Word processing programs have features that help you proofread your writing. Most computers have a word processing program with a built-in spell check feature. When you run a spell check, the computer highlights each misspelled word in your text. You have the option of changing each word or keeping it the same.

The spell checker is a great tool most of the time. However, suppose you wrote this sentence: *Larry new he had passed the test.* A spell check would not highlight the word *new. New* is an adjective. In this sentence, though, the word *new* is incorrect. The correct word in this sentence is *knew,* which is a verb. But the computer does not recognize that the word is misused in the sentence. It only highlights words that are spelled incorrectly.

Software that checks grammar is available. Some grammar checkers will highlight any homophone. The computer doesn't know if it is a mistake or not. Get to know the proofreading features in the computer software you use. But do not rely on them completely. You need to proofread your work carefully before using a spelling or proofreading feature. Check the verbs you have used for the following:

- The correct past and past participle forms of verbs, especially of irregular verbs
- The correct spelling of each verb
- The correct forms of helping verbs
- Subject-verb agreement

1) Find the error in each sentence below. Decide whether a spell check feature (not grammar check) would find the error. Write *yes* or *no.* Then correct each error.

   a) The birds flu to the nest.

   b) The nest was hid in the bushes.

   c) Kenny buyed a scooter.

   d) Sandy road her bike.

2) Use a computer to type the paragraph you wrote for the Lesson 3 Review. Run a spell check and/or a grammar check. What errors does the computer show? Correct each error. Then write a paragraph explaining how your computer helps you proofread.

Writing Project

Revising and Proofreading

Knowing how to improve your written work will help
you write more effectively. Through good writing, you can communicate your ideas
to others. Steps in the writing process can help you write. The steps include
brainstorming and jotting down your ideas, writing a first draft, revising and
proofreading, and preparing your final draft.

Look at the following paragraphs. Try to improve them. Write the paragraphs on
your paper. Then revise and proofread the paragraphs. Improve this essay by adding
adjectives. Replace ordinary verbs with vivid verbs. Combine short, related sentences
into compound or complex sentences. Correct sentence fragments and run-on
sentences. Take out any sentences that don't belong. After you have made all your
changes, rewrite the essay on your paper.

My Dream Vacation
by Armando Hernandez

If I could go anywhere in the world, it would be to Paris, France.
I want to see the Eiffel Tower I want to walk under the Arc de
Triomphe I want to visit the Louvre. The Louvre is a very large art
museum. It is in an old royal palace on the Seine River. Some of the
world's greatest artworks are there. Including the Greek sculpture
Venus de Milo.

There is one painting in the Louvre that I want to see more than
any other. One of the world's best-known paintings. The *Mona Lisa,*
a portrait by Leonardo da Vinci, shows a woman with just a hint of a
smile. Nat King Cole sang about this smile in his most famous song.
As a future artist, I want to study this painting and figure out what
has made it so special to people for hundreds of years.

Now describe your own dream vacation. Imagine that you could go anywhere in the
world and do anything you like. Be sure your paragraph tells who, what, when,
where, and why. After you finish your paragraph, revise and proofread it. After you
make all the revisions, write your final draft.

WORD BANK

comma fault

edit

first draft

proofread

run-on sentence

Part A On a sheet of paper, write the correct word or words from the Word Bank to complete each sentence.

1) The first attempt at writing a paper is a _____.

2) A _____ is the use of commas rather than end punctuation to separate sentences.

3) A _____ has two or more ideas written as one without conjunctions or proper punctuation.

4) When you revise something you wrote, you _____ it.

5) When you read a paper for mistakes in spelling, grammar, and punctuation, you _____ it.

Part B Read each group of words and write it on your paper. Write *S* if the group of words is a sentence. Write *F* if it is a fragment. If the group of words is a fragment, rewrite it to make it correct.

6) The book on the top shelf.

7) pulled up a ladder.

8) reached up to get the book.

9) She looked at the table of contents.

10) The book had the information she needed.

Part C Read each group of words. Decide whether each group is a correct sentence or a run-on sentence. Write *correct* or *run-on* on your paper. If the sentence is a run-on sentence, rewrite it to make it correct.

11) Lincoln is the second largest city in Nebraska it is also the state capital.

12) The main campus of the University of Nebraska is in Lincoln.

13) Lancaster, the city's original name, was changed to Lincoln in honor of President Abraham Lincoln.

14) The largest city in Nebraska is Omaha, the Missouri River forms its eastern boundary.

15) Omaha was Nebraska's first capital city, in 1867 Lincoln was chosen as the new capital city.

Part D Read the paragraph. The writer has used proofreading symbols to make corrections. On your paper, write the paragraph and fix the mistakes.

The Bowling Team
by Nathan Young

My parents bowl on Mondays with their best friend*s*,

Jim and Maureen Janoski. The name of their team ~~are~~ *is* the

"Pitiful Four." according to my dad, the team is living up

to ~~her~~ *its* name. So far, it is in ~~the most~~ last place. My mom

keeps saying that they should practice but the rest of the

team refuses "Why put pressure on ourselves?" said

maureen. "In last place, theres nowhere to go but up."

Understanding Paragraph Basics

Sometimes we can express an idea in a sentence. But often we need a group of sentences to express an idea. A group of sentences on a single topic is a paragraph.

Look at the photograph on the opposite page. What do you see? A tree, a road, wildflowers, and the sky. Those are the elements, or parts, from which the photograph is made. They are basic to the photograph. Without them, there would be no photograph.

Topic sentence, supporting sentences, conclusion—these are the basic elements from which a paragraph is made. In Chapter 14, you will learn how to create the basic building block of written communication—the paragraph.

Goals for Learning

▶ To write a topic sentence that expresses the main idea of the paragraph

▶ To express a point of view in topic sentences

▶ To write sentences that support the main idea of the paragraph

▶ To end the paragraph with a conclusion or summary statement

▶ To learn the differences among paragraphs that inform, persuade, explain, or tell a story

▶ To create and punctuate dialogue

Paragraph

A group of sentences about a main idea, or topic

A **paragraph** is a group of sentences about a main idea, or topic. Within your paragraph you introduce the main idea and develop it through facts, descriptions, and explanations.

When you write several paragraphs, you need to **indent** the first sentence in each one. Put five spaces at the beginning of the first sentence in a paragraph to indent it.

Before you begin writing, choose a main idea, or topic, that meets these criteria:

Indent

To put five spaces at the beginning of the first sentence in a paragraph

- You know something about the topic.

- You know enough about the topic to do the assignment. If you don't have the information you need, you must do research.

- You are interested in the topic.

Once you have chosen your topic and have done any research required, you are ready to write a **topic sentence.** The topic sentence tells the main idea of a paragraph. Before you write your topic sentence,

Topic sentence

The sentence that tells the main idea of a paragraph

- Decide the purpose of your paragraph.

- Think about the main point you want to make.

- Consider why you are writing the paragraph.

> **EXAMPLE**   I will always remember the first time my friends and I made snow angels. Freshly fallen snow blanketed the ground. The smooth, sparkling snow invited us to play. Each of us picked a spot. We lay down and waved our arms and legs back and forth. Afterward we admired our snow angels.

Activity A Reread the example paragraph about snow angels. On your paper, write another topic sentence that expresses the same main idea.

<table>
<tr><td>**Point of view**

The way a person views or thinks about something</td><td>**Point of view** means "the way you see something." For example, if 20 people are in a room, each one of them views the room in a different way. Your topic sentence should reflect your point of view. The sentence should let the reader know your opinion of the topic.</td></tr>
</table>

EXAMPLE	**Poor**	I like going to the movies.
	Better	Seeing an entertaining movie brightens up a weekend.

Both sentences express a point of view. The writer enjoys seeing a movie. The second sentence, however, is more interesting. The participle *entertaining* describes the type of movie the writer likes to see. The verb *like* is not a vivid verb. The verb *brightens* is better. It tells how the writer feels about seeing a movie.

Activity B Improve these sentences by making them express your point of view. Add strong adjectives and change the verbs. Write the new sentences on your paper.

1) Bird watching is an interesting activity.

2) Each year I look forward to spring vacation.

3) Pizza is a popular food.

4) My week at camp was fun.

5) The view outside my window is nice.

Title

The name of a written work

Usually, you will give a report or paragraph a **title.** Like the topic sentence, a title tells your reader what the report or paragraph is about. Choose a title that meets these criteria.

- A title tells the reader what the paragraph is about.
- It is short. (Titles may be words, phrases, or clauses.)
- It includes a vivid verb or a colorful adjective.
- It expresses a point of view.

EXAMPLE

Poetry Slams

Poetry slams are becoming very popular throughout the United States. A slam is a contest in which poets read or recite their poetry. A jury, composed of volunteers from the audience, gives each poem a score from 1 to 10. A poetry slam is like an Olympic event for poets.

Activity C Write a different title for the paragraph "Poetry Slams" on your paper.

Activity D On your paper, write a title for each of these paragraphs. Then write the topic sentence from each paragraph.

1) On the first warm day of spring, players flock to the nearest golf course. They have been waiting impatiently throughout the winter for this day. Now they drag out their clubs, search for their shoes, and buy a box of new balls. Their hands tremble as they approach the first tee. They take a practice swing and then make their first drive of the season.

2) Have you ever been to Boston, the capital of Massachusetts? Boston is a modern city with a rich past. Modern buildings and busy stores surround historic sites. You can walk along Freedom Trail and visit the Old North Church. You can see the cemetery where Paul Revere and Samuel Adams are buried. These are just a few of the sites that draw thousands of tourists to Boston every year.

On your paper, write a topic sentence for each subject. Express a point of view in each topic sentence. Include enough information to make the reader want to know more about the topic.

1) Finding a summer job

2) Eating healthy food

3) Spring break

On your paper, write a title for each of these paragraphs. Then write the topic sentence from each paragraph.

4)   During cold winter months, people long for warm weather. When the temperature rises, they dress in their spring clothes and head out the door. They tramp through the woods, take a spin on their bikes, or just sit in the sun. They delight in whatever they choose to do as long as they are not indoors.

5)   Did you hear about the mayor who put his city on a diet? He noticed that the people had put on a few too many pounds. The mayor declared a citywide cutback on all things fattening! He recommended that the citizens increase their exercise and eat more vegetables. "We all need a healthier life style," the mayor advised.

Body

The part of a paragraph that discusses and supports the main idea; the sentences can include facts, reasons, examples, descriptions, or explanations

A paragraph includes details that support the main idea. These details may be examples, facts, descriptions, or other information. This part is called the **body** of a paragraph.

Prewriting is the work you do before you write. You can start by making a list of details about the topic.

You can include any of these elements in your paragraph.

Facts	Reasons	Explanations
Examples	Descriptions	

Prewriting

Work to do before writing begins

Activity A Practice developing a main idea. Write the following topic sentence on your paper. Do some prewriting. Use the details given below to write three sentences. All of the sentences must be about the main idea stated in the topic sentence.

Topic Sentence

Finding a summer job requires determination and imagination.

Details

Many students are looking for work.

There is a limited number of jobs available.

High school students have little job experience.

High school students may not have the skills required.

Transportation is a concern.

Activity B Make a list of details using your own experience in finding a summer job. Use the topic sentence above or one of your own. Write three or four sentences that provide examples or details.

Activity C Read the following facts. On your paper, write a topic sentence for a paragraph about these facts. Your topic sentence should state the main idea and a point of view.

- Andrew Lloyd Webber is a composer.

- He composed several popular musical plays.

- He composed *The Phantom of the Opera*.

- He is the composer of *Cats, Starlight Express,* and *Sunset Boulevard.*

- *Cats* and *The Phantom of the Opera* are two of the longest running plays in Broadway history.

- He also wrote *Evita* and *Jesus Christ Superstar.*

- Some of his best-known songs are "I Don't Know How to Love Him," "Memory," and "Don't Cry for Me, Argentina."

Activity D On your paper, write a paragraph beginning with the topic sentence that you wrote for Activity C. It is important to stick with the topic. Sentences that are not about the topic sentence will confuse the reader.

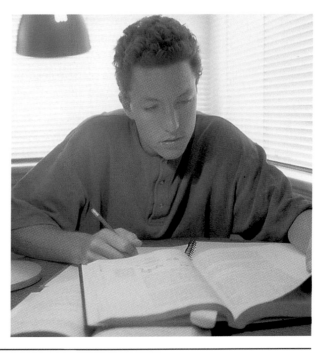

Prepare to write by making a list of details about the topic.

Activity E Write these paragraphs on your paper. Cross out the sentence or sentences that do not belong in each paragraph.

1)   Vegetarians get the calories and all the nutrients they need from diets that do not include meats. Vegetarians eat mainly foods that come from plants. They do not eat meat, fish, or poultry. Some vegetarians do not eat eggs or other dairy products. Is chocolate a vegetable? They get the vitamins and minerals they need by eating a variety of vegetables and foods made from plants. For example, they eat tofu and beans for protein.

2)   Many people enjoy reading novels for pleasure and relaxation. A novel is a long work of fiction with characters and a plot. Readers imagine the events and can lose themselves in the story. Poetry is also fun to read. A good writer creates characters that the reader remembers forever.

Spelling Builder

-Able *or* -Ible

The suffixes *-able* and *-ible* have the same meanings. Both can mean "can be," "suitable for," or "inclined to."
Here are some rules that can help you decide how to spell words with these suffixes.

- When the root word is a separate word, you spell the suffix *-able: readable, breakable, dependable.*
- When the root word is not a separate word, spell the suffix *-ible: terrible, possible, visible.*
- When the root word ends in e, drop the e and add *-able: movable, usable, likable.*

Add the suffix *-able* or *-ible* to each of the following root words. Then use the words in sentences. Check the meanings of the root words in a dictionary.

correct   cred   work   horr

Read each paragraph. On your paper, write the topic sentence. Then write the sentence that does not support the topic.

1)　　Bird watching can be an exciting and fun outdoor activity. National parks are ideal places to pursue this interest. To get started you will need binoculars. They will help you get a better look at these small creatures. The Audubon Society is an interesting group. Many people find that they become hooked on bird watching after just one try.

2)　　A fad is an activity that becomes very popular very fast. Its popularity can also fade away just as quickly. Fads of the past include pet rocks and hula hoops. Vanilla ice cream has been popular for a hundred years. One day everyone is buying them, and the next day nobody wants them.

Choose one of the sample topic sentences below, or write a topic sentence of your own. Then write a short paragraph—four or five sentences—that support the topic. Use prewriting to help you identify details to include in your paragraph. Provide facts, examples, or explanations.

- Popular music plays an important role in American culture.

- Before choosing a college, think about these important points.

- Eating a healthful diet helps determine a person's health.

Summary

A brief statement that repeats or restates the main points in a paragraph

Many paragraphs end with a **summary** statement that repeats or restates the main points in the paragraph.

A summary sentence often repeats the main idea in slightly different words.

> EXAMPLE
>
> Since I started using a computer, writing has become easier. With the computer, I can add and delete words. I can correct mistakes. I can even move sentences around. I can use the spell check to find and correct misspellings. With a computer, I don't need erasers. I don't have to recopy what I have written. A computer makes writing easier.

Activity A Read each paragraph and write a summary statement.

1) For many people, drawing is a relaxing activity. They enjoy using their imaginations. They like being creative. Each individual can draw what he or she sees in his or her own way.

2) Going camping is one way that people enjoy the great outdoors. Campers have responsibilities to nature, though. They should always stay on paths when hiking. They should be sure to put out any fires they use for cooking or keeping warm. Campers should not dig up or pick plants, and they should not try to get close to animals in the wild. They should clean their campsites before they leave.

Conclusion

A statement at the end of a paragraph that expresses an idea based on information in the paragraph

A **conclusion** is another way to end a paragraph. A conclusion is an ending statement that expresses an idea based on information in the paragraph. You take all of the facts in the case and draw a logical conclusion.

EXAMPLE

Not a Logical Conclusion

My favorite dessert is ice cream. I love all flavors. I like any topping. I could eat ice cream after every meal. I never can get too much ice cream. Last night my mother served ice cream. I decided not to have dessert because I didn't like the flavor.

Logical Conclusion

A computer is a very useful tool for students. You can use a computer to write and edit paragraphs and reports. You can play games on your computer. You can use it to do research on the Internet. You can even keep in touch with friends by e-mail. A computer can make working, learning, and keeping in touch easier.

Activity B Read these paragraphs. On your paper, write a logical conclusion for each one.

1) When the Wright brothers first took flight in 1903, their plane flew for a few seconds at about 30 miles per hour. By the mid-1920s, a very small passenger plane could fly about 135 miles per hour. The first large passenger jet began flying in the 1950s and could reach speeds of about 500 miles per hour. By the late 1970s, supersonic passenger jets could fly about 1,200 miles per hour.

2) Doing a few simple things can prevent most falls. Falls are a leading cause of accidental death and injury. First, pay attention when going up and down stairs. Second, keep floors free of clutter. Clean up spills. A tidy house prevents falls. Next, make sure stairs and doorways have good lighting.

Read each of the following paragraphs. On your paper, write a summary statement for each paragraph.

1) For many reasons, Angela thinks swimming is the ideal exercise. Very few swimmers become injured. Swimming tones many muscles at the same time. It is aerobic and so it is good for the heart. Opportunities for swimming are available in many neighborhoods.

2) Most people know it as the Statue of Liberty, but that was not its first name. The Statue of Liberty, a gift from France, has stood in New York Harbor for over 100 years. In 1886, the statue was dedicated as Liberty Enlightening the World.

Read each of the following paragraphs. What conclusion would you draw from reading this information? On your paper, write a logical conclusion for each paragraph.

3) Everyone should have emergency supplies. The family uses these supplies in case of a major storm or other disaster. The supplies should include a flashlight, a first-aid kit, food, and water.

4) Many libraries have book clubs. Book club members choose a book to read. Each month they meet at the library to talk about the book. They share ideas and opinions. These discussions increase everyone's understanding and appreciation of the book.

Select one of the following topics or choose one of your own. On your paper, write a paragraph that contains a strong topic sentence, details, and a summary or conclusion.

5) My life as a cat   My favorite color and why
My life as a dog   My favorite book and why
Why many people like baseball

You learned that sentences have different purposes. Paragraphs can have different purposes too. The most common purpose for a paragraph is to inform or explain. In a paragraph that informs or explains, the goals are

- To make something clear

- To help someone understand an idea

- To give the meaning of something

- To give reasons for something

Activity A Read this paragraph. It gives information. On your paper, answer the questions that follow.

> Kiribati is a small country of islands with fewer than 100,000 people. Made up of 33 islands in the middle of the Pacific Ocean, Kiribati covers just 277 square miles. That is just a little larger than the city of El Paso, Texas. The population density is 332 people per square mile. Most of the people fish or make handicrafts for a living. People also raise chickens and crops such as sweet potatoes and other root vegetables. Kiribati has a tropical climate. Some of the islands get over 100 inches of rain per year. Other islands receive about 40 inches. This small island nation would be an interesting place to visit.

1) What is the topic of this paragraph?

2) Which sentence is the topic sentence?

3) What are three details that support the topic sentence?

4) What is the writer's conclusion?

5) Write your own conclusion.

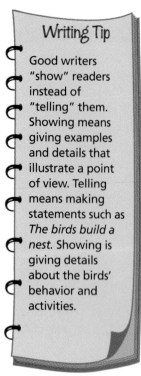

Writing Tip

Good writers "show" readers instead of "telling" them. Showing means giving examples and details that illustrate a point of view. Telling means making statements such as *The birds build a nest.* Showing is giving details about the birds' behavior and activities.

Answering Questions

Many times on a test, you must write an essay to answer a question.

Read the question below. Notice how the paragraph answers the question by giving details, facts, and examples.

Question

Why do so many people enjoy visiting national parks?

Paragraph Answer

People enjoy visiting national parks because the parks offer a change from their usual lives. Parks provide an opportunity to get back to nature. Visitors comment about the many birds and other wildlife. They delight in the trees and wildflowers. They enjoy a break from the pressures of their day-to-day routines.

Activity B Choose one of the questions below. On your paper, write a paragraph to answer it. Start with a topic sentence. Use adjectives and action verbs to make your answers clear to the reader.

- How can the average person eat five fruits and vegetables every day?

- Why is good grooming important on a job interview?

- What are some good ways to spend a rainy day?

- What are some ways that a person can stay healthy?

- Why do people visit amusement parks?

The How-to Paragraph

Some of the most popular books are "how-to" books. They tell readers how to do something or how to make something.

In a how-to paragraph, the topic sentence tells readers what they will do or make. The rest of the paragraph takes them through the steps they must follow. The final sentence is a summary or conclusion.

In a how-to paragraph, you can use sequence words such as *first, second, next, then,* and *finally.* These words help your readers know what to do and when to do it.

Activity C Read the how-to paragraph below. Then answer the questions on your paper.

> Yesterday, I got a sudden urge to bake a cake. I found a cake mix in our pantry. First, I read the directions. Second, I gathered the ingredients I needed—water, oil, and eggs. Then I turned on the oven, setting the temperature at 350°F. Next, I got the baking pan, a mixing bowl, and a measuring cup. Then I measured some ingredients, poured all of the ingredients into the bowl, and mixed them for two minutes. After flouring the pan, I poured the batter into the pan and placed it in the oven. Thirty minutes later, the cake was done and I took it from the oven. In no time, I was munching on warm cake. Who needs icing?

1) What is the topic of this paragraph?

2) How does the writer feel about this project? What is the point of view?

3) What sequence words does the writer use?

4) What is the final thing the writer did?

5) Write a different conclusion or summary statement.

Activity D Choose one of the following topics or pick one of your own. On your paper, write a how-to paragraph about it.

- Plant a garden
- Make a salad (or other food)
- Get from your home to the school
- Play a game
- Get ready for school in the morning

Requests for Information

When you write a request for information, be specific. Let the person know exactly what information you need. If your question is vague, the response you get may be incomplete.

EXAMPLE

Vague Question
What is the strawberry festival?

Vague Answer
When people eat strawberries.

Specific Request
Could you please tell me where the strawberry festival is? What is the date and time of the festival? What happens there?

Specific Answer
The strawberry festival is being held in the village park on June 3 between 8:00 A.M. and 5:00 P.M. People will be selling strawberries, jams, and pies. There will be a picnic and music for everyone to enjoy and games and rides for children.

Activity E Choose a partner in your class. Then follow these directions.

1) On your paper, write a paragraph requesting specific information about a topic that interests you.

2) Exchange paragraphs with your classmate. On his or her paper, write a paragraph answering your classmate's question. Be specific in your answer.

Paragraphs That Persuade

When you persuade someone, you convince that person to agree with your point of view. To persuade, you state your opinion. You also give reasons and facts that support your point of view.

Steps to Writing a Persuasive Paragraph

- State your opinion clearly.

- Use logical reasons to support your opinion.

- Use facts to support your opinion.

- Think about the other person's doubts. Try to overcome those doubts.

Activity F Choose one of these statements and use it as a topic sentence in your paragraph. Use your paragraph to provide reasons and facts. End your paragraph with a summary statement or conclusion.

- If you elect me president, I will be an excellent leader.

- Every classroom in this school should have computers for students to use.

- Without a doubt, everyone should exercise every day.

Read the paragraph below. Then answer the questions on your paper.

A Nest of Robins
by Neeru Peri

The poem "Trees" tells about "a tree that may in summer wear, a nest of robins in her hair." This morning I watched as a pair of robins built a nest in our evergreen tree. Back and forth they flew, bringing in bits of straw and grass. The branches of our tree are so thick that I could only catch a glimpse of the birds. I could hear their loud and lively chatter. Their enthusiasm was amazing. I am looking forward to the sounds of baby birds in the not-too-distant future.

1) What is the topic of this paragraph? Write it on your paper.

2) Write the topic sentence of this paragraph on your paper.

3) List the details that explain or tell about the topic.

4) Is the final sentence a summary or a conclusion?

5) What is the purpose of this paragraph?

On your paper, write a paragraph of your own. Tell about something that happened to you. Try to show the reader why this experience was important to write about.

A story tells about something that happened. **Fiction** is a story about imaginary people and events. **Nonfiction** writing is about *real* people and events. A writer can write a story in **first-person narrative** or in **third-person narrative.** In first-person narrative, a character in the story tells the story. In third-person narrative, someone who is not in the story tells the story.

Fiction

A story about imaginary people and events

Nonfiction

A book or an article about real people and events

First-person narrative

A story told by someone in the story

Third-person narrative

A story told by someone not in the story

EXAMPLE

First-person Narrative
I walked into a restaurant and sat down. Thus began a chain of events that I would long remember.

Third-person Narrative
The man walked into the restaurant and sat down. Thus began a chain of events that he would long remember.

Activity A The author told this story in first person. On your paper, rewrite it in third person. Use third-person pronouns such as *he, she,* and *they* instead of first-person pronouns such as *I* and *we.*

The Day We Lost Buddy
by Miguel Benetiz

My entire family panicked the day we lost my dog in the forest preserve. My job was to walk Buddy on his leash. In the woods, I took his leash off, and he bolted and vanished. I called and called him. Then I went home and got my parents. We searched for an hour. Then we heard a dog bark and some laughing. There was Buddy, begging for food at someone's picnic table. We all laughed.

You tell the events in a story in a certain kind of order. Stories are usually told in **chronological order**—according to time. Chronological order means to tell the events in the sequence, or order, that they happened.

EXAMPLE

- Yesterday we finished our shopping.

- In the evening we baked pies and completed other preparations.

- Today is Thanksgiving Day, and everyone is ready for a big dinner.

- Early this morning, we put the turkey in the oven.

- While the turkey baked, we prepared the side dishes.

- Finally, the meal was ready, and we sat down to eat.

Activity B On your paper, write the events in this story in chronological order.

My First Tennis Victory
by Emily Watson

On the last point, I hit an overhead for a winner. Winning a tennis tournament seemed like a distant or impossible dream. We had been practicing every day for weeks. Dreams do come true because we won every match all the way to the final. Even so, my friend Angela and I entered a tennis tournament as a doubles team. I grabbed it so hard that I could feel her bones crunching in my grip. I ran over to shake Angela's hand. "Hey," Angela yelled, "I may never be able to play again!"

Rule 5 If the quotation is a question, use a question mark at the end of the quotation. If the speaker's sentence expresses strong feeling, use an exclamation mark.

EXAMPLE

"Will I see you after practice?" asked Armando.

"No, I said I would talk to you after dinner!" said Angela.

Rule 6 Put the punctuation mark at the end of the quotation inside the closing quotation mark.

EXAMPLE

Angela said, "Practice ends at 5 o'clock."

Activity A Write these sentences on your paper. Punctuate them correctly. Add capital letters as needed.

1) What are you doing after school asked Emily.

2) Nathan replied I am going to the library.

3) Emily said would you get me a book.

4) What book do you want he asked.

5) She answered I need a book about frogs.

Activity B These quotations have punctuation mistakes. On your paper, write each quotation correctly.

1) "Can I help you," Emily said to a customer.

2) "Yes, I am looking for a special song" she replied.

3) I want a recording of a song my father likes.

4) Emily said "I'll help you find it."

5) "My manager knows every song ever written".

Rule 7 Start a new paragraph with each new speaker. You do not always need to identify the speaker.

> EXAMPLE
>
> "Why are you interested in getting a book about frogs?" asked Nathan.
>
> "I have a report due in biology class," Emily replied.
>
> "I should have guessed."

Rule 8 The speaker may say several sentences. Use quotation marks only at the beginning and end of the entire speech.

> EXAMPLE
>
> "I am writing a report about the types of amphibians. I am almost finished, but I need to check a few facts. If you could bring me a book about frogs, I would appreciate it. After band practice, I have to go to work for a couple of hours, so I can't get to the library."

Rule 9 When there are quotation marks inside a direct quotation, you use a single quotation mark for the inside quote. You also use single quotation marks around a title when it is written inside a quotation.

> EXAMPLE
>
> "I love the song 'You Are My Sunshine,' " said Meg.

Rule 10 You can identify the speaker within a quotation. Begin the second part of the sentence with a small letter.

> EXAMPLE
>
> "I think," **said Emily,** "that I have never heard that song before."

Writing Better Paragraphs

The spider in the photograph on the opposite page has made a web. The spider began with a few strands of silk. Then it added more and more strands. It made its simple web into a more complex web.

You know the basics of writing a paragraph. Now you will find out how to make your paragraphs better. Better paragraphs have livelier topic sentences. They use a variety of sentences. They create pictures with imagery and figurative language.

In Chapter 15, you will learn a lesson from the spider. You will take something basic—a paragraph—and make it into something more complex—a written piece.

Goals for Learning

▶ To identify ways to improve topic sentences

▶ To use adverbs, adverb phrases, or adverb clauses at the beginning of sentences

▶ To identify similes, metaphors, personification, exaggeration, and alliteration

▶ To use transitions to connect ideas

▶ To write sentences with active verbs

Better Topic Sentences

The best topic sentences grab the reader's attention. They make the reader eager to find out more about the topic.

To improve a topic sentence:

1) Get to the point. Take out unnecessary words.

2) Say something about the topic that the reader may not know.

3) Use strong adjectives and vivid verbs.

4) Add colorful details.

EXAMPLE

Poor   The paragraph is going to be about my new puppy that everyone in the family likes.

Better   Our whole family has fallen in love with Fluffy, our new cocker spaniel puppy.

Activity A   Improve these topic sentences by taking out unnecessary words. Add words that will grab the reader's attention. Write the new sentences on your paper.

1) This paragraph is about our family vacation in Colorado.

2) I think I will begin this paragraph by telling you that I just got a new DVD player.

3) Let me tell you about what I want to be someday, which is a music teacher.

4) I am going to write about the trip my friends and I took to the art gallery last week.

5) This paragraph tells about my new puppy.

One way to get the reader's attention is by asking a question. Notice the topic sentence in the paragraph below. It asks a question.

EXAMPLE

Cologne

Have you ever wondered how cologne got its name? Cologne is a fragrant liquid that is used like perfume. It was first made in a city in Germany over 200 years ago. The name of the city is Cologne! Its famous product became known by the French name *Eau de Cologne,* which translates as "water of cologne." The name has been shortened to *cologne.*

Activity B Read each pair of sentences. Decide which one is better as a topic sentence. Write *a* or *b* on your paper.

1) a) Our dog Buddy has some very peculiar habits.

   b) This paragraph is going to be about our dog Buddy.

2) a) Aren't some plants interesting?

   b) Have you ever heard of a meat-eating plant?

3) a) An avalanche is very dangerous.

   b) I will never forget the time that I nearly died in an avalanche.

4) a) The most famous painter of the twentieth century, without a doubt, is Pablo Picasso.

   b) Pablo Picasso is a famous twentieth-century painter.

5) a) Football is my favorite sport.

   b) If it is fall and it is Sunday, my family is watching football.

Activity C Write a short paragraph. Choose your own topic. Begin your paragraph with a question. The topic sentence should get to the point and grab the reader's attention.

Read each pair of topic sentences. Pick the one that is better and write *a* or *b* on your paper. Write a short explanation for your choice.

1) a) I want to tell you about a dangerous experience I had at the beach.

   b) One day at the beach, a terrible tragedy took place.

2) a) Our dog, Buddy, is the king of our home.

   b) This paragraph is about my dog.

3) a) Neeru Peri sings in the Wilson High School choir.

   b) Do you know Neeru Peri, lead soloist in the Wilson High School choir?

4) a) Do you know what Type II diabetes is?

   b) Did you know that Type II diabetes has been linked to heredity, inactivity, and obesity?

5) a) Eating too much fast food is bad for your health.

   b) Do not eat a lot of fast food.

Each of these topic sentences needs improvement. Rewrite each one to make it better.

6) Do you know something that is really funny?

7) The movie I saw was a romance.

8) We saw a play not long ago.

9) English can be an interesting subject.

10) Let me tell you about a scary experience I had.

Sentence Variety

Spice up your paragraphs by giving your sentences variety. Sentences with variety are more enjoyable to read.

One way that you can make your writing more interesting is by starting sentences with an adverb or an adverb phrase.

EXAMPLE	**Uninteresting**
Adverb	I sent Tanya an e-mail today.
Adverb Phrase	Tanya returned home from Switzerland last month.
	More interesting
Adverb	Today I sent Tanya an e-mail.
Adverb Phrase	Last month Tanya returned home from Switzerland.

Activity A Improve these sentences by moving an adverb or adverb phrase to the beginning of the sentence. Write each new sentence on your paper.

1) Beautiful handwriting is an art, according to many people.

2) Everyone applauded at the end of the concert.

3) Francis Scott Key wrote the words to "The Star-Spangled Banner" during the War of 1812.

4) None of the people in the school band is tone-deaf, according to Emily.

5) The concert began eventually.

Another way to start a sentence is with an adverb clause. Remember to punctuate introductory clauses correctly. Set off an introductory clause or long phrase with a comma.

 EXAMPLE   After they began reading the story, the students became more and more excited.

Activity B Improve these sentences by moving the adverb clause to the beginning of the sentence. Write each new sentence on your paper.

1) Nathan decided to be a scientist when he was a senior in high school.

2) Armando looked forward to spring because he could play baseball.

3) The team was behind until Armando hit a home run.

4) The family watched out of the window while the snow fell.

5) The students were dismissed from school after the closing bell sounded.

After school, some of the students had fun in the snow.

Grammar References

No one can remember every grammar rule. Grammar reference books provide help with punctuation questions, sentence fragments, run-on sentences, and more.

Suppose you are not sure whether to use a colon or a dash. The punctuation section of a grammar reference lists the rules for using each punctuation mark. Maybe you can't decide whether to use *its* or *it's* in a sentence. A grammar reference gives the meaning of each word. You can find many grammar references in a library. Use the index of the book you choose to find specific topics. For example, looking up *run-on sentences* leads to the following information in one grammar reference:

A **run-on sentence** is two or more sentences written as one without proper punctuation and conjunctions. Use one of the following ways to correct a run-on sentence:
> Make the clauses into separate sentences.
> Connect the clauses with a comma and a coordinating conjunction.
> Make one of the clauses a subordinate clause.

If you use a word processor, your computer probably has a grammar checker. When you run a grammar check, the computer indicates sentences that may have a grammatical error. It suggests changes to make to each sentence. A grammar checker can be helpful in pointing out possible problems. But remember—you are the writer! After a grammar checker points out a possible problem, look it up in a grammar reference. Then you can be sure there is really an error and if so, how to fix it.

1) Use the grammar reference entry above to check whether the sentence below is a run-on. If it is, use one of the ways listed in the entry to correct the problem.

> The library has many computers it also has a good reference section.

2) Proofread something you have written recently. Find a sentence with punctuation, usage, or grammar you are unsure of. Use a grammar reference to find out whether your sentence needs to be corrected. If it does, rewrite the sentence.

Rewrite these sentences so that they are direct quotations. Use correct punctuation and capitalization.

1) Nathan asked Emily to come to his party.

2) Emily asked him when it will be.

3) He told Emily the party will be on Friday night.

4) She said she had to ask her parents first.

5) Emily asked her father if she could go to Nathan's party.

6) Mr. Watson gave her permission to go.

7) Emily thanked her father.

8) She told Nathan she could come to his party.

9) Nathan told her the party started at 6:30 P.M.

10) Emily said that she'd be there.

Write a short story about something that recently happened to you or someone you know. Include some dialogue or some indirect quotations. Be sure to follow the rules for writing dialogue.

Using What You've Learned

Listen to a conversation between two people at home or on television. Write down some of their conversation. Then write the conversation in play format. Use the example on page 360 as a model.

Tell a Story Using Dialogue

Adding dialogue to a story creates interest. The characters
in the story speak to each other. They seem more real. Read the following story. Then
rewrite it to include dialogue. The first few sentences are done for you.

Example   Nathan and Armando were walking down the hall to class.
"The school play is in two weeks," said Armando.
"I was thinking of asking Emily to go to the play," replied Nathan.
"Do you think she would go with me?"

   Nathan and Armando were walking down the hall to class. The
school play was in two weeks. Nathan turned to Armando and said
that he was thinking of asking Emily to go to the school play. He asked
Armando if he thought Emily would go with him.
   Armando shrugged and said that he couldn't think of a reason
why she wouldn't go with Nathan. After all, Emily enjoyed the theater,
and she and Nathan were friends.
   Nathan agreed. It would be fun to see a play with Emily.
   Armando nodded. The two continued walking down the hall and
Nathan commented that Emily was in his next class.
   Nathan asked if it would be a good time to ask Emily then.
Armando said he thought that would be a good idea. Then Nathan
began looking through his backpack.
   Armando asked him what he was looking for. Nathan said that he
was making sure that he had two tickets to the play. He didn't want to
ask Emily and then not have tickets.
   Armando told Nathan that he had better find the tickets quickly
because Emily was coming down the hall and waving at them. Just
then, Nathan found the tickets. Armando wished Nathan luck and
went to his class.
   Nathan and Emily greeted each other and walked into English
class together. They sat down and took their books out. Then Nathan
turned to Emily and asked if she would like to go to the play with him.

CHAPTER 14 Review

WORD BANK

WORD BANK

body

chronological
  order

conclusion

dialogue

direct quotation

fiction

first-person
  narrative

indent

indirect quotation

nonfiction

paragraph

play

point of view

prewriting

quotation marks

summary

third-person
  narrative

title

topic sentence

Part A On your paper, write the correct word or words from the Word Bank to complete each sentence.

1) A group of sentences about a main idea, or topic, is a _____.

2) The _____ tells the main idea of the paragraph and expresses a point of view.

3) The way you look at or think about something is called a _____.

4) The name you give your report or paragraph is the _____.

5) The work you do before you write is _____.

6) A statement at the end of a paragraph that repeats or restates the main points is a _____.

7) A _____ is an ending statement that expresses an idea based on information in the paragraph.

8) Events placed in the sequence they happened is _____.

9) Words that people or fictional characters say is _____.

10) A _____ is a speaker's exact words, which are placed inside quotation marks.

11) An _____ is not a speaker's exact words. It is often introduced by the word *that*.

12) A book or an article about real people and events is _____.

13) A story about imaginary people and events is _____.

14) A story told by someone in the story is in _____.

15) A story told by someone who is not in the story is in _____.

16) When you _____ a paragraph, you put five spaces at the beginning of the first sentence in the paragraph.

17) The _____ of a paragraph discusses and supports the main idea.

18) The punctuation marks placed at the beginning and end of a direct quotation are _____.

19) A _____ is a story told in dialogue that someone wrote to be performed on stage.

Part B Read the paragraph below. Then answer the questions in complete sentences on your paper.

> Summertime is the season for part-time jobs. To me, working has two important purposes. First, I make money. I need cash for summer fun. My paycheck pays for clothes and fees for the water park and other activities. Having a job also gives me work experience. My summer job gives me an idea about what the work world is like.

20) What is this paragraph about?
What would be a good title for this paragraph?
What is the writer's point of view?
How does the writer feel about the topic?

Part C Choose one of the following topics to write about or one of your own. Follow the suggestions. Then write a paragraph on your paper.

Best Friends	School Cafeteria Food
A Day to Remember	Summer Fun

- Do some prewriting. List some details about the topic. Write a topic sentence that expresses the main idea and your point of view.
- Write sentences that include details, facts, and examples about the topic.
- Write a conclusion or summary sentence and a title.

Test-Taking Tip When you read test directions, try to restate them in your own words. Tell yourself what you are expected to do. That way, you can make sure you understand the directions.

Rewrite these sentences. Add an adverb, adverb phrase, or adverb clause at the beginning of each one. Write the new sentences on your paper.

1) The students arrived at school.

2) They had lunch in the cafeteria.

3) We bought bottles of juice.

4) Cold water is refreshing.

5) Our school building is 10 years old.

6) The car skidded on the ice.

7) We bought a present for Mr. Thomas.

8) The baby cried.

9) I saw Angela at the store.

10) The books crashed to the floor.

Vocabulary Builder

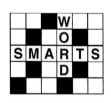

Onomatopoeia

Crash! Bang! Thud! What do these words have in common? They are words that sound like the sounds they name. Onomatopoeia means the use of words whose sounds suggest their sense. Some words imitate loud sounds. *Roar! Slam! Boom!* Some words imitate soft sounds. *Hiss. Peep. Swish.* We use words such as these to create images in our writing.

Use these words in sentences.

    screech   whine   snap   hum

Now think of three more words that imitate sounds and use them in sentences.

Transition

A change from one place or time to another

A **transition** is a change from one place or time to another. In paragraphs, we use adverbs to help the reader move smoothly from one idea to the next. Without smooth transitions, you take your reader on a bumpy ride.

Here are some transition words and phrases.

Transition Words and Phrases			
after	before	later	now
also	finally	meanwhile	soon
at last	first	next	then

In the early days of television, people had only a few channels. **Now** it is possible to have hundreds of channels.

Activity A Find the word or phrase that helps the reader understand the change in time.

1) Nothing happened for a while. Then suddenly things changed.

2) Emily was eager to hear about her college application. Meanwhile, she continued to enjoy her senior year.

3) Angela entered all of the local swimming meets for many years. Finally, her dream came true and she participated in the statewide meet.

4) We put all of the ingredients into the bread maker. Four hours later, the crusty warm bread was ready to eat.

5) Nathan was hungry all morning. By lunchtime, he was starved.

Here are other transition words and phrases.

More Transitions		
as a result	however	nevertheless
besides	in addition to	on the other hand
but	in conclusion	therefore
for example	instead	so

Activity B Add a transition word or phrase that will link these sets of sentences together. Write the new sentences on your paper.

1) Graduation day was growing closer. The day arrived.

2) The mall was having unbelievable sales. Shoes in one store were two pairs for ten dollars.

3) Emily wanted some new shoes. She had to work on Saturday.

4) Everyone looked forward to summer. Armando's family went fishing and camping.

5) The warm spring provided opportunities for outdoor activities. Angela and Emily decided to play tennis after school.

Activity C List the transition words and phrases in the paragraph below. Not all sentences have a transition.

The Optimist

As a beginning golfer, Mrs. Young had hopes of reaching high standards. When she wasn't golfing, she was reading about golf or watching it on television. However, nothing helped. In addition to hitting golf balls into the woods, she landed many of her best shots in water or sand traps. As a result, she became discouraged. Nevertheless, Mrs. Young is a persistent person. "I will never give up!" she announced to her family. "I will master this game." She ignored the grins on their faces.

1) Make a list of 10 transition words and phrases on your paper.

2) Read the paragraphs below. Find the transition words and phrases. Write them on your paper.

An American Singer

Marian Anderson was the first African American singer to become known internationally as a concert singer. She first sang in church choirs. Even then, people recognized she had an amazing voice. But because she was African American, she wasn't accepted into music school. Instead she took private lessons. In 1925 she won a competition to sing with the New York Philharmonic Orchestra. Then she went to Europe to study and sing.

In 1939 Anderson wasn't allowed to sing in Constitution Hall in Washington, D.C. So she sang on the steps of the Lincoln Memorial for an audience of 75,000. Later, she was the first African American to sing at the Metropolitan Opera in New York City. However, that was the only time she sang in an opera.

After she retired, Anderson was appointed as a delegate to the United Nations. Also, she received the Presidential Medal of Freedom, a Congressional gold medal, and one of the first Kennedy Center honors.

Active verb

A verb form that we use when the subject is doing the action

Passive verb

A verb form that we use when the action happens to the subject

Action verbs can be active or passive. When the verb is **active,** the subject is doing something. When the verb is **passive,** someone is doing something to the subject.

EXAMPLE		
Active	Armando kicked the soccer ball from one end of the field to the other.
Passive	The soccer ball was kicked from one end of the field to the other.

Sentences that are written with active verbs express energy. Sentences written with passive verbs slow down your writing.

EXAMPLE
S   V   Prep. Phrase
The birthday gift was selected by Mrs. Choy.
S   V   DO
Mrs. Choy selected the birthday gift.

To change a passive sentence to an active sentence, use the object of the preposition *by* as the subject. Change the subject to the direct object. Remove the helping verb *be.* (The form is usually *is, are, was,* or *were.*)

Activity A Change the verb in each sentence from passive to active. Write the new sentences on your paper.

1) The decision was reached by the committee.

2) The costumes for the play were designed by Angela and Neeru.

3) The winning goal was scored by Armando.

4) All of the winning songs are being played by the school band.

5) The best song of the evening was performed by Emily.

Sometimes the sentence does not have a prepositional phrase beginning with *by.* You have to figure out who did the action.

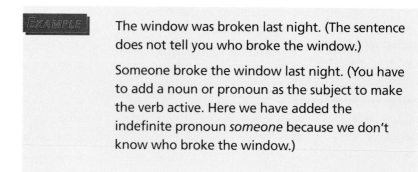

EXAMPLE

The window was broken last night. (The sentence does not tell you who broke the window.)

Someone broke the window last night. (You have to add a noun or pronoun as the subject to make the verb active. Here we have added the indefinite pronoun *someone* because we don't know who broke the window.)

Activity B Rewrite these sentences changing the passive verbs to active verbs. You may use an indefinite pronoun or a noun as the subject of the new sentence. You may add information to the sentence.

1) Emily was called on the telephone.

2) The e-mail that Armando received was sent by Michelle.

3) The birthday party for Neeru was planned by her friends.

4) Neeru was hired by the manager of the music store.

5) Angela's lunch was packed by her mother.

Michelle read and responded to Armando's e-mail.

Sometimes passive verbs appear in dependent clauses.

Passive	Have you seen the latest movie that was produced by Steven Spielberg?
Active	Have you seen the latest movie that Steven Spielberg produced?

Activity C Rewrite these sentences changing the passive verbs to active verbs.

1) The puppy that was found by Nathan was returned to Julie.

2) Did you find the book that was checked out of the library by Emily?

3) One time I tasted a cake that had been baked in Greece.

4) Because we didn't have one of our own, we used a ball that was owned by the bowling alley.

5) The paper that was thrown in our yard by the paper carrier got wet.

Spelling Builder

Prefixes per-, pre-, pro-

It is easy to misspell words with the prefixes *per-, pre-,* and *pro-.* Exaggerate the first syllable of *per-* words. For example, say "purrr-fect" for *perfect.* This will help you remember where to write the *r.* Mispronounce the first syllable in *pre-* and *pro-* words. For example, say "prē-dict" for *predict* and "prō-tect" for *protect.* This will help you remember when to write *e* and when to write *o.*

Choose *per-, pre-,* or *pro-* to complete these words. Write the words on your paper. Look up each word in a dictionary.

____duce	____form	____pare
____tend	____vide	____mit

Rewrite these sentences changing the passive verbs to active verbs. You may use an indefinite pronoun as the subject of a new sentence. You may also add information to the sentence.

1) Nothing is better than being served dinner at home.

2) The dinner was prepared by Mrs. Choy.

3) The recipe had been handed down in the family for generations.

4) Mrs. Choy was given the recipe by her mother.

5) Have you tasted the latest batch of General Tao's chicken prepared by Mrs. Choy?

6) The dessert was made by Angela's sister Julie.

7) Julie was chosen as one of her company's top employees.

8) During dinner, the cell phone that was brought by Emily rang.

9) The telephone was finally answered.

10) "I have been selected by the community college for a scholarship," Emily told them.

Write five sentences using these verbs. Make each verb active. Use any tense of the verb you choose—present, past, future, or perfect.

11) bounce

12) select

13) write

14) add

15) discovered

LESSON 5	**Creating Images with Writing**

Language that appeals to one of the five senses can bring writing to life. The five senses are seeing, touching, tasting, smelling, and hearing.

> **EXAMPLE**   On a cold day, Mrs. Choy feels as though her bones are creaking.
>
> He walked around on the brittle grass.

Activity A Write these sentences on your paper. Underline the words in each sentence that appeal to the senses. Then write the sense or senses appealed to.

1) The clouds floated across the sky like huge balls of cotton.

2) The scent of the bacon that we fried for breakfast lingered in the air.

3) We enjoyed the noise the bread crust made as we crunched it in our mouths.

4) After sitting all day at a desk, Mrs. Young thought someone was sticking hot needles into the back of her neck.

5) The children's delighted laughter as they fed the quacking ducks brought tears of joy to their parents' faces.

Activity B Write a sentence that appeals to each one of the senses on your paper.

1) sight

2) sound

3) touch

4) taste

5) smell

Simile

An indirect comparison that tells how one thing is like something else

Metaphor

A direct comparison that says something is the same as something else

Comparisons can give the reader a mental picture. We can use **similes** and **metaphors** to make comparisons. A simile is an indirect comparison that tells how one thing is *like* something else.

> EXAMPLE Nathan is like smoke. When you try to grab him, he evaporates.
>
> When angry, Armando roars like a lion.

A metaphor is a direct comparison that says something is the same as something else.

> EXAMPLE "All the world's a stage," wrote William Shakespeare.

Activity C Write these sentences on your paper. Underline the similes and metaphors.

1) The leaves on that tree are as green as an emerald.

2) "Your room is a pigpen," said Nathan's father.

3) My computer is faster than lightning.

4) She sings like a lark.

5) The news spread like wildfire.

Personification

Giving human characteristics to an object or an animal

Personification is giving human characteristics to an object or an animal.

> EXAMPLE The wind ripped up the street, whining past the plate glass windows.
>
> In summer, a tree may wear a nest of robins in her hair, according to poet Joyce Kilmer.
>
> "The fog came in on little cat feet," wrote poet Carl Sandburg.

Activity D Write these sentences on your paper. Underline the examples of personification.

1) The tree spread its branches wide, inviting us to seek shelter there.

2) The United States Constitution protects the rights of its citizens.

3) The shelves of the bookcase groaned under the weight of the encyclopedias.

4) The stars seemed to skip across the sky.

5) "The computer ate my homework!" exclaimed Emily.

Exaggeration

A statement that makes a situation seem bigger or more serious than it is

Exaggeration is a statement that makes a situation seem bigger or more serious than it is. In exaggeration, the words go beyond the truth to make a point or to add interest.

EXAMPLE   You can smell that garbage in the next state!

I saw a tree that was as big as a skyscraper.

Activity E Write these sentences on your paper. Underline the example of exaggeration.

1) I am so hungry I could eat a bear.

2) They served giant-sized hamburgers for lunch.

3) Emily sleeps so soundly that a tornado wouldn't wake her up.

4) That cake is so big it would take a week to eat it.

5) "I studied a million hours for that quiz," Efran claimed.

Alliteration

Alliteration
The use of two or more words together that begin with the same sound

Alliteration is the use of two or more words together that begin with the same sound. Alliteration makes writing more rhythmic.

EXAMPLE   She wiggled her toes in the soft silky sand.

Activity F Write these sentences on your paper. Underline the alliteration.

1) Nathan had never seen the sea so still.

2) Armando is a pleasant, polite person.

3) The sunshine shimmered on the sea.

4) There was a batch of buttery biscuits on the breakfast table.

5) The campers walked down the long, lonely trail.

Activity G Use each example of alliteration in a sentence.

1) fierce, foaming waves

2) sad-sounding sighs

3) the fat furry feline

4) first to fall

5) without wondering why

The sand crystals shimmered in the sunlight.

Identify the simile, metaphor, personification, alliteration, or exaggeration in these sentences. Write *simile, metaphor, personification, alliteration,* or *exaggeration* on your paper. If the words appeal to one of the senses, write the sense.

1) The neighborhood sounds floated in the window.

2) The sunset was a painting of many brilliant colors.

3) The houses huddled close together.

4) The president picked a particular person for the post.

5) The sheep's wool looked like lumps of gray cotton.

6) To the child, the bedroom was a dungeon.

7) We could see the clouds reflected in her sunglasses.

8) Her hair grew so fast she tripped over it when she walked.

9) To the young couple, the moon seemed to be smiling down at them.

10) The baby's skin was as smooth as silk.

Write an example of each of the following: simile, metaphor, personification, exaggeration, alliteration.

Using What You've Learned

Write a description of a favorite place. Use language that appeals to the senses so that your reader can see, smell, and hear what the place is like. Try to use similes, metaphors, personification, exaggeration, or alliteration at least once in your description.

Periodicals

Suppose you wanted information on whale research, current bicycle technology, or career trends. You could find the latest information on all these subjects in periodicals. *Periodicals* are publications that are issued on a regular basis. They are published once a month, once a week, or at other regular times. Magazines, newspapers, and journals are periodicals.

Popular weekly news magazines publish articles on many different subjects. When you go to the library, you will find periodicals that have very detailed articles on specific subjects. You will find magazines on every subject imaginable. There are magazines devoted to animals, travel, art, science, gardens, sports, movies, games, and cars. Suppose you were looking for information about a seabird called a puffin. Here is part of an article about Maine from the periodical *Down East:*

> The seven scraggly acres of Eastern Egg Rock rising out of the wind-whipped waters of outer Muscongus Bay are less than impressive at first glance. There are no trees or even any shrubs. The low-lying granite pile is all boulders and gravel, with barely enough soil to support scattered clumps of grass and brambles. But this is an island known around the world as the place where an impossible event happened twenty years ago—the place where ornithologist Stephen W. Kress persuaded a comical little seabird known as the puffin to make a home, raise a family, and establish a new colony for the first time since 1885.

Periodicals are valuable resources for reports and term papers. But in this wealth of information, how do you find the facts you need? The *Readers' Guide to Periodical Literature* indexes hundreds of periodicals. When you look up a subject in the *Readers' Guide,* you will find a list of articles on that subject and the periodicals in which they are found. You can use the *Readers' Guide* in print or online in many libraries.

1) In the paragraph about puffins, what transition does the author use? Write one long sentence and one short sentence the author uses. Write two vivid images the author uses.

2) Think of a subject you would like to research and write about. Use the *Readers' Guide to Periodical Literature* to find at least two articles on the subject. Write the titles of the articles and periodicals and summaries of the articles.

Paying Attention to Details

Good writers help you see what they see. They write as if
they are video cameras. In this activity, choose a place you have visited or a building
you know well. You will need to describe it.

Emily's Bedroom

My bedroom is a tiny, narrow space with one narrow
casement window a foot from the ceiling. The chintz
curtains block the small amount of light that could
otherwise enter. During the spring and summer months,
the window is often open. The neighborhood sounds
float into the room along with hazy lines of light.

1) Write a paragraph (five to seven sentences) telling about the place or building
you choose. Describe everything about the place or building that makes it
memorable or recognizable. Focus on important details.

2) Read your description to the class. Then ask the class these questions:

Did my description help you visualize the place or building?

Were there any specific words that helped you visualize the place
or building? If so, what were they?

Would you like to visit the place or building?

3) Exchange papers with a classmate.

4) Read your classmate's description.

5) Draw a picture of the place or building using the details your classmate
provided.

WORD BANK

active verb

alliteration

exaggeration

metaphor

passive verb

personification

simile

transition

Part A On a sheet of paper, write the correct word or words from the Word Bank to complete each sentence.

1) When you use an _____, the subject is doing something.

2) "As light as a cloud" is an example of a _____.

3) "He was a mountain of a man" is an example of a _____.

4) When you use a _____, someone is doing something to the subject.

5) "She's so slow a turtle could beat her" is an example of a _____.

6) Two or more words together that begin with the same sound create _____.

7) A _____ is a change from one place or time to another.

8) "The leaves danced in the street" is an example of _____.

Part B Improve these topic sentences. Remove unnecessary words. Add details, adjectives, and vivid verbs. Write the new sentences on your paper.

9) This paragraph describes Emily, my best friend.

10) Let me tell you about my recent visit to the science museum.

11) This is what happened when I went whitewater rafting.

Part C Improve these sentences. Move the adverb, adverb phrase, or adverb clause to the beginning of the sentence. Write the new sentences on your paper.

12) I saw Nathan yesterday.

13) We played baseball after school.

14) Our team celebrated after we won.

Choosing a Topic

report
organized summary of information about a topic

A **report** is an organized summary of information about a topic that you have researched. Writing a report requires planning and time. A good report requires a good plan. The first step in writing a report is choosing a topic.

Usually the teacher assigns a general subject for reports. When the general subject area is assigned, your next task is to decide on a topic. Each subject area has many interesting areas to write about.

Possible Topics

Pure Sciences	Social Sciences	Fine Arts and Recreation
Pond life	Government of Japan	History of golf
Microbiology	History of the stock market	Mozart and music
Discovery of aspirin	European education	Roman buildings

Suppose *music* is the assigned general subject. Music fits under the Fine Arts and Recreation topic. The history of guitars is a topic within that subject area. You could write a long book about the history of guitars. For your report, it would be better to choose a narrower topic, such as the guitar music of Eric Clapton.

EXAMPLE

General Subject Area Music
Topic History of guitars
Subtopic Guitar music of Eric Clapton

subtopic
division or part of a larger topic

A **subtopic** is a division or part of a larger topic.

Part D Add a transition word or phrase that will link the sentences together. Use a different transition word or phrase in each new sentence.

15) Emily put on her socks. She put on her shoes.

16) Armando saved money for six months. He could buy a new CD player.

17) Angela wants to go to camp. She wants to stay home.

Part E Rewrite these sentences changing the passive verbs to active verbs.

18) Thirteen Grand Slam titles have been won by tennis player Pete Sampras.

19) One hundred and seventy-six touchdowns were scored by Jerry Rice during his career.

20) A tiger shark weighing over 1,700 pounds was caught by Walter Maxwell in South Carolina.

Part F Write an example of each of the following.

21) simile
22) metaphor
23) personification
24) exaggeration
25) alliteration

Test-Taking Tip

When studying for a test, use a marker to highlight important facts and terms in your notebook notes. For a final review, read over the highlighted items.

Chapter 16 Preparing to Write a Report

Writing Better Paragraphs Chapter 15 **389**

CHAPTER 16

Preparing to W
a Report

The bees in the photograph on the oppos
building a hive. To do that, they must fo
a set of steps in a special order. When th
process, they will get what they want—a new hi

Writing a report is like building a hive. Like the
set of steps. You choose a topic and find inform
organize the information and begin to write the
follow this process, you will have what you nee
report—a suitable topic, solid information, and

Writing a report takes time and planning. In Cl
learn the steps in preparing to write a report. K
and following them will make the work easier.

Goals for Learning

▶ To identify report topics and subtopics wi
subject area

▶ To identify resources for finding informa
the topic

▶ To practice note taking and paraphrasing

▶ To organize notes and create an outline

▶ To describe the steps in writing the first

Activity A Identify the topic and the subtopic in each pair of topics. Write *topic* or *subtopic* on your paper.

1)
  a) South Dakota
  b) Schools and libraries in South Dakota

2)
  a) The United States Space Program
  b) Apollo missions

3)
  a) The Rose Bowl
  b) College football in the United States

4)
  a) The invention of aspirin
  b) Pain-killing medications

5)
  a) The Great Lakes
  b) Lake Superior

Activity B Choose one of the subject areas below. List all of the topics you can think of in that subject area. Then circle the three topics that interest you most. Next, choose one of those topics. Narrow it to a subtopic or title for a report.

Art	Literature	Science
Geography	Mathematics	Sports
History	Music	Technology

Check on the amount of information there is about your topic before you make a final decision. You want to have enough information for your report but not too much information.

EXAMPLE

Too Much	There are hundreds of books written about the topic. That would be too much to handle for one report.
Not Enough	There is only one book on the topic or no books at all.
Just Right	You find several books or magazine articles on the topic.

Write these general subjects on your paper. Under each one, write a topic that you could write a report about.

1) Government

2) Geography

3) History

4) Technology

5) Art

Read each pair of topics. Choose the subtopic and write it on your paper.

6) **a)** Computer applications

   b) Word processing

7) **a)** The digestive system

   b) What your stomach does

8) **a)** Improving your foul shot percentage

   b) Playing better basketball

9) **a)** Designing a stage

   b) Producing your senior class play

10) **a)** The most popular breeds of dogs

   b) Characteristics of a Labrador retriever

Research

Looking for information about a topic

When you have chosen a topic, you are ready to **research** the topic. Research is looking for information about a topic. You can find information in books, periodicals, and reference materials.

Encyclopedias, almanacs, and atlases are some well-known references.

- Encyclopedias provide general information about many topics.

- Almanacs are published every year. They contain facts and records for current and past years.

- Atlases are books of maps. They contain facts about cities, states, countries, and world regions.

You can also research a topic by watching events and interviewing experts.

Key word

Subject, topic, author, or publication title a computer uses to search for information

You can locate information about a topic through a computer search. Use a search engine or browser to find Web sites that offer information about your topic. Use **key words** to search for the information you need. Key words can be subjects, topics, authors, or publication titles. The search engine looks for the words you enter and gives you the search results. Suppose your topic is "Mammals that are in danger of becoming extinct." Some key words you could use are *mammals* and *endangered animals.*

Activity A Imagine you are looking for books about these topics. Write three key words for each topic on your paper.

1) The life of Edgar Allan Poe, a short story writer and poet

2) Soccer

3) The Mississippi River

4) Birds of the Amazon

5) Popular situation comedy television programs

When you have identified a book about your topic, look for the information you want in the table of contents. The index will give detailed information about where to find the information in the book.

Taking Notes

Make a list of the main topics you will use to search for information. Armando is thinking about opening his own art gallery someday. He has listed five possible main topics to include in his report. Armando has chosen a topic that he already knows something about. He often visits galleries.

Report Topic: Opening My Own Art Gallery

Main Topics: Reasons for Opening an Art Gallery

Initial Decisions

Setting Up for Business

Staying in Business

Spreading the Word

Armando will use magazine articles and books to get information. He will also interview someone who owns an art gallery. When he finds information, he will write it on note cards. On each card, he will write information about his source. He will use that information to prepare his bibliography. Here is one of Armando's note cards.

Reasons to start a gallery: To fulfill a dream, to have a place to work, to have a place to show artwork and to sell artwork

Otis, Michaelin, and Jean Ranstrom. "Opening your own gallery." The Artist's Magazine. Vol. 18, no. 7 (July 2001): 64–68.

Activity B On your paper, make a list of possible main topics to research for the following report topics.

1) Growing Vegetables

2) Famous Contemporary Artists

3) The 2000 Summer Olympics

4) The Stock Market

5) The International Space Station

Before you research your report topic, make a list of questions you want to answer in your report. For example, do vegetables grow better in full sun or full shade?

Activity C Write one question that you would want answered in each of the following reports.

1) Famous Musicians in the Past 50 Years

2) Downhill Skiing Competition in the 1998 Winter Olympics

3) Making a Water Garden

4) Famous American Writers in the Past 100 Years

5) Exploring Bird Watching

Many people enjoy bird watching.

Paraphrasing

Paraphrase

Express someone else's ideas in your own words

As you take notes, **paraphrase** the ideas instead of copying words and sentences. To paraphrase is to express someone else's idea in your own words. When the information is in the writer's exact words, use quotation marks around those words. The other information in your notes should be in your own words.

EXAMPLE

Attracting Wild Birds

"More Americans enjoy bird watching than any other hobby except gardening. There are several ways to attract wild birds to your yard. First, birds love water. You can install a birdbath or pond. Second, they need food. A bird feeder is a good way to attract birds. Third, they need protection from predators and the elements. Build birdhouses or plant trees and the birds will move in."

Paraphrase

Some ways to attract wild birds are (1) put in a birdbath or pond; (2) get a bird feeder; and (3) build birdhouses and plant trees.

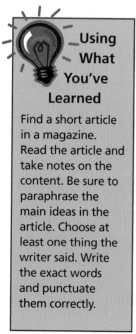

Using What You've Learned

Find a short article in a magazine. Read the article and take notes on the content. Be sure to paraphrase the main ideas in the article. Choose at least one thing the writer said. Write the exact words and punctuate them correctly.

Activity D Paraphrase the information in these paragraphs.

1) Sparrows are the most common birds in the United States. They often drive away other birds from feeders. Sparrows can live anywhere, in cities, suburbs, and the country. They eat plants and insects. Wherever you find birds, you will probably find sparrows.

2) The red-headed woodpecker has a completely red head. Its back is solid black. There are large white patches on its wings. They are easy to spot. A woodpecker can cling to a vertical tree trunk. It uses its long narrow bill to root out beetles, ants, and other insects. These birds are unusually beautiful.

Write your answer to each question in a complete sentence.

1) You want to find a book in the library catalog. What are three types of information you can use to look up the book?

2) You are writing a report about Sir Walter Raleigh, an English naval officer. What key words could you use to find information about him?

3) Armando wants to know the names of the largest art museums in the United States. Which of these references—almanac, atlas, or encyclopedia—should he use?

4) You are writing a report about the history of basketball. Write two possible main topics you could research.

5) Use the information below to prepare a sample note card.

Book Title: 100 Women Who Shaped World History

Author: Gail Meyer Rolka

Publisher: Bluewood Books

Date: 1994

"The charismatic and popular Queen Elizabeth I reigned for 45 years. Her reign ushered in an era of national achievement and economic prosperity. Elizabeth's reign established England as an international power. She was born in Greenwich, the daughter of Henry VIII and his second wife, Anne Boleyn."

When you finish your research, you will have many note cards. Before you write your report, you must organize your notes. Follow these steps to sort your note cards.

- Look at the main topic or subtopic listed at the top of each card. Put the notes on the same topics together.

- If you have only one card on a topic, see if it fits with one of the other topics.

- If you have a large pile of cards on one topic, you may need to separate them into subtopics.

- Some of your notes may not fit anywhere. You do not have to use all of your research information.

Activity A Write the main topics on your paper. Match the subtopics with the main topics. Write the subtopics under each main topic.

Main topics

1) How to attract wild birds   **2)** Create a water garden

Subtopics

a) Plants that grow in water   **c)** Birdseed mixes

b) Building bird feeders   **d)** Garden locations

Next, choose the order that seems to fit your report topic best.

Chronological Order	According to the time events happened
Order of Importance	From most to least important, or least to most important
Order of Size or Cost	From largest to smallest, or most expensive to least expensive

Activity B Nathan wrote a report about attracting wild birds. Organize the subtopics that he used into a logical order.

Building birdhouses and bird feeders

Kinds of birds in his area

Understanding what wild birds need

Investigating the local environment

First, organize your notes and decide on the order. Now, write an **outline.** An outline is a plan that lists main topics and subtopics.

Outline

A plan that lists main topics and subtopics

- Main topics are listed after Roman numerals.

- Subtopics are listed after capital letters.

- Smaller subtopics are listed after Arabic numerals.

- Whenever you divide a main topic into subtopics, there must always be at least two parts.

EXAMPLE		
Title	Designing a Birdhouse	
Main Topic	I.	Deciding on the species
Subtopics	A.	Species in your area
	B.	Choosing the design
	II.	Building the house
	A.	Buying the materials
Subtopics	1.	Weather resistant
	2.	Durability
	B.	Season the lumber
	C.	Treat wood with preserver
	III.	Mount the birdhouse

Activity C Rewrite the outline above. Make each part a complete sentence.

1) Write the main topics on your paper. Write the subtopics under the related main topics.

Main topics

    Early Life of George Herman Ruth

    Career Highlights of "Babe" Ruth

    Contributions to Baseball by Babe Ruth

Subtopics

    Babe Ruth's home runs change baseball strategy

    Babe Ruth is born in Baltimore in 1895

    Early career as a pitcher with the Red Sox

    Babe Ruth's popularity makes baseball the national sport

    Ruth becomes a home-run hitter with the Yankees

    Ruth attends school in Baltimore

2) Arrange these topics in an outline form with topics and subtopics.

    Breathing in Yoga

    How to Get Started with Meditation

    Rapid Breathing Exercises

    The Benefits of Meditation

    The Camel and Other More Advanced Postures

    The Complete Yoga Breath

    The Table and Other Beginning Postures

    Yoga Meditation

    Yoga Postures

Topic paragraph

A paragraph that introduces a report and states the main idea of the report

Refer to your outline as you write your report. You will find that an outline makes writing easier. Begin the report with a **topic paragraph** that tells your reader what the report will be about. This paragraph is the introduction to your report. Remember the three main parts of your report:

- The topic paragraph states the main idea.
- The body lists the main topics (I, II, III, and so on in your outline).
- The **summary paragraph**.

Summary paragraph

A paragraph that repeats the main points of a report and ends the report

Read the sample topic paragraph. Compare the sentences in this paragraph to the outline on page 401. Notice that the main topics are included. Subtopics will be discussed in the rest of the report.

 Topic Paragraph

> Before designing a birdhouse, answer these important questions. First, what kinds of birds do you want to attract? The answer to that question will help you answer the next question. What kinds of materials do you need? The last question is where to put the birdhouse in your yard.

The paragraphs that follow the topic paragraph must provide details that support the main idea. The details may be examples, facts, descriptions, or other information.

EXAMPLE

> To decide what kinds of birds you want to attract, check out the species in your area. Some birds live only in the eastern United States. Some live only in the West. Once you know what kinds of birds live in your area, you can figure out the type of birdhouse to build. About 50 types of birds use birdhouses for nesting. The birdhouse must be built to attract the specific bird you want to live in your yard.

End your report with a summary paragraph. A summary paragraph does not have to be long. It repeats the main points of your report and brings the report to a definite end.

Notice how this summary paragraph sums up the main topics of the outline on page 401.

 Summary Paragraph

Once your birdhouse is finished, your feathered friends will flock to your yard. You will have hours of fun watching them. The way they build a nest is amazing. You will especially enjoy seeing the tiny mouths of baby birds begging for food. Build your birdhouse right, and it will last for many seasons.

Spelling Builder

Homographs

What is a round object that children play with? A ball. What is a formal dance? A ball. How can that be? *Ball* (the toy) and *ball* (the dance) are homographs. Homographs are words that have the same spelling but different meanings. To tell which meaning is being used, you have to look at the context. The context is the words and sentences around the word.

Match one word with each pair of meanings. You will not use every word.

fleet	stroke	bear	rare
tire	light	story	school

1) large animal
   carry or support

2) place for learning
   group of fish

3) not heavy
   not dark

4) rapid
   group of ships

1) Write a topic paragraph to introduce a report on staying in shape. Use the outline below to write your paragraph. Write at least one sentence about each main topic.

> **Staying in Shape**
> I.   Choosing healthy foods
> II. Exercising daily
> III. Getting enough rest
> IV. Keeping a positive attitude

2) Look at the topic paragraph you wrote above. Think about the information that might have been included in the report "Staying in Shape." Write a summary paragraph that could come at the end of that report.

Vocabulary Builder

Words from Names

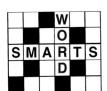

Some English words come from the names of people and places. Usually a place name is attached to something that comes from that place. For example, the word *denim* comes from *serge de Nimes,* meaning serge (a cloth) of Nimes. Over time *de Nimes* became *denim.* A person's name usually is attached to something that person invented or discovered. For example, the Earl of Sandwich didn't want to stop playing cards to eat, so he put meat between two slices of bread and created the sandwich.

Look up these words in a dictionary that includes information about the history of words. What place name or person's name does each word come from?

diesel	tuxedo	calico	pasteurize
limerick	bikini	poinsettia	maverick

Search the Internet

When you need information for a report or research paper, the library and the Internet have the facts you need. Computers make finding the information easier.

You can use an Internet search engine to find information. A search engine is a Web site that offers an index of other sites. Type the search engine name on your computer. Then conduct a key word search by typing in a specific subject. The search engine will provide a list of titles with brief descriptions about the subject. Look at the list of Web sites the search uncovers. Visit a few of the sites to gather information. Be sure to write down each site address and any other important details.

Here are some results from a search using the key words "shark attacks."

> **Top 10 of about 135,190 found in Web sites for: shark attacks**
>
> 1. Chances of a **Shark Attack** Despite what you saw in the "Jaws" movies, it really is safe to go in the water.
>   www.beach-net.com/Sharkattack.html [more from this site]
> 2. Shark Attacks-International Shark Attack File, shark attack statistics
>   www.flmnh.ufl.edu/fish/Sharks/ISAF/ISAF.html [more from this site]

You can conduct a search of the Internet in many libraries. Many libraries have computer terminals that are connected to the World Wide Web. You can also use those terminals to search the library's online catalog.

1) Write some key words you would use to find information about each of these topics:

   a) Finding organs for transplants

   b) How oil spills in oceans are cleaned up

   c) The latest U.S. population data

2) Write three topics you are interested in researching. Look up the topics on the Internet. Write down three sources of information from your computer search about one of the topics.

Writing Project

Preparing a Bibliography

The last step in writing a report or term paper is preparing the bibliography. The purpose of a bibliography is to tell your reader about the sources you used to write your report. It is an alphabetical list of those sources.

Look at the sample bibliography below. Notice that books, periodicals, and encyclopedias are all listed differently.

If you type your bibliography on a computer, use italics for book titles and magazine titles. Otherwise, underline titles. Use quotation marks around the titles of magazine articles and encyclopedia articles. Begin a bibliography entry with the author's name, last name first. If there is no author, alphabetize the entry by the title of the book or article. Copy the information from the front and back of the title page in the book.

Bibliography

"Birds of North America," World Encyclopedia. Vol. 2, 2001, 114–117.

Burke, Ken, ed. How to Attract Birds. San Francisco: Ortho Books, 1983.

Dennis, George. "How to Attract Blue Birds." Wild Bird Life 7 (July 2000): 45–46.

Rewrite and alphabetize the bibliographic entries below. Find the mistakes in each entry. Look for order, capitalization, and punctuation. Underline the titles of books and magazines.

> Beginning yoga. Harold Schmidt. *The Yoga Journal,* Volume 12, December, 2001, page 20.
>
> Weaver, Christina. *Tips on Having a Healthy Life.* 2000. NY: Best Books, Inc.
>
> Rob Kunzig. *A Guide to Yoga and Teens.* Boston: Yoga Books, 1999.
>
> Clifton, Chad. My Favorite Yoga Books. *The Yoga Journal,* Vol. 3, March, 2002, pages 30–32.
>
> Hudson, Jody. (Ed.) "The Complete Yoga Breath." The Yoga Encyclopedia. New York: Yoga Publications, Inc.

WORD BANK

key word

outline

paraphrase

report

research

subtopic

summary
paragraph

topic paragraph

Part A On a sheet of paper, write the correct word or words from the Word Bank to complete each sentence.

1) When you _____ a topic, you look for information about the topic.

2) A _____ is a subject, topic, author, or publication title you enter into a computer to search for information.

3) A plan that lists main topics and subtopics is an _____.

4) To _____ is to express someone else's ideas in your own words.

5) A _____ is an organized summary of information about a topic.

6) A _____ introduces a report and states the main idea of the report.

7) A division or part of a larger topic is a _____.

8) A _____ repeats the main points of a report and ends the report.

Part B Read each pair of topics. Choose the subtopic and write it on your paper.

9) **a)** The Nile River

   b) Rivers of the world

10) **a)** The history of Chicago

    b) The Great Chicago Fire of 1871

11) **a)** The invention of air conditioning

    b) Important 20th-century inventions

Part C Imagine you are looking for information about these topics. Write three key words for each topic on your paper.

12) Metric system of measurement

13) The Great Wall of China

14) Roman gods and goddesses

Part D Arrange these topics in an outline form with topics and subtopics. The title is *Home Computer Systems.*

15) CD-ROM Drive   Laser Printer

Data Storage   Desktop Computer

Ink Jet Printer   Types of Computers

Laptop Computer   Types of Printers

Zip Drive

Part E Write a topic paragraph to introduce a report about your favorite holiday. Use the outline below. Write at least one sentence about each main topic.

My Favorite Holiday

    I. What people do on this holiday

   II. How my family and friends celebrate this holiday

  III. Why this holiday is my favorite

Part F Think about the information that might be included in the report "My Favorite Holiday." Write a summary paragraph that could come at the end of that report.

Test-Taking Tip

When taking a short-answer test, first answer the questions you know. Then go back and spend time on the questions you are less sure of.

Appendix A:
The Writing Process

The word *process* makes writing sound as if it is a simple set of steps every writer follows. In fact, every writer follows his or her own set of steps. But every writer must answer the same questions: *What do I write about? How do I organize my ideas? What do I leave in? What do I take out? How can I make my writing better?* The following guidelines can help you when you write.

Prewriting

Choosing a Topic

Some writers think this is the hardest part of writing. Certainly it is a very important part. Without a good topic, you have nowhere to go with your writing. Here are some ways to look for a topic:

- Think about people you know, places you have seen, and activities you do.
- Think about memories or past experiences.
- Read newspapers and magazines. Listen to the radio. Watch television.
- Talk to other people about your ideas. They may offer suggestions.
- Draw a picture, map, diagram, chart, or web. One of the details may provide a good topic.
- Ask questions about a subject. A question can be a good topic to investigate.
- Choose a topic that you feel strongly about. It may be something you like. It may be something you dislike.

Developing a Topic

Once you have chosen a topic, you need to gather information about it or research it. Here are some kinds of details:

- Facts
- Reasons
- Sensory details
- Stories or events
- Examples

Where do you get these details? First, look back at anything you wrote when you were thinking about topics—notes, charts, webs, maps, and so on. To find more details, you might do the following:

- Research
- Interview
- Remember
- Imagine
- Observe

Before you begin to write your first draft, you need to answer two more questions.

- What is my reason for writing?
- Who is my audience?

Your reason may be to entertain, to inform, to persuade, or a combination of these purposes. Your audience may be your classmates, your friends, or any other group of people. Knowing your reason helps you focus your writing. Knowing your audience helps you choose the information to include.

Drafting

Now it is time to write your first draft. In a first draft, you put down all your ideas on paper. Some writers make an outline or a plan first and follow that as they write. Others write their ideas in any order and then rearrange them later. Use whatever method works best for you.

Try to write the whole draft at once. Don't stop to rearrange or change anything. You can do that after you have finished the draft. Remember, a first draft will be rough.

How can you arrange your details? Here are some suggestions:

- Main idea and supporting details
- Chronological, or time, order
- Order of importance
- Comparison and contrast

How can you begin and end your writing? A good introduction should tell readers what they will be reading about. It should also grab and hold their attention. You might begin with

- A story
- A fact
- A question
- A quotation

A good conclusion tells readers this is the end. Generally, it looks back at what has gone before. You might end with

- A summary
- A suggestion
- The last event in a sequence

Revising

Now it is time to revise your draft. When you revise, you try to improve what you have written. You decide what you want to change and how you will change it. You might add or take out words. You might rearrange sentences or paragraphs. Here are some tips for revising.

- Set your draft aside for a while. When you read it again, you will see your writing in a new way.
- Read your draft aloud. This will help you hear awkward sentences and see places where information is missing.
- Ask someone else to read your draft. Encourage the reader to tell you what is good and what is not.
- Ask yourself (and your reader) questions about your draft. For example,

    —Is my main idea clear?

    —Did I include enough details? Are there too many?

    —Are my ideas arranged in a way that makes sense?

Now, using your comments and your reader's comments, rewrite your draft. Then read your second draft and revise it. You may have to write several drafts before you have one that you like.

Proofreading

Once you have a draft you like, proofread it. When you proofread, you look for and correct mistakes in spelling, grammar, punctuation, and capitalization. After all, you want your reader to notice your ideas, not your mistakes. Here are some suggestions to help you proofread.

- Make a checklist of things to look for. For example,
    - —Are my words spelled correctly?
    - —Did I capitalize proper nouns?
    - —Did I write complete sentences?
    - —Do my subjects and verbs agree?
- Use a computer spell checker. But remember that it cannot catch some spelling errors.
- Ask someone else to proofread your work.
- Proofread more than once. Look for a different kind of mistake each time.
- Read your work aloud. You may hear mistakes.
- Set your writing aside. Proofread it later. You may see mistakes more clearly.
- Keep a dictionary and a grammar handbook nearby. You may have questions that they can help answer.

To make your proofreading faster and easier to follow, use proofreading symbols. Draw the proofreading symbol at the place where you want to make the correction. You will find some common proofreading symbols on page 327.

Publishing

Think of publishing as presenting and sharing your writing with others. Many writers get their writing published in a newspaper or magazine or as a book. But there are other ways to get published:

- Get together with other writers. Take turns reading your work aloud and discussing it.
- Send in your writing to a school or community publication.
- Give copies of your work to anyone who is interested, including family members and friends.
- Post your work on the classroom bulletin board.

Each time you write, think about the writing process you used. Ask yourself, "What would I do the same next time? What would I do differently? What parts do I need to work on?" Use the answers to these questions to help you the next time you write.

Glossary

A

Abbreviation—(ə brē vē ā´ shən) A short form of a word (p. 33)

Abstract noun—(ab´ strakt noun) A word that names something you cannot see or touch (p. 35)

Action verb—(ak´ shən verb) A word that tells what someone or something does, did, or will do (p. 120)

Active verb—(ak´ tiv verb) A verb form that we use when the subject is doing the action (p. 377)

Adjective—(aj´ ik tiv) A word that describes or tells about a noun or pronoun (p. 88)

Adjective clause—(aj´ ik tiv klöz) A dependent clause that describes a noun or pronoun (p. 305)

Adjective phrase—(aj´ ik tiv frāz) A group of words that tells *which one, what kind,* or *how many* about a noun (p. 206)

Adverb—(ad´ verb) A word that answers questions about a verb, an adjective, or another adverb in a sentence (p. 172)

Adverb clause—(ad´ verb klöz) A dependent clause that works like an adverb in a sentence (p. 301)

Adverb of negation—(ad´ verb ov ni gā´ shən) The adverbs *never* and *not,* which tell that an action in a sentence will not happen or that a state of being is not present (p. 178)

Adverb phrase—(ad´ verb frāz) A group of words that answers the question *how, when, where, how much,* or *how long* about the verb in a sentence (p. 209)

Alliteration—(ə lit e rā´ shən) The use of two or more words together that begin with the same sound (p. 384)

Antecedent—(an tə sēd´ nt) The noun that a pronoun replaces (p. 60)

Apostrophe—(ə pos´ trə fē) A punctuation mark that indicates a noun is possessive (p. 47)

Appositive—(ə poz´ ə tiv) A noun, phrase, or clause that is placed next to a noun to rename or explain it (p. 303)

B

Body—(bod ē´) The part of a paragraph that discusses and supports the main idea; the sentences can include facts, reasons, examples, descriptions, or explanations (p. 340)

C

Capital letter—(kap´ ə təl let´ ər) The uppercase form of a letter such as *A* (p. 10)

Chronological order—(kron ə loj´ ə kəl ôr´ dər) Events placed in the sequence that they happened (p. 354)

Clause—(klöz) A group of words with a subject and a verb (p. 218)

Collective noun—(kə lek´ tiv noun) The name of a group of people, places, or things (p. 27)

Comma—(kom´ ə) A punctuation mark (,) used to separate words, phrases, or clauses in a series (p. 219)

Comma fault—(kom´ ə fölt) The use of commas rather than end punctuation to separate sentences (p. 318)

Common noun—(kom´ ən noun) The name of a general type of person, place, thing, or idea (p. 30)

Comparative form—(kəm par´ ə tiv fôrm) The form of an adjective used to compare two people or things (p. 108)

Complement—(kom plə ment´) A word or phrase that completes the meaning of a verbal (p. 273)

Complex sentence—(kəm pleks´ sen´ təns) A sentence with one independent clause and one or more dependent clauses (p. 308)

Compound—(kom´ pound) Two or more sentences or parts of a sentence that are connected with a conjunction (p. 297)

Compound noun—(kom´ pound noun) Two words joined together to form one new noun (p. 27)

Compound personal pronoun—(kom´ pound per´ sə nəl prō´ noun) A pronoun made by combining a singular personal pronoun and *-self* or a plural personal pronoun and *–selves* (p. 65)

Compound relative pronoun—(kom´ pound rel´ ə tiv prō´ noun) A pronoun such as *whoever, whomever, whichever,* and *whatever* (p. 68)

Compound sentence—(kom´ pound sen´ təns) Two or more related clauses that are connected with a conjunction (p. 297)

Compound subject—(kom´ pound sub´jikt) Two or more subjects connected by a conjunction (p. 229)

Compound verb—(kom´ pound verb) Two or more verbs connected by a conjunction (p. 242)

Conclusion—(kən klü´ zhən) A statement at the end of a paragraph that expresses an idea based on information in the paragraph (p. 345)

Concrete noun—(kon´ krēt noun) A word that names something you can see or touch (p. 35)

Conjunction—(kən jungk´ shən) A word that connects parts of a sentence (p. 218)

Contraction—(kən trak´ shən) Two words made into one by replacing one or more letters with an apostrophe (p. 80)

Coordinating conjunction—(kō ôr´ di nāt´ ing kən jungk´ shən) A word that connects two or more equal parts of a sentence (p. 218)

Correlative conjunction—(kə rel´ ə tiv kən jungk´ shən) A pair of conjunctions that expresses a shared relationship (p. 228)

D

Declarative sentence—(di klar´ ə tiv sen´ təns) A sentence that states a fact (p. 16)

Definite article—(def´ ə nit är´ tə kəl) The word *the*, which is used to talk about a particular person or thing (p. 91)

Demonstrative adjective—(di mon´ strə tiv aj´ ik tiv) The word *this, that, these,* or *those* used as an adjective (p. 106)

Demonstrative pronoun—(di mon´ strə tiv prō´ noun) A pronoun that points out a particular person or thing (p. 74)

Dependent clause—(di pen´ dənt klôz) A clause that does not express a complete thought (p. 223)

Dialogue—(dī´ ə lôg) The words that people or fictional characters say to each other (p. 356)

Direct object—(də rekt´ ob´ jikt) A noun or pronoun that receives the action of a verb (p. 245)

Direct quotation—(də rekt´ kwō tā´ shən) A speaker's exact words (p. 356)

E

Edit—(ed´ it) To revise, improve, and correct a written work (p. 325)

End punctuation—(end pungk chü ā´ shən) A mark at the end of a sentence that tells the reader where a sentence ends:
• a period (.)
• a question mark (?)
• an exclamation mark (!) (p. 10)

Exaggeration—(eg za jə rā´ shən) A statement that makes a situation seem bigger or more serious than it is (p. 383)

Exclamatory sentence—(ek sklam´ ə tôr ē sen´ təns) A sentence that expresses strong feelings (p. 16)

F

Fiction—(fik´ shən) A story about imaginary people and events (p. 353)

First draft—(fėrst draft) The rough, unedited copy of a written work (p. 325)

First-person narrative—(fėrst pėr´ sən nar´ ə tiv) A story told by someone in the story (p. 353)

First-person pronoun—(fėrst pėr´ sən prō´ noun) A pronoun that refers to the person who is speaking (p. 62)

G

Gerund—(jer´ ənd) A verb ending in *-ing* that is used as a noun (p. 272)

Gerund phrase—(jer´ ənd frāz) A gerund and its complements (p. 281)

H

Helping verb—(hel´ ping vėrb) A verb that combines with a main verb to form a verb phrase (p. 123)

Hyphen—(hī´ fən) A short dash between parts of a word (p. 28)

I

Imperative sentence—(im per´ ə tiv sen´ təns) A sentence that gives a command (p. 16)

Indefinite article—(in def´ ə nit är´ ti kəl) The word *a* or *an*, which is used to talk about a general group of people or things (p. 91)

Indefinite pronoun—(in def´ ə nit prō´ noun) A pronoun that does not refer to a specific person or thing (p. 77)

Indent—(in dent´) To put five spaces at the beginning of the first sentence in a paragraph (p. 336)

Independent clause—(in di pen´ dənt klôz) A clause that expresses a complete thought (p. 223)

Indirect object—(in də rekt´ ob´ jikt) A noun or pronoun that receives the direct object of an action verb (p. 249)

Indirect quotation—(in də rekt´ kwō tā´ shən) Not a speaker's exact words; an indirect quotation is often introduced by the word *that* (p. 359)

Infinitive—(in fin´ ə tiv) *To* plus the present tense of a verb (p. 123)

a	hat	e	let	ī	ice	ô	order	ù	put	sh	she	ə	a in about
ā	age	ē	equal	o	hot	oi	oil	ü	rule	th	thin		e in taken
ä	far	ėr	term	ō	open	ou	out	ch	child	ᵺ	then		i in pencil
â	care	i	it	ò	saw	u	cup	ng	long	zh	measure		o in lemon
													u in circus

Infinitive phrase—(in fin´ ə tiv frāz) An infinitive, its complements, and any words that describe it (p. 277)

Interjection—(in´ tər jek´ shən) A word or phrase that expresses a feeling and is not related to other parts of a sentence (p. 231)

Interrogative pronoun—(in tə rog´ ə tiv prō´ noun) A pronoun that asks a question (p. 71)

Interrogative sentence—(in tə rog´ ə tiv sen´ təns) A sentence that asks a question (p. 16)

Irregular verb—(i reg´ yə lər vėrb) A verb whose past tense and past participle are formed in different ways (p. 128)

K

Key word—(kē wėrd) Subject, topic, author, or publication title a computer uses to search for information (p. 395)

L

Linking verb—(lingk´ ing vėrb) A state-of-being verb that joins the subject with an adjective, a noun, or a pronoun in the predicate (p. 258)

M

Metaphor—(met´ ə fôr) A direct comparison that says something is the same as something else (p. 382)

N

Nonfiction—(non fik´ shən) A book or an article about real people and events (p. 353)

Noun—(noun) A word that names a person, place, thing, or idea (p. 26)

Noun clause—(noun klȯz) A dependent clause that works like a noun in a sentence (p. 302)

O

Object complement—(ob´ jikt kom plə ment´) A noun or an adjective that follows and refers to the direct object (p. 254)

Object of a preposition—(ob´ jikt ov a prep ə zish´ ən) The noun or pronoun that follows the preposition in a prepositional phrase (p. 196)

Outline—(out´ līn) A plan that lists main topics and subtopics (p. 401)

P

Paragraph—(par´ ə graf) A group of sentences about a main idea, or topic (p. 336)

Paraphrase—(par´ ə frāz) Express someone else's ideas in your own words (p. 398)

Participle—(pär´ tə sip əl) A verb that can be used as an adjective (p. 272)

Participle phrase—(pär´ tə sip əl frāz) A participle plus any words that complement or describe it (p. 285)

Passive verb—(pas´ iv vėrb) A verb form that we use when the action happens to the subject (p. 377)

Past participle—(past pär´ tə sip əl) The verb form used to form the perfect tenses (p. 128)

Perfect tenses—(pėr´ fikt tens´ ez) Present perfect, past perfect, and future perfect forms of a verb (p. 124)

Personal pronoun—(pėr sə nel´ prō´ noun) A pronoun that refers to a person or a thing (p. 62)

Personification—(pər son ə fə dā´shən) Giving human characteristics to an object or an animal (p. 382)

Phrase—(frāz) A group of words that work together (p. 294)

Play—(plā) A story told in dialogue that someone wrote to be performed on a stage (p. 360)

Plural noun—(plùr´ əl noun) The name of more than one person, place, thing, or idea (p. 38)

Point of view—(point ov vyü) The way a person views or thinks about something (p. 337)

Positive form—(poz´ ə tiv fôrm) The form of an adjective used to describe people or things (p. 108)

Possessive noun—(pə zes´ iv noun) A word that shows ownership or a relationship between two things (p. 47)

Predicate—(pred´ ə kit) The word or words in a sentence that tell something about the subject; it always contains a verb (p. 13)

Predicate adjective—(pred´ ə kit aj´ ik tiv) An adjective that comes after the noun or pronoun it describes (p. 89)

Predicate noun—(pred´ ə kit noun) A noun or pronoun that follows a linking verb and renames the subject (p. 258)

Preposition—(prep ə zish´ ən) A word that shows a relationship between a noun or pronoun and other words in a sentence (p. 196)

Prepositional phrase—(prep ə zish´ ə nəl frāz) A group of words made up of a preposition, an object, and adjectives and adverbs that describe the object (p. 196)

Present participle—(prez´ nt pär´ tə sip əl) A verb form that shows continuing action (p. 133)

Prewriting—(prē´ rī ting) Work to do before writing begins (p. 340)

Progressive verb phrase—(prə gres´ iv vėrb frāz) The form of a verb that ends in -ing and uses a form of be as a helping verb to show continuous action (p. 133)

Pronoun—(prō´ noun) A word that replaces a noun (p. 60)

Proofread—(prüf´ rēd) To read a paper for mistakes in spelling, grammar, and punctuation (p. 326)

Proper adjective—(prop´ ər aj´ ik tiv) A proper noun used as an adjective, or the adjective form of a proper noun (p. 94)

Proper noun—(prop´ ər noun) The name of a particular person, place, thing, or idea (p. 30)

Q

Quotation marks—(kwō tā´ shən märks) The marks (" ") placed at the beginning and end of a direct quotation (p. 356)

R

Regular verb—(reg´ yə lər vėrb) A verb whose past tense and past participle are formed by adding -ed or -d (p. 128)

Relative pronoun—(rel´ ə tiv prō´ noun) A pronoun such as *who, whom, whose, which, that,* and *what* (p. 67)

Report—(ri pôrt´) An organized summary of information about a topic (p. 392)

Research—(ri sėrch´) Looking for information about a topic (p. 395)

Run-on sentence—(run on sen´ təns) Two or more ideas written as one without proper punctuation or conjunctions (p. 316)

S

Second-person pronoun—(sek´ ənd pėr´ sən prō´ noun) A pronoun that refers to the person who is being spoken to (p. 62)

Sentence—(sen´ təns) A group of words that expresses a complete thought (p. 8)

Sentence fragment—(sen´ təns frag´ mənt) A group of words that does not express a complete thought (p. 8)

Series—(sir´ ēz) A group of more than two words, phrases, or clauses (p. 219)

Simile—(sim´ ə lē) An indirect comparison that tells how one thing is like something else (p. 382)

Simple sentence—(sim´ pəl sen´ təns) A sentence with one subject and one predicate (p. 295)

Simple tenses—(sim´ pəl tens´ ez) Present, past, and future forms of verbs (p. 123)

Singular noun—(sing´ gyə lər noun) The name of one person, place, thing, or idea (p. 38)

State-of-being verb—(stāt ov bē´ ing vėrb) A verb that tells something about the condition of the subject of a sentence (p. 154)

Subject—(sub´ jikt) The word or words in a sentence that tell what the sentence is about (p. 12)

Subordinating conjunction—(sə bôr´ di nā ting kən jungk´ shən) A word that connects a dependent clause to an independent clause in a sentence (p. 223)

Subtopic—(sub´ top´ ik) A division or part of a larger topic (p. 392)

Summary—(sum´ ər ē) A brief statement that repeats or restates the main points in a paragraph (p. 344)

Summary paragraph—(sum´ ər ē par´ ə graf) A paragraph that repeats the main points of a report and ends the report (p. 403)

Superlative form—(sə pėr´ lə tiv fôrm) The form of an adjective used to compare more than two people or things (p. 108)

T

Tense—(tens) The time when an action takes place (p. 123)

Third-person narrative—(thėrd pėr´ sən nar´ ə tiv) A story told by someone not in the story (p. 353)

Third-person pronoun—(thėrd pėr´ sən prō´ noun) A pronoun that refers to the person or thing that is being talked about (p. 62)

Title—(tī´ tl) The name of a written work (p. 338)

Topic paragraph—(top´ ik par´ ə graf) A paragraph that introduces a report and states the main idea of the report (p. 403)

Topic sentence—(top´ ik sen´ təns) The sentence that tells the main idea of a paragraph (p. 336)

Transition—(tran zish´ ən) A change from one place or time to another (p. 374)

V

Verb—(vėrb) The word or words in a sentence that express action or state of being or link ideas (p. 13)

Verb phrase—(vėrb frāz) A main verb plus a helping verb (p. 125)

Verbal—(vėr´ bəl) A verb used as another part of speech (p. 272)

a	hat	e	let	ī	ice	ó	order	ú	put	sh	she	a	in about
ā	age	ē	equal	o	hot	oi	oil	ü	rule	th	thin	e	in taken
ä	far	ėr	term	ō	open	ou	out	ch	child	ᴛʜ	then	ə i	in pencil
â	care	i	it	ó	saw	u	cup	ng	long	zh	measure	o	in lemon
												u	in circus

Index

Part D Add a transition word or phrase that will link the sentences together. Use a different transition word or phrase in each new sentence.

15) Emily put on her socks. She put on her shoes.

16) Armando saved money for six months. He could buy a new CD player.

17) Angela wants to go to camp. She wants to stay home.

Part E Rewrite these sentences changing the passive verbs to active verbs.

18) Thirteen Grand Slam titles have been won by tennis player Pete Sampras.

19) One hundred and seventy-six touchdowns were scored by Jerry Rice during his career.

20) A tiger shark weighing over 1,700 pounds was caught by Walter Maxwell in South Carolina.

Part F Write an example of each of the following.

21) simile

22) metaphor

23) personification

24) exaggeration

25) alliteration

Test-Taking Tip

When studying for a test, use a marker to highlight important facts and terms in your notebook notes. For a final review, read over the highlighted items.

Preparing to Write a Report

The bees in the photograph on the opposite page are building a hive. To do that, they must follow a process, or a set of steps in a special order. When they follow that process, they will get what they want—a new hive.

Writing a report is like building a hive. Like the bees, you follow a set of steps. You choose a topic and find information. Then you organize the information and begin to write the report. If you follow this process, you will have what you need to write a good report—a suitable topic, solid information, and a logical plan.

Writing a report takes time and planning. In Chapter 16, you will learn the steps in preparing to write a report. Knowing these steps and following them will make the work easier.

Goals for Learning

▶ To identify report topics and subtopics within a general subject area

▶ To identify resources for finding information about the topic

▶ To practice note taking and paraphrasing

▶ To organize notes and create an outline

▶ To describe the steps in writing the first draft of a report

Play

A story told in dialogue that someone wrote to be performed on a stage

A **play** is a story told in dialogue that someone wrote to be performed on a stage. The dialogue does not need quotation marks. It is introduced by the speaker's name followed by a colon (:). Sometimes stage directions, which tell an actor what to do, follow the speaker's name. These directions are placed in parentheses.

> **EXAMPLE**
>
> **Manager** *(turning to Emily):* You can leave early.
>
> **Emily:** Thank you.
>
> **Emily** *(to herself):* I wonder if Nathan was able to get the book I needed.

Activity E On your paper, write the following dialogue in play format.

Example   "Mr. Thomas, do we have a test this week?" asked Nathan.

Nathan: Mr. Thomas, do we have a test this week?

"Yes," answered Mr. Thomas. "There will be a test on Friday."

"Is it on Chapter Two or Chapter Three?"

"Both," replied Mr. Thomas.

"Both!" Nathan exclaimed. "Won't that be difficult?"

"Not if you start studying now."

"Will the test be multiple choice?"

Mr. Thomas replied, "Yes, there will be multiple choice and two short essay questions."

"Thanks, Mr. Thomas," said Nathan. "I'm going to start studying now!"

Activity C The quotations have punctuation mistakes. On your paper, write each quotation correctly.

1) Emily said. I am looking for a song called "You Belong to My Heart."

2) "Do you know who recorded it" she asked the manager.

3) "No," the manager said, "but we can look on the computer." "I am sure we will find it there."

4) "There it is! Emily spotted the name of the song.

5) "Thank you for helping me" the customer said.

<table>
<tr><td>

Indirect quotation

Not a speaker's exact words; an indirect quotation is often introduced by the word that

</td><td>

A quotation can be either direct or indirect. An **indirect quotation** does not use the speaker's exact words. It is often introduced by the word *that*. You do not use quotation marks in an indirect quote.

</td></tr>
</table>

EXAMPLE

Indirect Quotation
The customer said that she could not sing at all.

Direct Quotation
The customer said, "I cannot sing at all."

Activity D Write each of these indirect quotations as a direct quote. You may change the words around in the new sentence.

Example   The manager said that the store was not very busy.
            "The store is not very busy," the manager said.

1) The manager told Emily that she could leave early.

2) Emily thanked her manager.

3) She had explained that she was going home to finish her science report.

4) Nathan dropped by and told Emily that he had her book on frogs.

5) Nathan explained that he was happy to help Emily.

Dialogue

The words that people or fictional characters say to each other

Dialogue is conversation. It is the words that people or fictional characters say to each other. The speaker's exact words are a **direct quotation.** Place **quotation marks** at the beginning and end of the speaker's exact words. Follow these 10 rules when you write dialogue.

Direct quotation

A speaker's exact words

Rule 1 Put quotation marks around the speaker's exact words.

> EXAMPLE   "Time is money," said Benjamin Franklin.

Quotation marks

The marks (" ") placed at the beginning and end of a direct quotation

Rule 2 Capitalize the first word of a quotation.

> EXAMPLE   Franklin also said, "Early to bed and early to rise makes a man healthy, wealthy, and wise."

Rule 3 You may identify the speaker at the beginning of the quotation. Use a comma to separate the speaker from the quotation. Use an end punctuation mark at the end of the quotation.

> EXAMPLE   Angela said, "I am going to practice."

Rule 4 You may identify the speaker at the end of the quotation. Use a comma to separate the speaker from the quotation. Put the comma inside the quotation marks.

> EXAMPLE   "I will see you after practice," said Armando.

1) Write a paragraph telling about something interesting or funny that happened to you. Use first-person pronouns such as *I* and *we*. Begin your paragraph with a topic sentence. Add some details. End your paragraph with a summary statement or conclusion.

2) Rewrite the paragraph you wrote above in third person. Use third-person pronouns such as *he, she,* and *they.*

Vocabulary Builder

Words About Books

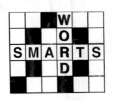

When you discuss different types of books, it is helpful to know the words people use to identify them.

Fiction—A story about imaginary people and events

Nonfiction—A book or an article about real people and events

Novel—A long work of fiction

Short story—A short work of fiction

Autobiography—Someone's life story written by that person

Biography—Someone's life story written by another person

How-to book—A book that tells people how to do something

Write the answers to these questions.

1) Which is longer—a novel or a short story?

2) If you wrote a story about yourself, would it be an autobiography or a biography?

3) If you wrote your life story, would it be fiction or nonfiction?

4) What subject could you write a how-to book about?

5) Name one book, other than a textbook, that you read last month. What type of book was it?
